KENNY EGAN

MY STORY

with Ewan MacKenna

Paperweight

First published in 2011 by Paperweight Publications, Level 4, Building 5,
Dundrum Townhouse Centre, Dublin 16, Ireland.

9780956913463
Kenny Egan - My Story

9780956913470
Kenny Egan - My Story e-book

Printed and bound by
CPI Group (UK) Ltd, Croydon, CR0 4YY

Paperweight Publishing Group, Level 4, Building 5,
Dundrum Townhouse Centre, Dublin 16, Ireland.

www.paperweightpublications.ie

Kenneth Egan is a member of the Irish amateur boxing team and one of the country's most successful athletes. A 10-time national champion — twice at middleweight and eight times at light-heavyweight — the Clondalkin man has twice been a European bronze medallist and famously captured a silver medal in the light-heavyweight division at the 2008 Olympic Games in Beijing.

A native of Athy, Co Kildare, **Ewan MacKenna** is a sports journalist who formerly worked for the *Sunday Tribune*. His previous titles are *'Darragh: My Story'* and *'The Gambler: Oisín McConville's Story',* which was short-listed for Sports Book of the Year at the 2008 Irish Book Awards. He was also a runner-up in the Sports Journalist of the Year category at the 2008 National Media Awards.

Front cover photo: Gary Ashe/Allpix
Back page photo: Patrick Bolger
Edited by Des Gibson
Designed by Ciaran Farren

Acknowledgements

I would like to take the opportunity to thank all those from the world of Irish boxing, who helped with my career and without whom this book would not have been possible. It is only fitting that I begin with my first coach, the late and great Noel Humpston, as well as Gerry Fleming and all the coaching staff in Neilstown BC.

The Olympic dream would never have been realised without the vision of Gary Keegan, Billy Walsh and Zauri Antia, and I'd also like to thank all the High Performance team, including John Cleary, Gerry Hussey, Scott Murphy, Johnson McEvoy, Sharon Madigan, Orla Samson, Conor McCarthy and, of course, all the lads on the Irish boxing team, many of whom are mentioned in this book.

Furthermore, I'd like to thank everyone involved in the AIBA, the City West Leisure Centre, Pat Hickey and, of course, the Irish Sports Council for their continued support and assistance.

There are too many friends to mention, but thanks too to Ken Bogle, John McKeown, Rory Burgess, Christy and Breda Beirne, Jack and Marian Brennan, Declan Doyle, Lucy Kennedy, my biggest fan Paddy Mulhall and Sharon McHugh for her support during the difficult times.

I wanted this book to be both a personal and honest account of my life, and on that note I would also like to thank all those involved with Alcoholics Anonymous. Going to the AA was the best move I ever made.

I'd also like to thank Des Gibson and all those at Paperweight Publications for giving me the opportunity to tell my story, and to Ewan MacKenna for his tireless dedication in penning this book.

Finally, and most importantly, I'd like to thank my wonderful parents, Paul and Maura, who mean the world to me, and to William, Paul, Tony and John, who are not only my brothers but my best friends.

- **Kenneth Egan**
November 2011

Contents

Foreword

My first introduction to Kenneth Egan was in Athy, Co Kildare, at the training camp ahead of the Sydney Olympic qualifiers, where I was assistant coach to Nicholas Cruz. Kenneth's own coach, the late Noel Humpston, had asked if he could get his fighter some sparring with the Olympic squad of the time. At the tender age of 18, he was a bit green and lacked the physicality of his senior opponents. However, he showed the types of skills that were to be his trademark for the next decade as he represented his country with distinction, time and time again, around the world. Indeed, not long after, and as a 19-year-old, Kenneth reached the heights of the top eight at the World Senior Championships in Belfast in 2001.

But personally, my first time to work with him as national coach was in 2002 on an ill-fated trip to Poland. It was my first time to be selected as coach to the national senior team and it was something I was really looking forward to and I was deeply honoured to have been selected. We travelled to Wisla in Poland to an Olympic training centre where we were to have a joint camp for 10 days, incorporating a couple of one-day internationals.

During the first international Kenneth fought one of the better Polish boxers. He seemed to be in fear of his opponent, and after being dropped by a body shot and receiving a standing count of eight, I threw in the towel. I remember thinking to myself that, despite all of his talent, Kenneth lacked balls and I felt at the time they were something that he could never grow. We lost the international with some very poor performances from an experienced Irish team but worse was still to come.

That night some of the team went on a drinking binge, Kenneth included. We were to have another international a couple of days later, so we had some extremely harsh words and continued to train for the competition. On the day of the weigh-in some of the team could not be found and Kenneth was one of them. I was disillusioned, disgusted and sickened by the fact that these guys were representing their country and behaving in this manner. As the fight day arrived, Kenneth and a few others went missing again. We waited in the changing room for Kenneth to turn up, and I was so furious that I got some boxing gear off the rest of the team and decided to take on Kenneth's man myself.

It was only when the Polish management stepped in and prevented me from entering the ring that the contest was called off. I remember saying to Brian McKeown, who was the coach with me at the time, that if I don't knock the Pole out in the first to throw in the towel because I wouldn't have the conditioning to last the three rounds.

On our return I duly sent in my report to the officer board of the IABA and a disciplinary hearing was called. Three of the team were suspended from their funding for six months and Kenneth was one of those. As a consequence, you can imagine when I was employed as head coach of the newly formed High Performance Unit in 2003 that my relationship with Kenneth would not have been the best, but at least he knew where I stood.

I recall saying to Kenneth shortly after he won his silver in Beijing that if he had not been taken to task over his behaviour in Poland in 2002, that glorious day would never have happened. I felt my reactions and disgust at what had happened were instrumental in the decision by Gary Keegan to select me as head coach. This turned out to be the start of the transformation of the Irish boxing team under the guidance of Keegan — from a culture of drink, amateurism, low self-belief and under-performance on the international stage, to one that has now helped transform amateur boxing into the most successful international sport in the country.

Kenneth Egan has played a major part in the success story of boxing over the past decade. And during that period my relationship with him has transformed from disdain on his part to one of mutual respect and deep friendship, bordering on the sibling status.

Throughout his journey Kenneth has had many highs and many lows, and every part of his character has been challenged. Thankfully, he has come out the other side a better person, and he continues to battle with his demons on a daily basis. In this book you will see the real Kenneth Egan: the professional, the dedicated achieving athlete who is first in the gym and last to leave. You will see a guy who, when he lost, would be the first person back to put right his mistakes. You will see a fun-loving, sometimes naïve person who struggled to cope with the fame and adulation of Beijing and how it nearly ruined his life. You will see how Kenneth has turned his life around, taking himself from heading to the gutter to remaining as one of the top athletes in Ireland and giving himself a chance to qualify for the London Olympic Games. And you will see the Kenneth I've been honoured to work with in my time despite the bad start and the many challenges.

- **Billy Walsh,**
Head of High Performance Unit,
Irish Amateur Boxing Association

PART 1

"Kenneth Egan is probably one of the best human beings that I've worked with, I've spent time with and I've had a relationship with. I would describe him as an absolute role model because, while he's not perfect, he's managed to achieve something special even with the faults he's had. I admire that in him so much. He's an ordinary guy who has done extraordinary things. He's special in terms of his willingness to make mistakes, to fall on his face, to get up again and walk back through the door and say, 'Right, I'm going to give it another shot'. I think it's a fundamental requirement and ingredient of every champion."

Gary Keegan, Director, Irish Institute of Sport

CHAPTER 1

Sunday, March 1, 2009

10.00am

Strange the things that wake you up from the shallow haze of a drunken sleep. Sometimes it's the mundane; a spear of light breaking through a gap in the curtains to bring you back to the reality of day, a reality that you keep trying to run away from but can never escape. Other times it's the difficulty of trying to swallow down a throat that's dry and scorched from shot, after short, after beer. On more than a couple of occasions recently it's been the realisation in the middle of the night that there's a cloaked, faceless figure standing high at the end of the bed, casting a black shadow over me, before I pull the duvet over my head, pull myself together and remember that it's just the alcohol that's making this happen.

This morning, it's none of those. Instead it's the simplicity of a bead of sweat breaking free from my fringe and trickling past closed eyes. Eventually it causes them to open, red and sore and tired, not just of last night, but of life. I lie there confused and angry, miserable and lonely, and for a few seconds I feel the heaviness of my head, the pain in my temple, the horrible clamminess of my body on sheets that are damp from yet another night of drink that's been trying to escape through every pore. Then I remember where I am and suddenly the situation seems worse than any hangover.

I look around a twin room in the Chelsea Hotel on West 23rd Street. I can see a few clothes scattered on the ground through the murkiness of my vision and the stale greyness escaping the curtains. But they are not the clothes I was wearing yesterday. Those clothes? I'm still wearing them because I stumbled into bed just a few hours ago unable to even undress before passing out.

Across from me lies Stephen O'Reilly, a friend from back home, snoring and oblivious to what I've done and what I'm going through. For him this is just a holiday and a way to forget a broken relationship. He was going out with a girl for close to seven years and shortly after I came back from Beijing it ended. I'd known him to say hello to but actually knew his brother Alan better. Yet all of a sudden he was around constantly. Some mates I'd see one day and then not for another week. He was there all the time. I guess we need each other, even if this trip for me is the continuation of ruination. This is what I've become and I can neither stand it nor stop it.

I wipe my forehead and feel an infection taking hold of a burn around my eye. Then I remember Friday night, stumbling and falling into the lift and dragging my face down the carpet on the wall. There's some blood on the pillow too. If I was just an average bloke it would seem a funny incident, one to tell the lads and to earn a pat on the back for. But it's becoming common and that means I'm not an average guy. Deep down I know I've a problem but right now it seems easier to drink it away than to face up to it. So I pull off the duvet and manage to stumble to my feet because it's time to escape again.

So this is Kenny Egan, the role model. This is Kenny Egan, the hero. This is Kenny Egan, the athlete. This is Kenny Egan, the Olympian, the medallist. Sometimes I wish Beijing never happened because it seems cheap to sell yourself for just a single piece of silver.

I take a look at my phone and it's still off. Drink makes you a coward. It makes you nervous. Every time a message beeps or a call rings you jerk uneasily in case you've done something wrong. You feel your heart beating too quickly and moisture on your skin. You become paranoid over something so normal. You think everyone knows you are in trouble and are going down a dangerous road. They might just be calling to say hello but for some reason you think they want to stop you when you don't want to be stopped. At first you ignore attempted contact but just knowing people are looking for you plays on your mind and creates slivers of guilt. So eventually you just take out the battery and pretend you are free from your problems. Short-term thinking. Solving the symptom but not the disease.

Enough introspection, I lean over and shake Stephen and he groans. *"Alright buddy, how's the head?"* I say, putting a brave face on to smother my feelings. But those feelings won't be there for long as I head to the bathroom to get myself ready to go again. There's a better way to smother them. Another day propping up a bar and throwing it all away. *"Come on Steve, it's Sunday in New York and the clock is ticking."*

We've been here three nights and already I feel like the old and unshorn men that line the streets of a New York night after a life of this. My body aches and my muscles scream as they slowly turn to fat, day by day, but it was only Thursday when we did the unthinkable and left Ireland without telling a soul. It was then that I stumbled half-cut from the night before into the Irish Permanent and took out €5,000. From there I wandered in the front door of my house and told my Mam I'd see her later as I whipped my passport into my pocket without anyone noticing. Stephen, meanwhile, went off and collected the money he'd received from selling his Mini and we hit Dublin Airport to see which destinations on the departures screens took our fancy. Nothing excited us. That is, until we saw New York, and glanced at each other with daring eyes that were willing us to go all out and hit the big time.

Was this when this madness started? I don't think so. No one knows, but for me it feels like I've been changing since late August when I led the homecoming of the Irish Olympic team through Dublin Airport with that medal around my neck and was greeted with hysteria. Kids cheering. *"Kenny, Kenny, Kenny".*

My name is Kenneth, always was up to that point, but that homecoming was the beginning of a new chapter and a different person. Ever since I came back from those Games I've found it hard to handle. You train all your life to just get there, never mind win a silver, but no one ever tells you what comes next. For me it's been openings of shops and shopping centres, followed by after-parties, followed by invitations to night clubs, followed by women. Everywhere I go there's a free drink and a free compliment and some girl looking to get into bed so she can climb whatever social ladder she is hanging from.

I know all that isn't for me but the next day I always do it all again, living a false and hollow existence because there is nothing to replace what went before. They say this is what being a celebrity is all about, but part of me is just looking to fill the void after achieving my lifetime ambition. When your only dream becomes a reality, what do you do then? Nobody can give me an answer to that and maybe it's that uncertainty which drove me here and has led me to this hotel room.

On Wednesday I went into Dublin city centre with Stephen to do a gig and pick up a few easy euro. It was an advert promoting a competition for free tickets to the upcoming world title fight in The O2 arena. That's just three weeks away and I'm on the undercard. But that is a worry for another day. On Wednesday all I had to do was stand in front of the camera. It should have been simple. I brought my silver medal with me, hung it around my neck and was given a quick and easy line to recite. *"Hello, my name is Kenny Egan, Olympic silver medallist. If you can answer the following question you are in with the chance to win two tickets to the Bernard Dunne-Ricardo Cordoba world title fight."* That was all and yet I couldn't even do it because I was shook, edgy and nervous.

There was a cameraman there and this guy with a light. *"Cut, cut, cut."* After a while I got pissed off, became agitated, and said I'd give it one last go. Finally I got it right but I was like an idiot and got angry to hide the embarrassment. I said to Stephen, *"Come on, we'll get out of here"* and headed for The Quays in Temple Bar. Knowing what was coming down the tracks, I put my medal in a box. I put the box into an envelope and asked the barman to keep it safe. It went from there. By that night we were in a club. By the following morning we were in the airport.

I knew I had a scheduled fight on Friday night in the international against the USA. Captaining my country should be big but that Olympic medal has made me bigger in my head. Besides, I've fought that American before and he's no great shakes. I could have told our head coach Billy Walsh I was injured or sick and he would have covered for me missing the bout, but I was drunk and as I said, drink makes you a coward and running only makes things worse. I'll have to face that soon and I know there must be 1,000 missed calls on my phone from Billy, from my Mam, from the media. But I will not be answering now because I'm in the bathroom, staring myself down in the mirror. I look at the graze on my eye. I wish it was from the fight back home and I hadn't done all this but I've made my decision and I'll need to go to a pharmacy shortly. First though I'll try to wash away the stale smell and brush away the stale taste.

On Thursday when we went to Aer Lingus, the girl behind the booking desk looked at us like we weren't right in the head. We had no bags and no jackets, and were just standing there with no more than a T-shirt on our backs, a passport and a wad of money in the pockets of our jeans.

"New York please, two returns leaving today, back on Tuesday."

"Are you sure?"

"Very. Why?"

"No reason. Okay, that'll be €1,400."

"Not too bad a price, eh Steve?"

And from there we ran up the stairs giddy, into the bar, mixing a round of new drinks with the alcohol from the previous night before stumbling towards the gate. On the air bridge I quickly dialled the number of Michelle McCormack, a bar girl who I met just a couple of months ago when on a trip to New York to look at offers of turning professional, who happens to be the daughter of the Iron Man from Rhode, former Offaly fullback Paddy. I told her we were on the way. She laughed. I asked her to book us into a twin room at a nearby hotel, which she did. I was a long way from professional on this trip but it didn't matter because as we sat down on board the Airbus A330 I was recognised. I was still the man, I was still the celebrity.

The steward from Galway liked his boxing. He came to say hello and returned a few minutes later with a bag full of shorts and mixers and shoved them under the seat. Next thing there was another admirer. This time it was an air hostess in her early 50s who came down and said that my mother must have been so proud of me. Selfish and stupid, I rang Mam's number and told the stewardess what to say.

"Hello Mrs Egan, I'd just like to let you know that I'll be taking good care of your son for the next seven hours."

And then I hung up and turned off the phone, leaving my mother in turmoil, not knowing where I was, who I was with, or where I was going. I was just getting a kick out of it. Nobody knew what had happened to me but I was already tipsy so I didn't care. I'd become the most selfish person you could ever meet. The blinkers were on, and when that happens there's only one way and that's my way.

There he was again. Kenny Egan, the role model. Kenny Egan, the hero. Kenny Egan, the athlete. Kenny Egan, the Olympian, the medallist, the man who sold out for a piece of silver that's still sitting behind a bar in Dublin.

By Thursday afternoon we were on the ground in JFK, hailing a big yellow taxi. We drove towards the high-rises in Manhattan, the lights climbing into the sky, banging on the Plexiglas. We were shouting at the driver to turn up Lady Gaga's *'Poker Face'* and screaming out the words, dancing drunk and clueless as the buildings became taller and our excitement grew, not knowing what trouble we may be causing at home, not caring about the air hostess ringing Mam.

That's what I become with drink and I even convince myself sometimes that I am in the right, yet here I am now picking at the scab that's growing over my graze, looking at the green infection replacing the bloody cut and staring at my own poker face. But it's not just the graze that's a sign of where I'm at in life. It's my flaky, spotty, dehydrated skin. When I rub my hands through my hair there are bits of scalp in my nails. But it's just temporary. It's just temporary. It's just temporary.

They say alcoholics are the greatest liars in the world, but I'm hardly that. Alcoholics have a serious problem. Me? I'm just on a bit of a bender. It'll pass. It's just because of the Olympics and that won't last forever. I repeat this as I get into the shower and the hot water washes away the night before. *"It's just temporary. It's just temporary. It's just temporary."* But as I close my eyes, it happens again. In recent weeks when I shut them in the shower I see these ghostly faces flashing towards me. They are evil and I stumble backwards but regain my footing, finish up, dry off, brush my teeth, gel my hair and suddenly I'm ready for another day. Part of me knows it's going to be just like all the other days but I tuck away that feeling.

When *'Poker Face'* finally ended in the cab on Thursday, we decided we'd head straight to see Michelle. She works in a place on Seventh Avenue called *Seven* and we figured, since we had no luggage, the hotel could wait. I don't know what it is about New York, but just seeing the steam coming up out of the roads makes you think there's no point in wasting time checking in to a room that you only booked for minimum hours of sleep anyway. A few pints later and we finally made it to the hotel, but not our quarters. Instead we took our key cards, put some money in the safe at reception, hit a lap-dancing club where I treated Stephen before we finally collapsed, exhausted, into bed late that night.

Next thing I knew it was Friday and I was talking to myself again. *"It's just temporary. It's just temporary. It's just temporary."* While my teammates were getting ready to take on the US back in Dublin, in the best physical condition a human can be in, I was facing into the fact that I needed some socks, jocks, razors, shampoo, toothpaste, a toothbrush and hair gel just to get away from living like an animal. A hangover was killing me but at least the other guy was still beside me so we finally faced up to the reality that a drinking session that had started in Temple Bar had ended up in New York and we headed out into the unknown.

I don't think I'll ever forget the cold as long as I live. We were weak and underdressed for a New York winter and the wind was whipping down the broad streets, cutting us in half as the slush soaked into our runners. It was bitter but we carried on, at one point sheltering ourselves in McDonald's and cramming in a cheeseburger because like it or not, we knew it wouldn't be long before we were back in a bar for the day and the chances were there would be no more food for quite a while. Why go sightseeing or to a restaurant when we can drink? That's all this trip was ever about. I might be hurting myself but as long as there's laughter and another round then that hurt disappears. The worry about what's happening back at home disappears with the alcohol.

And that's the way Friday played out. More rounds. More laughter. More hiding. We went back to the hotel room, changed and off we went. By the evening we said we'd treat our bodies to a shower but got as far as the lobby, only to hear some laughter from the hotel bar. Drink on board, we both decided we needed to be part of this. Always looking for more, more, more. In we went and there was this guy with a terrible haircut. Lovely fella, but Friar Tuck written all over him. I started offering him $100 to get a normal cut but all the convincing in the world didn't get a yes out of him. And then there were the two lads in the corner. That's where we whiled away the night and the craic was unreal.

The two lads were bikers, with skinheads and goatees, about 6'5" each and carrying 20 stone of muscle. Good looking lads, and when we got talking to them we found out they worked for Nike. And then we discovered that they were boyfriend and boyfriend and that's when the slagging started. *Jaysus lads, who gives who the good news, we can't work it out?* Sure we moved on to shorts and shots until I finally said I've enough, I'm up to bed, leaving Stephen behind until he decided he could take no more either. I crawled into the lift, slipped or tripped or stumbled and that's when I opened my face up. I don't know how I found the room. I was on autopilot, fell flat on the bed, clothes still on and the lights out again.

Just like last night. Just like every night. But now I dry my horrible skin, make my way back into the bedroom, pull back the curtains and pull open the window to let out the stale stench and decide it's time to go again. The cold hits quickly and I shiver and my body tells me it's too weak and that I need to stop but there's only one cure for that. This drink will not beat me. Stephen is up and he's getting ready and it's okay because we are nearly on the move. He says I should check my phone so I put in the battery, turn it on and messages come flooding through, the beeping cut off by a call. I give him the phone nervously. He answers. I panic.

"No, Kenny is not here, sorry."

"Who was it?"

"Reporter."

"What did they say?"

"Nothing, forget about it. Turn that thing off."

So I do. We are shaky now for sure, but shortly we'll be in a bar and while the first and even the second will be a struggle, after that we'll be back in form, back laughing. Back hiding. The same as yesterday. Yet another Groundhog Day. I bet people back home think I'm doing all this for attention, how every night out and every girl and every newspaper headline is about becoming famous. I don't want that. I'm a boxer and I just want to be Kenneth Egan but no one can see that and no one wants to help.

Everyone waits for Saturday night but recently I've been so exhausted after a week of boozing, I've been winding down while the world is having its fun in moderation. But Stephen reminded me yesterday morning of where we were and that there was no point in feeling sorry for ourselves, or worrying about the trouble we were causing back home. That would be there anyway when we got back, so for now I might as well be hung for a sheep as a lamb. That in mind, first off we went to *Seven* where we met Michelle and her friend Lauren, a stunner who I stared at in a drunken state just as much as I stared at my pint. From there the four of us took off to the *Mean Fiddler*. But it was the same night as all the other nights recently.

I go through different feelings as often as I go through different drinks. One moment I'm feeling sorry for myself as I lean against a bar and want to cry. But then something funny may happen and I hop back on cloud nine and order another, stronger round in celebration. Up and down. Never plain sailing. Never the normality and comfort everyone else in the club seems to enjoy. The comfort that I crave.

I was feeling sorry for myself last night when I turned to Michelle and told her that while I was in New York, I'd love to see James Moore, a former amateur teammate who won bronze in the 2001 World Championships in Belfast and later emigrated to go professional. She smiled, turned my body to the dance floor, pointed and said he's right over there. So I stumbled across the dance floor and hugged James and arranged to meet him around lunchtime today. But that's still three hours away. How to fill the time? How to fill the time? How to fill the time?

Stephen is a bit of a technology geek so he takes his iPhone out and opens up the Twitter account he set up for me just a couple of days ago. I'd never heard of it but he reckons it will be bigger than Facebook and we could have some fun and get some publicity out of it. Just as drink is bad for me and I can't say no, this is something similar. Already he's put up a picture of an American Apparel bag, dropping clues as to our whereabouts and then we wrote, *"This could be my last Tweet for a while. Cannot say any more!!!! Kenny Egan has left the building. Take care y'all!!"* And so we continue our fun, looking at the responses and laughing away.

I glance at my watch for a second and decide I better run to the pharmacy before we head out again. It's 10.28 and leaving that stagnant room behind, I somehow manage to convince myself that the worst part of the day is now behind me.

CHAPTER 2

10.30am

Out the bedroom door, into the lift, through the lobby while asking at reception for the nearest pharmacy, down the steps and into the biting cold of West 23rd Street. The freeze briefly numbs my headache and the fresh air soothes my throat and opens up my lungs. For a moment I feel human so I pause and look at the concrete that seems to make its way forever up towards the clouds. No matter how many times you end up in New York you always seem to walk around with your neck tilted upwards in awe. Standing here I remember what my Mam used to tell me.

"Travel the world. Don't be foolish. Don't get tied down with kids too young. There is a great big planet out there." I guess she forgot to tell me to put the brakes on at some stage and that moderation is good no matter what the thrill.

Looking around, it's strange how beautiful a concrete surrounding can be. Not back home though. Not when we moved from Neilstown into a new housing estate in Clondalkin when I was just four. But nowadays as I look into myself too much for answers while standing beneath the towers of granite and glass, searching my soul for answers, I take stock of how good my childhood had been. Back in Clondalkin as a kid there were no worries, no stresses, no self-destruction. People who aren't from working class areas would probably look down on what we got up to in our younger years, but they didn't understand and still don't. We had to occupy ourselves and while we were up to no good for the most part, it was never meant in a bad way. It was never malicious, never hurt anyone and it made us happy.

In the heart of Manhattan, some more privileged children walk past enjoying the freedom of their weekend, knowing that tomorrow they'll be back in a classroom. But I was never one to be confined like that. I remember one time I went on the hop with another lad. There was a convent up at the top of the road with a swing and we used to chill out there. But this particular time when we looked down at the nearby field, there were a load of gardaí walking through it in single file, searching for something. We thought we had better hide so we climbed up this tree and they walked right under us, one by one, with us looking down at them with the school bags on our backs. I don't know what possessed the last copper, but he stared upwards to see our shocked faces. *"Get down here now. What are you doing, are you on the skip from school?"* And when I did come down, he caught me a dig in the stomach that I wasn't expecting. *"Get your arses back to Moyle Park."*

Sure we walked back into the village, got some lunch and headed for the convent again because you can't just go on the mitch for a few classes and then stroll back in. But as we were walking, the same copper drove by us, only this time he had given up and just shook his head.

It wasn't the first time I'd been caught. I remember that occasion clearly as well. I walked into the house and there was my Dad asking how was school. *"Fine,"* I replied. *"You liar,"* he roared and he gave me such a kick up the hole that I flew up the stairs. *"Get up to that room."* It turned out the school principal had rang. He was a man that would have been ringing the house all the time, asking whether Mr or Mrs Egan were able to come down for a chat at the school. There were five boys in that house so the requests were frequent but both my parents were too busy working. They simply couldn't leave their jobs in the Green Isle Hotel to see him. My Dad, Paul, was a chef and my Mam, Maura, a waitress, so they had to earn money to feed the five of us and generally try to keep us out of harm's way.

Mam's a Kilkenny woman. She had five brothers and one sister, while Dad had 11 in his family. She met him in the hotel when she was 18 and reckons he's been there so long now that he must have a share in the place. But while he stayed cooking away in the same kitchen, Mam fell pregnant with Willie before going back to work in the Royal Hospital for 11 years. When that place closed down she moved on to work at the CityWest Hotel. As for grandparents; Mam's mother, Mary, worked in a drapery shop in Kilkenny. She had loved wrapping parcels and every Christmas she'd be getting stressed because her kids weren't wrapping the presents perfectly. Her father, James Brennan, was a farmer and he had a small little place in the countryside but then fell into bad health and they moved into the city. As for my Dad; his father, Willie, had a shop in the Coombe selling vegetables. He died a young man, 54, from a brain tumour. Dad's mother, Maureen, never married again. She's still alive but she's in a rest home, and suffering from dementia. She was very bad when I was at the Olympics and her condition has deteriorated since. Her body is fine but she has the mind of a child, and doesn't even recall being married at all. It's very tragic.

From Moyle Park for my Junior Cert exams, I switched to Kylemore College for my Leaving Cert. But I skipped school a lot around the time of All-Ireland Championships, because I had to make the weight and boxing always came first. I'd tell Mam I was off to class for the day and I'd leave with a bag on my back but there were no books in it. Instead it was there to carry my sweat gear and off I'd go running. A lot of people outside boxing think you just get into the ring and fight. Far from it. It's a lifestyle choice and this was the lifestyle I was choosing even at that age.

****

But right now I'm in the middle of a different lifestyle that seems to have chosen me, without giving me a chance. I reach the pharmacy and the hangover returns, thankfully with a little bit of sense to go along with it. As I show the girl at the counter the area around my eye, I tell her I'm an athlete and that we get drug tested. *"We can't fail the tests or we lose everything"*, I tell her. So the two of us stand there confused, unsure of what is acceptable, neither willing to take a risk. Strange that I'm worried about being a boxer when I've abandoned my team, my training, my fitness and my reputation to run away and drink it up, but that's where my mind is at. In the end I get some stuff I know won't heal it up right but having come this far, I'm glad to take anything just so I can get out of here and back to Stephen and a bar.

Out the door, down the steps and into the biting cold of West 23rd Street. The freeze briefly numbs my headache and the fresh air soothes my throat and opens up my lungs. For a moment I feel human again so I pause and think about better times.

Mam always said I was the worst of her five boys but I never thought that was true until now. She'd laugh when she said it though, remembering when I was barely old enough to walk, but old enough to cause trouble. Seemingly I had a habit whereby every time I saw a little girl out with a pram, I ran and kicked it over or every time I saw a baby with a hat I'd swipe it off its head.

But she didn't mind because I was seen as special and was spoiled from the time I was knee-high. She didn't know she was pregnant with me when Keith, the youngest at the time, died in his cot at three months. After that she couldn't sleep and thought it would happen with me so people took turns watching over me, night after night. It was always in her mind that the worst would happen and that catastrophe was just around the corner. I probably didn't help because I was always falling over and breaking some sort of bone.

By the time I was four I'd gone into the neighbour's paint shed, got all sorts of colours, and went up and down the road with two brushes deciding the cars needed some brightening up. Not happy enough with that, I got back and saw some white spirits on a shelf, liked the look of it and finished my spree having my stomach pumped in Crumlin Hospital. Not long after, I had another brainwave and let the air out of everyone's tyres. And come my first Communion I spent the morning of it in my suit on a bike only to come clean off it and snap my arm. Instead of church we headed for Our Lady's Hospital.

We'd only moved from Neilstown because my Mam always wanted a bigger house with a downstairs bathroom. Us running wild probably wasn't the best way to make a good impression on the new neighbours. But there was no need to worry, Mam loves it there, despite us running wild as youngsters. And in truth no one really minded us either. For months after we arrived most people were still asking Mam just how many kids she actually had because they'd never seen us all together.

That's what made it a nice estate despite the title it was given. Officially it's called the Dutch Village, but because you come down the Monastery Hill to it, a lot of people called it the 'Kip in the Dip'. It didn't bother us though. In fact, it was like a badge of honour. Living just around the corner from Boomers pub, an estate bar with regulars only, added plenty of value to the house in our minds. It certainly did for my Dad too. One Christmas Eve he went out for a few pints and held off putting together our presents until he came home. A few hours later he was on the living room floor with a spanner fitting wheels and handlebars to bike frames. I always told him there must have been more than just a few pints in him because while he was in bed hungover early the next morning, I was cycling down the street when suddenly the handlebars started shaking. I'd no control over where I was going at high speed or how I would stop for that matter. It was a familiar sensation these days.

I pass a man looking drugged-up, sleeping rough on the side of the New York street. It doesn't matter the landscape, this is a universal problem. There were little phases when different drugs would come and go back home too. When ecstasy came in all the E-heads were hanging around the shops. That trend went and you had heroin coming in. Many of the addicts in the area died and it seemed that with their passing the scourge of heroin abated too. Nowadays it's alcohol in Clondalkin, a lot of young lads drinking down the fields. But there isn't too much crime. Years ago you'd see the odd burnt car but the open spaces are blocked off now so that is a phase that's ended as well.

There were always plenty of ways to make a quick buck growing up too. When we moved in first, a lot of the area was a building site and the tennis courts hadn't been turned into areas for bonfires at Halloween yet. There used to be the Kit Kat summer camps and myself and the brothers used to look after the nets, putting them up every morning, taking them down every evening. For that we'd get £30. As time passed though, we found other ways to earn money and plenty of ways to spend it.

With no boxing to keep me out of trouble in summer, myself and my mates were over in the fields, the area Park West is now, robbing horses off the Travellers there. We almost got as much of a thrill crossing the M50 as we did taking the animals, that is until one day my brother Willie walked down the road with this stallion that must have been over 17 hands high. It was huge and he was strutting around with this proud face until the next thing it starts shitting its way up the middle of the street. My Mam and Dad came out, beat the head off him and made him go up and clean everything that had come out of the horse. He was out there for ages and we were all loving it.

In later years we were back doing deals with the Travellers, spending money we'd somehow got our hands on. We'd buy these old cars for £100. We didn't steal them but the Travellers certainly had because you could have started them with an ice cream stick in the ignition. We'd rally them around industrial estates until we got bored and then sell them on for £50, accepting the loss for the fun we'd had and then we'd go off trying to earn more. Always scheming.

When I was about 18, I met up with Kieran Mulcahy, a friend of my brother Willie's from the Army who had to leave because of a blood condition. So he got into gardening. My younger brother John works with him now but one Christmas myself and Kieran had a brainwave, thinking it could make us more than the usual loose change. It was so cold that there was nothing growing and with no gardening to be done we agreed we'd sell Christmas trees. So we got this trailer, about eight feet by six feet, with steel sides on it and we found a place in Wicklow selling the trees at four quid a pop. Bingo. We reckoned we'd get about 100 into the trailer and make a killing.

Wasn't long before we hit a snag. When we got there and were loading them into the cage we got about 20 in before I was up on top of them jumping, trying to make more room with branches snapping off under my weight. By the time we were done there were about 30 in so we drove home and met Rory Burgess, the owner of Boomers, who also owns a shopping complex in the village. He told us there was a little unit that was just built, where we could store trees there and sell them. So we put up a few signs, stood there in the cold all day and got the odd neighbour coming in.

There was one guy though, Robbie Mahon, who picked a tree and we brought it down to the house and set it up for him. We were walking out of the living room when I saw this trail of needles and it dawned on me then that they were shed trees, as opposed to the non-shed we had promised. A few weeks later he saw my Mam and Dad in the bar. *"See that son of yours,"* he shouted over. *"Tell him I've a bare twig down in my sitting room in a stand and I'm going to kill him."* The whole estate must have thought we were gangsters.

On other occasions work was more legitimate. When I left school I did a bit of building and labouring, mixing cement, and general donkey work. It was all hard graft. I was only on £1,200 a year through boxing so my Mam, who by then was working at CityWest, got me a part-time job in there at the big events.

Myself and my brother Tony served Tiger Woods and his wife when they were over. The manager knew we were mad into sport, so she put me on his table. His wife was gorgeous and I'm not sure what it says about me but that's my lasting recollection.

But even such occasions aside, it was a great place to work. It was only a five-hour shift, you'd set up the room, have your lunch and spend two hours serving. The best part though was when we used to go up to the canteen before we started and there must have been 60 or 70 women, mothers and daughters, all ages, and the moaning out of them. There were only a few lads and we'd sit there listening to, *"My Johnny did this,"* and, *"Wait till I tell you about Jack"*. They were a nagging shower. And they'd be talking about some other one in the corner who got paid this much for doing a nixer. They seemed like they were programmed to whinge. It was very funny. And it was good money, of which more and more was going towards nights out on the town. But at that age, there was nothing abnormal about that.

When we were 15 we used to walk down the canal to Inchicore because it was the only place we'd get served in an off-licence. At first, the beverage of choice was Amber Gold, two-litre bottles of cider. Then our taste buds matured and myself and a guy called Owen McMahon, more commonly known as Mahuna, would make money in summer cutting grass. We would tell our folks we had barely been paid anything and sneak off to the off-licence with about 40 quid in the back pocket. With that we turned our attention to Bacardi Breezers. It was tasty and we couldn't stomach beer so we'd sit over in Castle Park with a tray each.

Soon after, that wasn't enough and we got adventurous. We used to go to the Daniel O'Connell on the quays for a load of pints and from there to what was once McGrath's at the top of O'Connell Street where there was a nightclub. I robbed my brother Paul's passport, and even though he looks like me with dark hair and a similar face, I still cut his picture clean out of it and put my own passport picture in. I did a great job too, so suddenly instead of being 16 I was 20 and that opened up the city to me. That was all well and good until one day he was looking for his passport before a trip to Holland. He picked up mine and saw my head and threw it back down. So he picked up his, saw my head again and went bananas. I explained myself and gave him the £50 to get a new one.

We did the whole dance scene too. We would hit all the main spots, the Ormond, the Temple Theatre and then get the Nitelink home, which was the wildest part of it all as we snaked down through Ballyfermot and Neilstown at 4am surrounded by all sorts of headcases. By that stage I was a regular ecstasy taker and tried my share of cocaine too. Both were easy to get hold of. We used to have bottles on the bus, take a few tablets and dance the night away. I knocked all that on the head in 2000 and haven't gone near that scene since. With boxing going well I got onto the Carding Scheme, which provides High Performance athletes with grants. Having worked so hard to get there and with money so scarce, as well as the ever-present prospect of drug testing, I've never touched anything like that since.

It was probably for the best too. That stuff messes with your head. I was at a house party one time and the guy had a big conservatory, and we were drinking away all night in it. There was condensation dripping onto the floor and as the sun came up I was sitting on a chair and was getting annoyed. Believing I was on the Nitelink bus, I started asking everyone who was still conscious, *"What time is this bus leaving at anyway?"* I looked up and could see empty cans floating past me. I didn't know where I was. Alan O'Reilly, Stephen's brother, was asleep on the floor. They were the young years and I was glad there was boxing, to keep me off the streets and out of trouble. The lads I was with weren't bad guys either, I just needed something else to occupy my mind.

But what have I got now?

I snap out of my daydream to the sound of an ambulance howling past, of vibrant New York streets full of people with purpose. A group of guys in their early 20s with English accents stroll past, on holidays, the way I used to be. Drinking at night but able to stop in the day. I went away on my first holiday when I was 18. About eight of us went over to Crete and while I'd travelled abroad to box this was a shock to the system. Literally. So much so that after two weeks of it, I swore I'd never do that length again because it was too hard on the body, even at that age.

On that occasion there were eight of us but we only booked an apartment for four. We landed into reception and while the guys were checking in, I ran into our place and went to the toilet on the shower floor before hopping back out. Finally the guys made it in, were looking around, talking about how nice the place was until one pulled back the shower curtain and let out a roar.

"Ah lads, there's steam coming out of it. It must have been the people here before us. That's rotten."

We went mad for the two weeks. Ran wild. The second last night we were all in the same place, half of us kipping on the floor when I got this baton in the ribs and looked up. The Greek police were in the apartment, one standing over me, glaring at me. I was half naked and the old woman who ran the place was there shouting about how these Irish drink too much and about how there were extra people staying and we'd have to pay more if we wanted to remain there. We didn't care less and just laughed them off.

The brother, Tony, was with us that time and as we were waiting to leave for the airport to go home, I was feeling bad and mentioned that we didn't even buy our Mam anything to bring back from our holiday. So we were sitting there drowning in our guilt in reception, waiting for a bus, when I looked in behind the counter and there was this lovely vase looking back at me. I gave Tony the nod, whipped it into a bag and it's still in my mother's house to this day.

I went back to Crete five years in a row with different groups. Another year there were just three of us — myself,

Martin Nolan and Gareth Sallinger. We were in a little apartment. Martin was quiet, wouldn't really chat to too many women but I was lucky enough, or unlucky enough, to have some girl in the room a few nights on the trot. One morning we saw Martin asleep on the doorstep and he lifted his head with an imprint of the doormat carved into his skin. *"I'm after spending £540 for the week and I haven't slept in a bed once."* Sure the room was always engaged and he was too shy to tell me to get out.

Another time one of the lads, Mark O'Dwyer, was drinking ouzo, the local short out there. He got up the next day and walked out of the apartment but he suffered some kind of allergic reaction and his head swelled up. He was like some corpse you'd see in the Liffey, pulled out in a suitcase. I asked him what happened, but he hadn't a clue. He was dribbling out of his mouth. I told him he'd better get back into bed and he stayed there for the rest of the week.

I could always balance those trips with boxing because it was summer and there was little happening in the gym, and the Worlds or Europeans were before any holiday. Besides, you build up a level of fitness you never lose at the very top end of sport and you could always sweat it out of you when you got back. And in later years we thought we were maturing. We'd promise ourselves that we'd go over and eat well and really enjoy it, spoil ourselves and have a few drinks on the side. But we always ended up eating burgers and pizzas at the bar. Those were great days though but they ended in 2004 when I was walking down the main street and some kid roared, *"Alright mister."* I thought at that moment I was getting too old for it. I nipped it in the bud with that.

I'm too old for this now as well, but I can't simply 'nip it in the bud' anymore. So I climb up the steps, back into the hotel and out of the biting cold of West 23rd street. A group of women pass. Well-dressed with Gucci bags and designer shoes. This is a long way from *Club Diva*, a nightclub at the Red Cow Hotel in Dublin, but I still miss that life despite the so-called glamour of this one. When I used to pop over to that nightclub, which my friends called the *Cattle Market*, no one bothered you. It was local, it was innocuous, but it was fun. And there were always women, but not like the ones that have started to come my way lately. The girls now, who just want to create a story to tell and end up with their picture in the newspapers.

There were stories before but no one cared then. Except my Mam maybe. It got so bad that she had an empty bottle of Windolene that she filled with water to spray on whoever was sprawled out beside me in the house the next morning. That didn't always work though, so one morning I woke to see her pulling a duvet off this girl and throwing a basin of water over her. There was a taxi waiting for her outside, and Mam dragged her down the stairs, threw her out the door into the front garden and her clothes shortly afterwards. The driver was sitting in his cab staring at all this with a smile on his face, watching her get dressed. And my Ma would tell me again and again that there were rules in the house and I needed to learn them.

So I learned. Not just that there were rules, but how to get around them. I'd tell girls to take their heels off in the porch because of the noise they'd make on the staircase, and besides, half of them couldn't walk in heels anyway. But it wasn't just my fault. I reckon I picked up those bad habits off my brothers and their friends. When I was 14 and still trying to grow some bum fluff on my chin, there was one night Willie was up in the room with this girl, and Kieran Mulcahy, the Christmas tree man, was on the couch with another. Mam got up and went nuts. She threw Willie out with no trousers while Mulcahy ran to the toilet with his girl but they never got away. It got so bad that Mulcahy's girl tried to escape out the window but Mam hauled her back in by the legs.

Again she warned us that we were never to bring anyone home, especially if they were living in the estate. When we did it again she told my father that he had to put his foot down and put a stop to it. He just laughed and said, *"Boys will be boys"*.

And on it went, with Mam going crazy, and us always trying

it on. My younger brother John brought a girl back to the house one night and had his van, a big white Hiace, parked parallel to the garden, with my BMW in the drive. Next morning I was looking out the curtains to see what she looked like when she went up to my car thinking it was his and tried to open it. *"No, no,"* he roared, *"that's my baby over there",* pointing to the Hiace. God knows what he told her the night before.

Finally I think Mam gave up and decided to have some revenge. One New Year's Eve myself and Tony were out all day. I don't think we even saw midnight but we stumbled back into the house with a blow-up doll covered in chalk from a game of pool we tried to have with it. Mam told us afterwards she had to endure us talking for hours, Tony rambling on about how when he would have kids he'd bring them up to the graveyard to save a few quid. He would tell them that Santa Claus was buried there, the Easter Bunny here, and the Tooth Fairy over in the corner. The next morning we remembered none of this but we were awoken to Mam shouting at us to get downstairs.

"There's some slapper at my kitchen table for breakfast, which one of ye was it?"

We had two single beds with a locker in between. We jumped out of the bed at the same time and clashed heads. Next thing we ran down the stairs to declare our innocence only to see this blow up doll with a wig and a bikini. Mam started laughing and told us that was for all the years of having to put up with us.

That was when drink was fun. Back then it only caused laughter and never impinged on work or family or relationships. But being here now, crossing the lobby of the Chelsea Hotel, standing in this lift, heading back to the room, I can claim none of that now. I've dug a hole and all I know is how to keep digging. So I get Stephen and throw on some aftershave. And from there it's out the bedroom door, into the lift, through the lobby, down the steps and into the biting cold of West 23rd Street.

KENNY EGAN: MY STORY

CHAPTER 3

11.30am

The 1920s heavyweight champion Jack Dempsey once said that a man in his position at the very top owed everybody something, and that he could never pay back for all the help he got. But sitting in Jack Dempsey's Bar on West 33rd Street, that saying doesn't rest easy. Here I am, a man supposedly at the top of his career, and I'm acting like everyone owes me something and that I've no one to pay back. But instead of contemplating the ills of my mindset, I pull up a stool at the outstretched mahogany bar. Myself and Stephen get comfortable and we settle in for the long haul.

"Two pints, please." A slow start. *"Two more of the same there."*

And so it goes but for the first time on this trip, these drinks don't seem to be making things better. Quite the opposite. They are making me nostalgic, aware of where I came from, how hard I worked to earn my medal, how this might just be the ultimate result of all that effort.

Maybe it's that which is most depressing. Years of being sheltered and secluded results in this lifestyle? Where is the reward for hours and hours of tortuous dedication? My boxing success didn't just start when people turned on their televisions during the Olympics or showed an interest when I came through arrivals in Dublin Airport with a medal. It didn't start at the qualifiers or even back when the High Performance programme was formed. It started when I was eight, as my eldest brother Willie would come in and ask, *"Ma, have you got subs."* That's a long road to travel to end up at a destination like this.

My old coach Noel Humpston used to collect my older brother Willie outside the house every Monday, Wednesday and Friday to bring him training. I was only a pup and I got curious so finally they brought me over one night. But it was the strangest introduction to boxing you could imagine. I walked into the hall of the St Peter Apostle Primary School. It was empty and there were loads of elephants and giraffes painted on the walls looking at me. This was boxing? Or more precisely it was just our club as I'd slowly come to understand. For 30 years those organising it had to get out the bags and hang them, erect the ring and then take it all back down when they were finished.

Noel took me under his wing but there were ups and downs and for a long time I never took it seriously, even when I saw Michael Carruth winning gold at the Barcelona Olympics of 1992. Granted, that was the best thing since sliced bread but I never thought in a million years that I'd be in an Olympic final, I never set myself a target, I just wanted to get into boxing and see how it went. So I tried and tried and tried but when I was just 10, an older guy in the club came over and gave me a smack right into the stomach as I was putting on my gloves. I ran into the toilets crying. I didn't want to say it to anyone so I just sat there embarrassed by my tears and thought maybe this boxing game wasn't for me. He was probably only messing but I was terrified. Anyway, eventually I dried my eyes and stuck with it and a couple of years later when I got older and hairier I got my own back.

These were the bumps on the road and all for what? For a destination like this?

"Two more of the same there please..."

A lot of guys came into the club just to stay fit and they'd go around the country having these club bouts but they never got near the Irish team. Willie was different though. He was the main man about our place, with all these national titles from boy and junior right up to intermediate. He never won a senior title though. He was beaten twice going for it and Noel

Humpston was putting an awful lot of pressure on him, telling him he had to win one for the club because we never had a senior champion. In the end Willie got sick of it and when he was 18 he joined the Army.

Once that happened his career with Neilstown was finished but he took up boxing again and won a silver medal in the Military Games in Rome in 1995. A guy by the name of Andrey Gogolov beat him 7-5 in the final. He was a Russian, a great fighter because they have all their top guys in the army. For years after it Willie always told me about the body shots this guy threw. Serious punches. And he was a southpaw, the same as myself. I saw him later on in a tournament in Finland and again he threw the left hand to the body and I just watched and took it all in. That's the shot that won me the Olympic medal. In fact, 69 per cent of my points came from that left uppercut to the body in Beijing. You had to choose your moment, to find the opening, but once there was a gap, it was so clean, so perfect. Such is the circle life travels in. In fact, Gogolov boxed in my first World Championships in Belfast and went on to win the gold medal at middleweight.

But long before World Championships and Olympic Games and left uppercuts there was a lot of pain and near misses and that's what bothers me about my place now. I came through all that. I kept going. Took the punches on the chin, came to accept the defeats that left a pain deep in my gut. Ran miles, sweated litres, skipped meals, ditched school, passed over girls. And for what? This bar, this trip, this drink, this guilt?

"Another two there when you're ready..."

You officially start boxing at 11 and are finally allowed into the ring to fight. One of my first times was a club show just before my first All-Ireland. It was Neilstown against Darndale and it was every bit as glamorous as that sounds. I don't know the guy's name and I don't think I'll ever find out either, but I was in the toilets getting ready and he came in after me. *"I'm gonna bate the head off you,"* he said, staring me down in the corner. Didn't happen though. I went out and I gave him such a hiding to claim my first official win. He was trying to be the hard man but it didn't work. And I went from there to bigger things but they were not always better.

As a kid, when you entered into underage All-Ireland tournaments you were fighting in the National Stadium and you think it's the centre of the universe. You hear the names of guys from towns and counties you imagined were in a different time zone. Ireland seemed massive and you were convinced this was actually important. But in my first three years at it, I reached the final each time and lost the lot — twice to Gerard McAuley, a fine fighter out of Belfast, and the other time to Collie Barrett, who was Olympian Francie Barrett's nephew. After each defeat I said 'this is not for me' because it was heartbreaking. You are so young but you are still looking at your diet and it is hard going. For instance, the All-Irelands were always on around April so I never got to eat my Easter egg until they were over. You were always looking to take off a kilo and you thought it was really serious, that you were the business, that winning would change your life. But instead I lost and nothing changed.

These were the bumps on the road and all for what? For a destination like this?

"Two more Steve..?"

And when nothing changed I always threw a strop and talked of packing it in. But you always get the itch to go back to the Neilstown club. It was worth it too because finally at my fourth attempt, I won. Kenneth Egan, All-Ireland champion. I got my little certificate and was delighted with myself. I was 14 at that stage and I've won an Irish title every year since. But while I thought that first title made me a superstar, it's funny how other people view what happens in boxing when all you can see is how to get better and how to keep winning.

Take my Mam for instance. After that first national title, on the Monday, she rang up the *Irish Daily Star* boxing writer Gerry Callan, and lost her temper on the phone because he had only printed the names of the finalists. *"You should be ashamed, all those kids wanted was a name in the paper. There's kids losing*

all week, but you never mentioned those who lost early." He made
the mistake of asking her who she was and what business it was
of hers, and by Friday all the names were printed. I don't think
she ever told him who it was phoning, but luckily for him he
didn't have to deal with her on too many occasions because by
the time I was 15 she'd watched me box for the last time. In
the stadium one night she heard the mother of the guy I was
fighting roaring from a few seats down. *"Take his head off."* She
told my Dad they were leaving. He tried to stay but she won that
battle as well.

At that stage in my career, I was an orthodox, right-hand
fighter. But Noel saw something more important than All-
Irelands, he saw something in me for the long run, and asked me
to switch hands. It was a little awkward to get my head around
but I felt great on my feet and boxing is all about balance and
footwork. I felt so much more comfortable moving so I stayed
that way. Suddenly I was a right-handed southpaw. In sparring I was changing so I went through a phase of switch hitting
but finally I stuck with it and I've been southpaw ever since. A
normal southpaw has his power in the backhand but people get
me all wrong. My power is in my right, in my jab, and all my
work is done with my lead hand.

So from winning All-Irelands in the orthodox position, I
went to winning them southpaw. And from sitting in the back
of Noel Humpston's car, I moved to the front as Willie gave up
and joined the Army. Myself and Noel would drive up to Mrs
Duffy who lives on the main Neilstown road. He'd tell me to
run across the green, go in and get the key to the school and
he'd do a U-turn. But every time there was a *"Hiya Ken, is Noel
out there, can you ask him to come in for a minute?"* I'd run back.
"Noel, she wants you." And off he'd go on a rant, wondering what
now and I'd sit in the car laughing as he stomped across the
grass to listen to some story about the gate being left open or the
lights being left on.

It was like clockwork and so were my victories. By 16 I
had won the juniors and headed over to Cardiff for my first

international against Wales. The other guy was 6'3" and I was wondering how I was going to get out of this alive. You always get nervous before big fights and against that guy I was looking at him thinking he couldn't be the same weight as me. But nerves are great, they make you respond quicker. You don't have fear but it's the nerves that ignite you. Everything you do in training comes out at the first bell with those nerves and it's like kicking a ball for soccer players. It just happens, and I got over him, and suddenly I was travelling a lot to places like London and Bedford, thinking they were exotic. By 1998 I even went to the European Cadet Championships in Jurmala, Latvia.

Nicholas Cruz was coach at the time and he travelled with us. Now there was an interesting character. After the Irish Amateur Boxing Association had asked for help to prepare an Irish team for the Seoul Olympics of 1988, Cuba answered and sent us the head of their Higher Institute for Physical Education. Nicholas probably anticipated some racism but was overwhelmed by the friendliness of the Irish people and left stunned by the sporting rubble he found instead of the top-class facilities he had grown up with.

As part of the team's conditioning he took them to Kerry for a training camp but found nothing but a ring on the ground floor of the hotel. In the end he borrowed a sledgehammer and tyre from a nearby yard and used them for cardio and strength work; he smashed rocks and used the smaller pieces as dumbbells; he used trees for chin-ups; and he had his team doing squats up and down the dunes on a nearby beach. Then he went looking for a masseuse to the amusement of higher powers.

Then came 1992 and Carruth and McCullough and when he returned to Cuba shortly afterwards, even Fidel Castro was talking about him. His family presumed he was a million-aire after his success in Europe and asked how much he had received. He told them he got a few hugs and plenty of satisfaction. They laughed. Nicholas was being serious. He had been promised payment but as far as I'm aware he received very little. Yet for some reason, when Ireland came calling again, he left everything behind. In 1996, he was giving a seminar to coaches and boxers in Puerto Rico. He had done too good a job in Barcelona and his bosses were happier to send him to a fighting wasteland rather than back to our shores. Before he'd left for the nearby Caribbean islands he'd told his wife if he didn't come back he'd be in Ireland and she cried. He defected.

He was married for 10 years with a daughter aged seven and a son aged just one. Most days here he'd walk to a local post office with a letter in his hand, knowing that it would be intercepted before it ever reached them. And within a couple of years in Ireland he'd grown into a dark shadow of his former self. He wasn't treated so well here either, was on poor money, slept in the back of the National Stadium, regretted leaving so much behind and one night he picked up a rope he found lying next to one of the rings. He wandered out to the door of the stadium, took a look at the trees and picked out the biggest branch. Thankfully he didn't go through with it and he recovered by working with prisoners and teaching them discipline through the sport of boxing.

On that trip in 1998 we didn't know any of Nicholas' personal problems. I guess we were just too young and too selfish at the time, presuming our performance in the ring was all that mattered. But he was still a great coach and despite the troubles that must have been torturing him in the background and he helped Paddy Hyland and myself to medals. I won a bronze out there after being beaten by a Ukrainian and over the years as I've been going through the ranks, you fight guys you'd never see again. That Ukrainian has disappeared altogether. So it's great that I have stuck at it for so long and I got my reward in Beijing. Or did I?

What became of them, I now wonder, as the glass in front of me nears empty? Do they have it better than me now, despite me staying the course and crossing the finishing line?

"Throw on another two there when you've a minute."

I tried other sports along the way through my teens. I played a bit of soccer with the lads down the fields. One time the whole estate organised a five-a-side competition and while I wasn't good enough to play on proper teams, basically because I wasn't great with the offside rule and had no interest, I was put in goal. The goals were only small and in the first game I stood there thinking, 'this will be easy'. But there was a lad down the other end, Tom Ryan, like an egg with legs. The sidelines were full with locals and he kicked the ball out as hard as he could, it was coming towards me, I ran out and said I'd catch it. But all I could see were their players running in my direction, the ball bounced in front of me, went over my head, I turned around and chased it back but it went in. Standing there I was thinking the sooner I got back to a boxing ring the better.

But it's all good winning All-Irelands from 11 to 18, but what if it ends there? What if you don't win a senior? The early years aren't really important in the greater scheme. There are so many lads out there winning junior and intermediate and then it stops. On top of that, Noel had always wanted that senior title that Willie couldn't provide and while I felt the pressure of that, I was still delivering. So much so that I did the Leaving Cert Applied course because I wasn't spending enough time in school.

I was very good at carpentry when I was in Moyle Park but that was about it and back at home, I have a mirror and a chair in the house that I made. I was good with my hands, and even if I wasn't the smartest, at least I had that. We had a young woodwork teacher, Mr McNulty, and he'd come into the school in his yellow-reg Calibra and we thought this thing was amazing. He was really proud of it too, was always talking about the engine size and this and that. He was a lovely man but now when I have bad days like this, and when I drink and get depressed, I wish I'd gotten a trade. I wish I'd become a carpenter and wasn't totally reliant on boxing. Instead, when I could have been doing something like carpentry, I was more interested in something my brother never quite achieved. I know that once I did achieve that, there was no going back.

As it happened I won junior, intermediate and senior titles

within eight months and got caught up in that torrent of success. Only Wayne McCullough and Bernard Dunne had achieved that so it wasn't bad company to be keeping. But Noel never saw it. Sadly, he passed away in 1999.

I was in the ring at the National Stadium training for the World Junior Championships in Hungary, but someone came in and mentioned that he was after having a turn, was sick, something wrong with his head. I sparred that evening but wasn't right, got punched around and I got out of the ring, had my shower, went to the canteen and Dave the chef came over to me. *"Jesus Kenneth, I'm awful sorry for your loss." "Ah yeah, no bother,"* I replied. I don't know why but it didn't register. I was still thinking I'll check in on him in the hospital and cheer him up but then my parents told me. It happened so quick. He hadn't been ill before but got this cyst on his brain and that was it.

He was a really serious man, a very proud guy. One time in the car he was asking me would I ever be interested in turning professional. I didn't think I was good enough for that. I thought to go that route you had to be the best of the best. Now I know anyone can do that, but still, he was glad when I said I didn't think it was for me because an Olympic Games was what he was looking for. It was nine years after he passed that I did make it that far but by then he was long gone. He wasn't around even to see the senior title he dreamed of. That affected me greatly because he was there right the way through, for years after setting the place up in Neilstown, coaching with kids every night, organising club shows, driving it forward. He was the heart and soul of the place, but he missed the club's finest moment.

He even missed going to visit George Foreman's club in Texas, a trip we went on shortly after Noel died. I was due to fight but my ankle swelled up on the plane so I couldn't box but all the young lads did and I ended up doing the corner. It was still worth the journey just to meet Foreman though. He brought us to one of his restaurants, fed us all, was bringing down the iced tea himself, and then brought us to a church beside his house. He's there every Sunday morning, playing guitar with this huge towel in his hand wiping the sweat off his face. He had this blue shirt covered in damp patches and all the black guys were standing up shouting Hallelujah. It was great craic.

****

By 2001 I wasn't going to enter the intermediate championships but my brother Willie told me that I might as well try them to get to senior. So I did and won and I entered the seniors as a 19-year-old, a complete underdog. Still, I knew I was getting better. I got into CityWest and Willie was acting like my coach, and did a lot of pad work with me. Things were changing on the sparring front too. Years ago he had me on my knees all the time, catching me with great body shots but there was one time we were down in Avoca, and I punched the head off him. There was blood coming out of his nose and into his mouth and I actually felt very sorry for him because it had dawned on him that times had moved on. He said, *"That's it, enough."* And I haven't sparred him since. He's six years older and by then was carrying a bit of a pot belly. His last fight was in Waterford not too long after that, at a club showdown, and while he won, they had to squeeze him in through the ropes.

But if beating Willie was a tremor, sparring Kevin Walsh in Athy shortly after was an earthquake. He was the 2000 senior champion and that was a big deal for me, because I was thinking this would be a good gauge of how long it would take me to get to the top. Next thing I was thumping him and had him in trouble. I left that ring saying to myself, "I've a good chance of winning this middleweight title" and even more so when I beat Walsh in the first round of the 2001 seniors and made it to the final to face Conall Carmichael, a knockout merchant from Holy Trinity in Belfast. RTE used to show a clip at the start of their coverage of him flooring Ian Tims but thankfully it didn't happen to me and I beat him 11-6. We brought the cup back to my local pub Boomers and filled it up with all sorts.

But my cup here is nearing empty and so is my resilience. I don't want any more but I don't know what else to do and as we put on two more, I look at Stephen. Suddenly I feel my body shaking and my eyes welling up and it all comes out. For a while now I've known it but just couldn't admit it. Now I do. I break down in tears. *"Steve, this drink is killing me."* He tells me he'll help me whatever way he can but he's in limbo after his break-up too. *"What are we at man?"* I say. *"We have to go back to all that stuff at home in a couple of days, only we've made it much worse."* All he can respond with is that we'll deal with that when we get to it, but we might as well enjoy this now.

Sometimes he's great to have here. But right now when I am hitting rock bottom and I know there is trouble at home, never once does he say that I am drinking too much. Someone needs to tell me but does it come back to everybody owing me something? Is it his place to even say that? He's not my father or my mother or my brother. Besides, I'm sure he has his own troubles and maybe he is afraid to say it because if I stop his party will be over as well and he'll have to face his reality. I've never asked him about how he feels. So why should he ask me?

At least he takes my attention off my misery for a short while. He reminds me that James Moore will be here in a while and he points out a Rod Stewart look-a-like that's sitting further down the mahogany bar. There is my lift again, the little thing that brings me back on track and makes me want to continue the session. We get talking to him and he has this American accent at first, but the more we talk, the more a twang from home comes out until he admits he's from Limerick. We hit the jukebox. *'Maggie May'. 'You Wear It Well'. 'Do Ya Think I'm Sexy?'*

With that we are singing and dancing and asking the guy for a photo but he refuses. Our commotion brings another photo request. This time it's an Irish couple who tell me I've made the Six-One News back home. One of the main stories. I barely made it that high up for getting to an Olympic final. I ask if they are joking but it's all true. Seemingly there's more too. There's a Gift Grub sketch out and Stephen gets it up on his iPhone. It's a skit of Joe Duffy trying to find me on Liveline. He calls me but only gets my voicemail.

"Hi, you've reached the voicemail of Kenny Egan. If you want to get off with me, press one. If you want me to turn up at an opening, press two. If you want me to turn up at an opening and get off with me, press three. If you want to arrange a photo of the above, press four. To box, press five. Please leave a message after the bell. Ding, ding."

Stephen and I both laugh but I turn down the photo request because it's gotten more out of control than I ever thought. I have to call Mam. That's a hard thing to do and I shiver when I hear the foreign dial tone and then her petrified voice. First thing she asks is if I'm alright. Then she tells me I had better come home straight away. I tell her I'll be back on Tuesday but that's not good enough, she says she wants me back now. She thinks I can just come back this second but she settles for Tuesday in the knowledge that I'm alive, even if I'm far from okay.

I hang up and after that conversation there's a few moments of an awkward silence. Finally Stephen reiterates that we're here now and might as well enjoy it. *"Besides,"* he says, pointing at the clock that's about to strike one, *"James Moore will be down any minute. He can have a chat with you about it all. It will be alright."*

I agree, this path seems easier as I flag down the barman.

"Two more of your finest there. We're running a bit dry over here."

CHAPTER 4

1.00pm

A man walks into a bar. Myself and Stephen look past our pint glasses, along the polished surface of the mahogany, and see James Moore staring back at us. There's no joke here though. It's obvious to me he's not the same person that left Irish shores and the amateur programme quite some time ago. Granted, he was always a serious character who loved a good row in the ring and always fancied it toe to toe, but he seems absent-minded and a little distant now, distracted by his own circumstances. He shakes our hands and the half-cut state of the two of us in the middle of the day briefly brings a smile to his face. *"You didn't waste time. How many have ye had?"* he asks.

But after that there's not much call for humour. Life hasn't worked out for him as he expected. He's lost a couple of fights in recent times, his perfect record and decent ranking disappearing with much of his confidence. Because of all that, it turns out that he's been wondering more and more if he's made a mistake turning professional and coming over here. Besides, these days he's making his money like an ordinary Joe, pouring drinks and serving up food as opposed to throwing punches. And it's far too late to go back. He seems trapped.

He looks at me with a hint of jealousy that proves he doesn't know the real Kenneth Egan these days, and also proves that I am getting better at hiding how I feel. In 2001, '02, '03 he was champion and then Henry Coyle came along in the 2004 seniors and beat him to a proper shot at the Olympics. That was a huge upset because no one saw it coming. That win saw Coyle go and lose two qualifiers and when James was only given his chance in the final qualifier, it was too little, too late. He went to the pro ranks without going to an Olympics but here he is sitting with someone who has an Olympic medal. For him, it must feel like that's the result of a choice he made and got horribly wrong.

He doesn't expect it but I mirror his expression of jealousy. So here we are, two men who thought they had it all going for them but who quickly learned self-doubt, and have slipped into a self-absorbed world of pity. Where else would you find such characters at one o'clock in the day but in a bar?

He asks me about this trip, life after Beijing, the reaction back home, how my world has changed, and I bluff it. From somewhere I summon positive words and tell him it's all good. *"Sure you know yourself, living the dream."* Everyone has their problems. It's just that everyone doesn't realise as much and I get away with playing the role of the man who has it made. I've become good at that. I get bigger and louder on the outside while I shrink and shrivel on the inside. However, I can only lie for so long, so rather than admit this life isn't all it's made out to be, I make sure to change the conversation quickly. To better times. Bygone times. To times that help me cope with the present.

"You remember the 2001 World Championships," I say as I call him a drink.

I know he'll like this because it was then in Belfast that he had his eight minutes of fame. A load of us made it to the quarter-finals then, including me, but he went one better and took home Ireland's only medal, collecting a bronze at welterweight in a tournament where Cuba beat up the rest of the world. That was when boxing was fun, because we were innocent, even if we weren't all that good.

"How many medals did we win again?" he retorts, knowing the answer well. I laugh as we live out the present thinking of the past.

But for me, just making the last eight was some achievement and we both know it, not only because of the average place I had reached as a fighter, but because of circumstances beyond my control as well. After Noel Humpston passed away there was no structure to fall back on, so between 1999 and 2003 there was this void that meant there was little chance of improvement. Like most of that team, I was fighting on with heart, not with head, in a typically valiant but flawed Irish way that meant while I may have gone down in flames, I still went down.

"Ah yeah, but who has the Olympic medal?" I remind him, pushing away thoughts of the chaos it's brought me.

Around that time in 2001, I was training in the Stadium the odd day and in my own club the rest of the time. But I didn't even have transport, so my Dad would drop me to CityWest before he went back into work at 10 in the morning and I'd get the 69 bus home from there when I was finished training. It only came once an hour though and it was like that for two years, wandering around with a bag on my back, staring down the road and mistaking lorries for buses. But even that was the easy part because when training was at the National Stadium on Dublin's South Circular Road, it was two buses each way — the 51 and then the number 18. I had to train but this is what I went through and it was against this background that I was fighting in Belfast.

Funny thing was I had been driving before that. When I was in Kylemore College I had this white Toyota and I'd go into school in it thinking I was great. Sure I was underage and had no insurance and the fumes out of this thing must have opened a hole in the ozone layer over west Dublin. A few years on, I was introduced to John McKeown from Nivea and he set me up with a car through a sponsorship deal, although the bad habits I collected as a kid saw me fail my driving test first time around.

And aside from the poor transport and support structure, there just wasn't the coaching structure around me either. In fact, it wasn't around for anyone in Irish boxing. An ex-boxer by the name of Gerry Fleming took over and he did great things in my club, but he'd admit himself he wouldn't be the most technical coach. He was a great volunteer and a great man for organising stuff and he did exactly what Noel did; getting fights for kids, registering them, keeping them busy and off the street. That was important because Neilstown was a rough area, a lot of drugs and robbed cars, although it's calmed down in more recent years. There was never enough outlets for young people there so what Gerry was doing was invaluable to the community, but in terms of where I was at in my career back then, I needed something more.

It's so strange then that things went so well at those first World Championships. After winning the senior title in February, I went to the Four Nations between Ireland, England, Scotland and Wales and won that too. I was flying and thought I was now a serious fighter, although the things I've learned since have showed me I was nothing special around then.

We trained down in Limerick in the National Coaching and Training Centre before those Worlds, getting a £50-a-day allowance but at least the company was valuable. Carl Froch was part of the camp, long before he went on to win a world professional title. As was David Haye, long before his world heavyweight crown. You wouldn't have recognised him because he was skinny back then and was only a pup without the arrogance that came later. But even then you could see he had a touch of class, although I can bet the Reynolds brothers, Alan and Stephen from Sligo, who were part of the Irish team and around Haye's weight, didn't see it that way as he smacked them around a ring. He actually went on to win silver at those championships, eventually losing out to Odlanier Solis in one of the greatest fights you'll ever see. Haye was 9-2 up within a minute and was close to a knockout, but he was 31-17 down when the referee had enough of it in the third.

If our performance in Belfast would turn out to be relatively impressive, the accommodation wasn't. We stayed in Stranmillis College and you wouldn't raise chickens in the place. The Cubans landed and they don't come from anywhere fancy but they refused to stay there. They decided they'd leave and find a hotel and the Yanks were the same. We said we'd stick with it though as it was only for two weeks, although some of us regretted that call when we saw breakfast. When we got up the first morning, there was a big greasy fry awaiting us. And it went on like that. Rashers, sausages, pudding, eggs. During the World Boxing Championships?

By the finish we had six in the quarter-finals. I got beaten by a Cuban called Yordanis Despaigne but I was still proud. My parents even came up for a few fights. With my younger brother John doing his Leaving Cert they didn't want to leave him at home alone, so they were commuting up and down. The night of that quarter-final they were trying to get a bus up except there was too much traffic. So they had to go over and ask a neighbour would they mind driving to Belfast. *"Do us a small favour?"* my Ma asked. It wasn't exactly like asking for a lend of some sugar or a drop of milk. Of course they said yes, but she still wouldn't watch it. She just wanted to be in the vicinity because it all seemed such a big deal.

Willie was there for the lot of it. He was almost my coach at that stage and stayed on my floor. He even took a week off work from the Army. These days he's a sergeant and loving it because I reckon the higher you get in that place the less you do. From the time I was eliminated, we were on the gargle. I was delighted with reaching the last eight and one morning myself and John Paul Kinsella, a small flyweight of 51 kilos, came back to the room. I knocked on the door, stuck the head in and there was Willie lying on the floor with this girl.

"What's the story?"

"You know yourself. Go on, I'll talk to you later."

So I did go on. I walked away from the room with the best intention of leaving him at it, but saw this fire extinguisher on the wall of the hall and had an idea. I grabbed it, turned back towards the room, but as I looked up, full of mischief, there was Willie standing at the door, shaking his head. I don't know what it says about me that he was possessed to double-check that I was gone so he could continue in peace. I asked him much later and he said it went too quiet for his liking.

But with everyone eliminated except for James Moore, we were getting up to more and more devilment. Late into the second week we went down to the Wellington Bar one morning to get rid of some sore heads from the night before. There was a big gang of boxers and coaches and we started ordering drink early and fast. With the bill mounting and the barman getting agitated, someone let a roar out to put it on the Irish Amateur Boxing Association tab. With that the pace picked up, as did the price of the drinks of choice. Someone in the staff must have made a call though because it wasn't long before the IABA president Dom O'Rourke walked in the door and let a thundering roar out of him. *"Cancel that tab."* He had a huge, angry head on him and we all broke down laughing.

As the best boxers in the world got ready for their final bouts, we were happy with just having been competitive and we were living it up on the back of that. Noel Montieth, a lightweight from Belfast, threw us a barbecue in his back yard. Willie thought he knew everything, appointed himself as head chef and then threw a bottle of lighter fluid onto the coals, nearly burning the whole house down. The back yard was full of smoke and Noel had to find his way through it to shut the door and save a fair amount of furniture. Those were good days. James Moore was there that day, just as he's here now. But while we've both grown and followed our dreams, neither one of us looks very happy about it.

We get talking about others on that team and what became of them. Guys like JP Kinsella who never made it big after missing out on a medal by a point in Belfast but got on with life and got into coaching and settled down. Guys like the Reynolds brothers who kept taking the big hits and coming back for more. Guys like John Duddy who has made it to a point in the professional game and has a perfect reputation, unlike the one I've been getting back home while on this trip. I think of Duddy and how he dealt with disappointment and kept on going. He had it from the day he was born. He got his name from his uncle John 'Jackie' Duddy. He too was a boxer and on January

30, 1972, some things about the Derry air must have reminded him of stepping out onto the canvas. The noise, the frantic excitement, the heavy breathing, the adrenaline and buzz and suddenly, the sharp shock of pain. At just 17 years of age he was there on Bloody Sunday and he was the first to be shot. Initially those around him thought that it was a rubber bullet until they saw the look of anguish in his face. His life was ended that day. And so John came into the world, sharing that name but he has made life look easy. How did he deal with all that? And why can't I? Why am I feeling sorry for myself?

"You remember that trip to Poland," says James, speaking of 2002.

"How could I forget it?"

"You blamed your hand."

"It was my hand."

"Yeah, yeah."

The incident he's talking about was one that got me and my funding suspended for quite a while. After the seniors that year we travelled to Eastern Europe for a set of internationals, one on a Thursday, the other on Saturday. Times were beginning to change in Irish boxing because, up to that point, different coaches would go on different trips. But Billy Walsh came on this trip and introduced consistency. Billy had been in Belfast at the time of the World Championships and had enjoyed our memorable barbecue. There was a friend of his, Matthew O'Gorman, a brother of the former Wexford hurler Larry, and he was a big man at the time and had travelled up to Belfast to order T-shirts. So Billy said he'd go with him and take in the boxing. First off they went into this clothes shop though, and the woman behind the counter was asking Larry did he want large or extra large.

"Do you have FM?" he asked.

"What's FM?" asked the woman.

"Fucking massive."

Nicholas Cruz had asked Billy in 2000 to be his assistant for the Olympics but that Polish trip in 2002 was his first time to go away as a coach and it was a huge honour for him. I lost on the Thursday and by Saturday myself and Stephen Ormond had gone missing, or that's what they said had happened. I don't know about Stephen, but I had hurt my hand and wasn't up to another fight. But Billy walked by this bar and saw me with a pint in front of me. His face said it all, but that didn't stop him storming in and firing a volley of furious words. I tried to explain what happened, said I'd damaged something in my hand, and that there was a lot of pain over one of the knuckles where the ligament kept slipping. He argued, and I argued back telling him that he wasn't a doctor. I didn't know him well at this stage and the two of us weren't exactly impressed with each other.

In fairness, what he did next impressed me as much as it amused me. He was 38 at that stage and the Pole I was supposed to be fighting had a major sponsor coming to look at him. So Billy wasn't going to give him a walkover and at one stage I walked past the dressing room and couldn't believe what I saw. Billy was there, with his large moustache squeezed into a head guard and he had his hands taped up. He was so angry about my perceived lack of pride in the Irish jersey and the fact that he had paid someone to cover for his job back home, that he decided he would fight for Ireland himself. Meanwhile, I was busy propping up a bar in his eyes.

He got some gear off the other lads and filled his mouth with cotton wool to act as a make-shift gum shield and was ready to go. Brian McKeown was the other coach and Billy told him that if he hadn't knocked out the Pole by the end of the first round, he was to throw in the towel. He was going out the door, and Oleg, the Polish physio, saw him and started shouting down the corridor. *"Billy, no. No, Billy. No. No. Please Billy, no."* In the end his begging worked and Billy took the gear off without a punch being thrown.

It was funny at the time, but after that there was a big fall-out. On past trips, all of that would have been ignored but even before the High Performance Unit, Billy saw the need for the culture to change if Irish boxing was ever to become a force to be reckoned with. Looking back, he was dead right at the time be-cause even at the airport before leaving Poland, I was sitting with some of the lads drinking pints in our Irish gear while watching the 2002 World Cup. But back then I couldn't believe Billy was being so strict. By the time I'd arrived home Billy had filed a report to the IABA, who suspended my money for six months. I wasn't even informed of the decision and, in fact, didn't find out until the day envelopes were being handed out, and there was none there for me. With no sports grant, I wasn't earning a penny and work wasn't easy to come by even though I was senior champion at the time.

Over the years as boxers we accepted that we weren't rec-ognised, although now I wish that was still the case. If you were a GAA player who had won an All-Ireland you would be a hero in your home town. But we trained just as hard, succeeded as much but just had to accept our place. So instead of dreaming of something big coming along on the work front while my money was withheld, I went back to being a part-time waiter at CityWest. There would be times when I'd be working at weddings up there in little slacks and a dicky bow with all these auld ones getting gargled and grabbing me by the arse. *"How are ya son?" "Jaysus you are gorgeous son."* It was actually good fun and Christmas parties were the best because I always asked to be put on the Peter Mark table as most of the girls there were stunners.

But after every gig up at CityWest I'd be waiting on my money to come back from boxing. I asked what was going on but I was told that there was a lot of stuff that needed sorting out for it to return, and I couldn't get a cheque until they held a central council meeting. I told them again and again my hand was hurt but drink and my behaviour was brought into it. I spent a long while working away in CityWest until finally I was cleared and all the money was paid back. But that wasted energy cost me a place at the European Championships in Russia that year and that hurt the most.

It could have gone wrong for me and Billy at that point. In

hindsight, he was the one in the right, but it took time to get to know him and to learn to respect him and what he had achieved. I didn't realise it then but he had been there for my spar with Kevin Walsh in 2000 in Athy and as we grew closer in the gym he admitted he was there in 1996 to see me lose at underage. Or as he likes to put it himself, *"When Kenneth was this big star in the making and some young lad came up from the country and beat him."*

****

To take the focus off me, I remind James Moore that he had a run in with Billy when he was trying to lay down the law as well.

"Remember you couldn't handle the technical stuff?"

"Ah, it wasn't that bad," he laughs.

But it probably was. Billy was trying to introduce more and more methodical coaching and James was getting frustrated. He took off his gloves, threw them away, and said *"fuck this".*

"Billy told you to get back in the ring or get out the door of the gym and stay out."

James goes quiet. So I fill the silence.

"You were quick enough getting back in."

We both giggle.

In fairness to James he was that bit older than me and was more set in his ways. He always just wanted to get into the ring and scrap, and he could get away with it for the most part because he had this great engine. That was his way and he found it hard to change. But if James's attitude was understandable, so was Billy's. And the more I got to hear about his back story, the more I liked the guy. We all knew he was a boxer from his battered nose and we knew he had won a few national titles. But that was where our knowledge of Billy Walsh stopped until little bits trickled into place over the years.

His family was from Wexford with a strong GAA background, and his aunt was an All-Ireland camogie winner. As for Billy, he was a hurler and a footballer but was a bit wayward and when a boxing club started up in school, his father went to the Christian Brothers and asked them to take him on board. He excelled at boxing just like he did at any sport he played. He boxed his way to an Irish under-14 title the same year he was playing hurling and football for his county. By the time he was a minor he was captain of the footballers and owned four Irish titles in the ring. But then came a roadblock in his GAA career. He happened to be on the minor hurling team that lost to Kilkenny after being five points up with six minutes to go in a Leinster final. They'd beaten the same team at under-14 when he was in the middle of the field in 1977 in Croke Park and they won by two points. But he couldn't take the loss the following year, so at the final whistle he slammed his hurl into the ground and said he was going to the Olympic Games. He wasn't hanging around to be relying on 14 other fellas any longer.

It turned out to be a good call. He won the intermediates at 18 despite breaking a hand in the semi-final. Then he won the seniors the following year and with six spots available for the Los Angeles Olympics of 1984 he was well placed. One Saturday evening in May he had his sweat gear on in the gym trying to make 64 kilos when an announcement came over the radio that the team had been picked. His name wasn't on the list so he took off his gear, walked out of the gym and didn't come back until October. The decision to leave him out of the team completely floored him. But the more we got to know Billy Walsh the coach, we realised how strong Billy Walsh the boxer had been. And ultimately, how strong Billy Walsh the man really is.

He would have had his 21st birthday at those Games and watched on as a British fighter called David Griffiths made the third round, a guy he had knocked out before. So he retreated to GAA, and won a county football medal with Sarsfields, and got beaten in a hurling final replay lining out with Fayth Harriers.

He lost his boxing title for two years but was back in time for selection for the Seoul Games four years later. But that was another disaster that haunts him to this day. The day the High

Performance programme started for us, Gary Keegan laid out what he'd give us in terms of strength and conditioning in return for our commitment. He then asked Billy to tell us his personal story about those 1988 Olympics. Billy's eyes flooded and he cried. He started off telling us how he stood in the middle of the pitch for the opening ceremony, how it was the greatest day of his life and how he and Mick Carruth were hugging each other and telling each other that they'd made it. From there it went downhill.

At that time no one was travelling abroad to exotic locations. People were lucky to get as far as Spain. As for Asia, few had ever even heard of it. It was fantastic. He had been out there for the pre-Olympics six months earlier and fought a local guy called Song Kyung-Sup and knocked him out cold. There were 401 host nation competitors at the opening ceremony. Billy could barely distinguish the difference until he somehow spotted this guy, Song, and reckoned he must be damn good if he could come back for more after the punishment he'd taken. Next thing they drew each other in the first round and Billy, who never cut, started bleeding and the referee stopped the fight.

He was the first Wexford man to make the Olympic boxing team and there were great celebrations and fundraising back home for him. There was huge pressure resting on his shoulders after all the goodwill. Later, I'd understand that from my own experiences. There were no phones out there either to call home, so Telecom Éireann had telegrams with good luck messages that athletes would collect in the office each day. Problem was, the messages Billy was getting were *'Please ring home'* because they all wanted to know what was happening and if he was okay. He'd tell us how he cried for a week, because he was thinking at 25 his career was over. His wife was two months pregnant and he needed to get work and get money.

Soon after he came home, he and his teammates went out one night after winning the football league, and ended up in the chipper. He swears it never happened but the lads started a rumour that he dropped his pants around his ankles, bent over

OK, so let's get the embarrassing
pictures out of the way... here's one
of me as a toddler with Mam

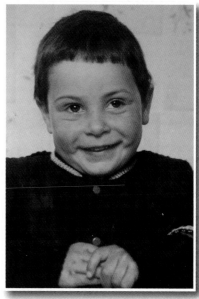

... and here I am in my early school
days, and left, standing to
attention on my Communion Day

Messing around the back garden with Dad, John and Tony after I smashed my wrist when I took a fall off my bike aged nine

... taking a well-earned break with my brothers John (left) and Tony

Looking, eh, sharp for my Confirmation back in 1995

Taking on George Foreman during our trip to Texas in 2000

Lining out with the lads from the club during the Texas trip which was an amazing experience, and (below) with Joe Frazier in Philadelphia

Slugging it out in the ring aged just 14, and (below) having a laugh in the dressing room during an away club match in Waterford

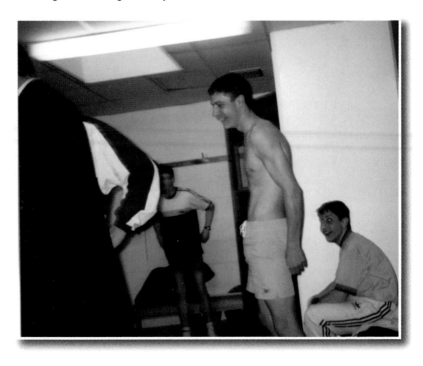

Receiving the trophy from Michael Carruth after winning my first Seniors in 2001, and below, then celebrating with all the lads from Clondalkin who have always been a huge support to me

A proud time as I line up for my first senior international with (from back, left to right) Michael Roche, myself, James Moore, Eanna Falvey, Stephen Reynolds, Alan Reynolds, (front) Michael Kelly, JP Campbell, Damian McKenna, Liam Cunningham and Noel Monteith

I didn't realise that back home had gone Olympic crazy and that the family house was mobbed. Here's Mam keeping her fingers crossed for me before my first fight

and started singing, *"I was in Seoul, take a look at my hole."* But he was far from finished with boxing. He went back to the club, and took up coaching. They had one guy called Tom Connors who was going to the seniors at light-flyweight and Billy was sparring him and knocking lumps out of him. Three weeks before those national championships, Billy started to feel out of shape and decided to go out jogging with Connors. At the start he couldn't keep up but after a few days Billy started to catch him and then eventually beat him.

Then, the night before the seniors, they went to Michael Carruth's club, in Drimnagh in Dublin, to check weights as was tradition. He weighed himself out of curiosity and came in at 70 kilos. The next morning Billy entered the light-middleweight section and incredibly became the 1989 champion with a couple of knockouts along the way.

He was working for a guy called Mick Miller and asked him initially for Fridays off which was not a problem. After those Senior Championships Mick asked what his plans were because he'd heard Billy had been picked for the national team to go to the States. Billy had no intention of travelling to the US and said he just wanted to keep his job but Mick told him to go, that he would still get paid and he could work the hours when he came back. And soon he was boxing his best. He was picked for the European Championships but didn't go with a baby due. But he did go to the World Championships in Moscow.

Nicholas Cruz was over at that stage and had the team training in Billy's home club of St Ibar's/St Joseph's in Wexford town. Billy would get up and go for a run on the beach and afterwards while the rest of the team went to train in his backyard, he had to skip the session to go to work. He'd work from nine till half four and meet the team again. Those few hours of training that were lost may well have been the difference between winning a medal and the disappointment he encountered. At those championships he saw Carruth win a bronze medal but Billy lost his quarter-final to a guy from Cairo called Salem Karim Kabbary. Seemingly, later that night Billy was the butt of the jokes from the rest of the squad in the nightclub as they sang *'Walk Like an Egyptian'* by The Bangles in his direction.

But, in fairness to him, Billy kept going. He seemed to keep going forever. He won the senior Irish title in 1990 but in 1991 Carruth moved up a weight and Billy moved down, so the two of them were drawn together in the first round of the Senior Championships. Billy stopped him, but was again beaten at the quarter-final stage of the European Championships. At least he won gold at the first EEC Championships in Denmark but that was a title that never meant a whole lot and Carruth was picked to go to the World Championships. But that wasn't the end of the saga. When Billy got off the plane from the EECs he was asked if he could go to Australia the following week because Carruth had broken his hand. Off he went. Quarter-finals again.

By 1992, he and Carruth were in the national final fighting for a place in the Olympic qualifiers, when Billy lost a tough battle. Some people found it hard to call, some told him that he won, others told him he lost. But history says he lost. There was no bitterness though because they were best mates. When it was over they hugged and said thank God that was the end of it because they could be normal again. Mick was younger and Billy was team captain and years earlier the two had shared a room on foreign trips.

In fact, Billy was in Carruth's sitting room the morning of that 1992 Olympic final. RTÉ invited him up to do an interview. He didn't let on at the time, but he wasn't confident of Carruth's chances. Juan Hernandez was in the other corner and was a 6'2" southpaw welterweight who seemed untouchable. Billy looked around the room and was dreading what was coming, wondering would everyone be in tears by the end. Noel Humpston was sitting beside him that day and as the final progressed Billy couldn't believe it. Carruth was one up after the first, level after the second and the Cuban coach was getting more and more agitated.

We all know what happened next, and that golden moment

spurred Billy into yet another comeback. While he was coaching, a guy in his club told him he was in great shape, and with the maximum age limit being increased back up to 35, Billy decided to have another shot at the title. He went abroad for his first fight in four years and lost, losing to his namesake Billy Walsh from Cork, and broke his nose, and was then beaten in the first round of the National Senior Championships. At that point the show was over. At least his dad was happy because he'd always told him never to try to make a comeback, but Billy was stubborn and thought he was different to everyone else.

He brought all that experience to us as a coach. That skill, that stubbornness, that will to win and, most of all, a real taste of national pride. James Moore saw some of it before he left. I saw plenty of it over the years, and from a guy I had a shouting match with in Poland, he became a father figure in terms of boxing. My problem is that I need something else now and I probably need a different side of Billy. I know he can help me with this drink problem but first of all I'll have to admit my problem to him, and myself. I'll have to tell Billy that the drink's gotten out of hand, and that I'm sorry for running away and letting down the team. But that's going to be the hardest part. Maybe he will already know that there is this side of me because of what happened back in 2002. Or maybe he doesn't. Maybe he just put that down to getting away for a day or two after defeats, tournaments, after hours at the gym. I start arguing in my head with myself over how I should tell him. Or even, if I should tell him at all. And then I remember that Billy told me of a similar story of a friend of his, who has now been off the booze for a decade.

I froze as he told me the story because I could relate to every sentence, every word, every occasion of binge drinking, and of letting people down. Did he tell me this story for a reason?

Billy's pal was either on the drink or off it. Billy told him on a couple of occasions that he was killing his relationships around him because he was going out at eight in the morning, not eating, and falling in the door that night in bits. He just couldn't stop, Billy told me. His last bender lasted six months and he drank every day of it. Billy told him a couple of times if he wanted to go for a few in the evening it wouldn't be a problem, but he needed to cut back. His pal told him it wasn't like that. It had to be all or nothing.

And that's racing through my head as I take another gulp of beer and keep fighting the monster. But I don't give it away. Instead Stephen sits there as James and I talk about the good old days like two guys that saw too much, too soon, and suddenly feel very old.

CHAPTER 5

3.00pm

It's a strange and cloudy feeling to have been drinking so much, so early. New faces enter the bar, bright and bubbly, full of smiles and conversation. I exhibit none of that. I turn to look for the Irish couple that earlier asked for a photo and explained about the TV news back home, but they've already left. Their empty glasses and any trace of their presence whisked away without me even noticing. It's little moments like this which remind me that time is passing quickly while I sit still. And it makes me wonder how they can be content with just a couple of drinks, how they can just stop and head out to enjoy the daylight and fresh air. They clearly had something more to look forward to aside from the next round of drinks.

The world races by but it's like it's happening around me and I'm not a part of it. Instead I'm here at the stagnant centre, never stirring, just feeling my head getting heavier, my eyes struggling to focus. Meaningless sounds that never have registered previously begin to bother me as I get anxious and agitated. Sounds like someone speaking too loudly, the sirens of a police car wailing past or a song on the jukebox that I don't like. And despite the early time on the clock, there's always that worry that at some point today my body won't be able for any more drinking.

Then what? Go back to the hotel room? Take a shower? A nap? Try have a night's rest? Those things bore me and if I sleep away a few hours, it's a few hours closer to the end of this trip. And that's a few hours nearer to having to face the problem I've created at home. Maybe even my own alcohol problem for that matter, and I'm not ready for any of that yet.

I've often believed that I've hollow legs as far as alcohol's concerned, but today is taking its toll. The beer doesn't go down easy now with each swig getting smaller and each pint taking longer. So I stare behind the bar, squinting to make out one bottle from the next as I contemplate moving on to a beverage that might provide me with a quicker, sharper boost. James and Stephen are still here and the conversation has skipped away from boxing, but looking up and down the shelves on the wall, I get a flashback to the walls of the stadium and the words written there. The meaning of the sayings, the names painted underneath.

"The little things should be taken seriously and matters of great importance should be taken lightly."

–Andy Lee, 75kg Olympian and European bronze medallist.

"Pain is temporary but glory lasts forever. A warrior's body may want to give up but his spirit will carry him forever."

–High Performance Junior Squad.

"It's God who arms me with strength. He makes my feet like the feet of a deer, he trains my hands for battle; my arms can bend a bow of bronze. You give me your shield of victory, and your right hand sustains me; you stoop down to make me great - Psalm 18, 32-35."

–Katie Taylor, 60kg World Champion.

"Confront and overcome all your obstacles, success awaits at the other side."

–Darren O'Neill, 75kg.

"Prepare to fight, get ready for war."

–Paddy Barnes, Olympic Bronze Medallist.

"The man who truly believes he can win, can."

–Michael Carruth, Olympic Champion.

"Failing to prepare is preparing to fail. The harder you train in the gym, the easier it will be in the ring."

–Darren Sutherland, Olympic Bronze Medallist.

"Performance is my goal. If I perform to my best, I achieve my

goals."

–John Joe Joyce, European Bronze Medallist.

"Don't follow your dreams, chase them."

–Eamonn O'Kane, European Bronze Medallist.

"Nobody is a natural. You work hard to become good and then you work harder to become better."

–Ross Hickey, European Bronze Medallist."

All were written for boxing but all seem strangely applicable to my life outside the ring. I spent so many hours in that place and have seen all those phrases so often that they've stuck with me. And with my mind making its way around the High Performance gym on the South Circular Road over 3,000 miles from here, I come across my own saying that sits proud against the whitewash.

"Accept your mistakes but learn from them."

–Kenneth Egan, Olympic Silver Medallist.

I think about that for a minute and reflect. If I don't accept them, how do I learn from them? It seems harder to do that in life than in boxing. And what if it takes longer? It was 2003 when the High Performance Unit set us on the path to success but even that took an age to produce results. I went through so much to get to Beijing, I couldn't handle going through much more to get to sobriety. It seems an impossible journey, but then again, so did ours as a boxing team when we were introduced to Gary Keegan over six years ago.

Our first trip under that programme was to the World Championships in Bangkok that July of 2003. But the programme was so fresh that none of it had really kicked in and we were raw, as were the coaches and the arrangements. Indeed by the end of it, we were still wild and while it was an honour to be there, once we were beaten it quickly became a holiday and not a time or a place to look back and question our mistakes.

After the World Championships in Belfast in 2001, I came home and was watching 9/11 unfold on the news. Two years on and things still weren't good when the Americans travelled as a national team. But we were put in a hotel with them and a couple of other countries, instead of with the Eastern Bloc teams, and we were very worried, and hoping nothing went off. It was nervy stuff and there was quite a bit of security around us all. We had a bit of a training camp with the English there, but that was it, and there was serious humidity to adapt to. In the end I made it to the quarter-finals, losing out to the eventual gold medallist, Yevgeniy Makarenko from Russia. He was superb, 6'4", and an absolute animal and I wasn't anywhere near experienced enough to beat him. But once that was out of the way, it was time for some fun. That's the way we were still thinking. Enjoyment, rather than reflection on the failure to win a medal again.

Myself, Alan Reynolds and James Moore went for a walk to the market one day and I bought five DVDs for 50 cent each and put them in my back pack. By the time I was at the end of the road my bag was empty. I'd say there was some other stall selling the same discs for 50 cent not long after. But we were arrogant too, believing that just being an international athlete gave us certain rights, even if we hadn't achieved much in the ring. Once we had all been beaten, myself and a handful of others on that team hired out an entire floor of the hotel before we hit the town one evening, just in case we managed to bring back some women.

Turns out we did return with plenty of women but it put a dent in a few wallets. This gorgeous looking girl came over to me, really tall, straight black hair, and I took a shine to her and took her back to my room. At one stage I went into the bathroom for a second, but made the mistake of leaving the main door a little open, and when I walked back out another of the lads was in my bed having sex with her. I thought she had liked me, but she just wanted to ride a boxer. Once I caught them, all I could do was stand in line and wait my turn to get in. At least I've learned a little when it comes to women over the years since then, even if I'm foolish when it comes to controlling the rest of my life.

When I was a junior and came into the Irish set-up, Nicholas Cruz was over it all. There was one ring down the end of the gym and the rest was just floor space with bags on either side. So we spent a lot of time working on those bags and skipping and just hanging about but there was little time in the ring. Boxers from all over the country would come down on Saturday mornings and spar. You'd be there for hours waiting to get just one round in. Sometimes it started with heaviest first but if Nicholas started calling flyweights and lightweights, you knew you were in for a long day sitting around.

It was called squad training and there were two sessions at 11.00 and 14.30 or 15.00, with your lunch in the canteen in the middle. That was it then. Off you went after a day spent waiting to box. The national set-up was in no-man's-land and none of that was Nicholas' fault either. He was a nice guy doing his best while being treated badly, but higher up there was no structure, no plan, no real forward thinking. There was little Nicholas could do about it. It was years of that which led to performances like Bangkok where we left the arena without so much as a podium place between us.

In that regard, the High Performance was a blessing. Without it I wouldn't have achieved what I did and wouldn't have won what I did. That goes for anyone who ever performed well in an Irish vest in recent times. And it all began one day when Gary Keegan wandered in, wearing his suit and tie, and announced he was starting the High Performance Unit.

He mapped out what a world-class boxer looked like, which turned out to be Makarenko, and one day in the gym when we all came in, he got a line of red tape, ran it across the floor, stood on one side, while we all stood on the other. Then he started talking.

"I have shown you what world class might look like. I've shown you what it doesn't look like. We've all been brought together here to become world class, to take on a journey. None of us are there yet, including me. We have all just been identified as people who have the potential to go to that space. I want to take that on and I'm making a choice and a commitment to actually take this journey on and do everything I can in order to succeed."

From there he told us all he'd remove every excuse from the system, and said anyone who wanted to join him could cross over the tape but once we did, we had to take on a new way of existing and an athletic lifestyle with a proper code of conduct. There was even a contract for us to sign up to which told us what they'd deliver for us as athletes and then what we had to give back. For instance, up to that point there were four or five internationals a year. Soon that would change to 15 or 20 a year and we'd be mixing with the top nations. I had no hesitation as I liked what I was hearing. I was on a grant at the time and getting paid to train, so I said: let's get serious about it and see what I can make of myself. I stepped over the line, signed the piece of paper and that was it.

****

Gary had a five-year programme detailing what he wanted to achieve. We had an Olympics one year away, which was too soon, but off we went, training full-time at the National Stadium five days a week. That was the start of something special and there were thousands of hours of blood and sweat spilled before we reached the levels that everyone saw in 2008. That makes me nervous now because I worry there could be thousands of tears spilled before this new journey takes me from this bar to home and on to help. And I hope eventually to be able to deal with a life both me and the High Performance Unit have created. It's daunting looking up at the mountain. Sometimes it's easier to just turn away.

Gary had been part of the sport for 20 years before he came along to us. It was his family and his community. He always talked about the importance of boxing because while we were the guys coming out at the top, there were so many others in the urban areas that got a chance to actually learn some discipline, to achieve fitness and to get some structure into their lives while being kept busy a few evenings a week. He was clearly passionate about boxing's impact on struggling and poorer areas but that's all we knew of him initially.

But here he was, coming in from the other end. Here he was looking at an international perspective, looking at what was happening at the top of Irish boxing that caused us to be where we were. We had managed to qualify just one boxer for the Sydney Games and were looking like we were only going to achieve the same for Athens. Our performance as a nation at the highest level had been diminishing over the years and it was something we didn't seem to notice. Sometimes you can sit there and say we don't have the talent, or that the potential isn't there and we are doing the best with what we have. But maybe that was an excuse and a question had to be asked. Gary was the one to ask it. Was it something to do with how we were viewing our international opponents? Was it something to do with what we were doing ourselves?

It was an Irish Sports Council initiative called the Athens Enhancement Programme which got the punches rolling. They launched it in 2001 and boxing didn't actually get onto the list until 2003. The Irish Government decided to invest in high performance sport, particularly around the smaller Olympic events, and eventually boxing was considered. Soon they became interested in us because boxing had a history of success at Olympic level so they felt that was a high level we could return to in the near future and they'd get their money's worth. So in March 2003, Gary got the go-ahead.

Much like we found out about Billy's background in parts, the same was true of Gary and how the programme was formed. Once there was funding, he thought about how he wanted the structure to work. He decided that it had to be led by an Irish coach, Billy Walsh, so that someone from our island would, down the line, be recognised as world class and that would leave a legacy for the Irish system. He hated the thought of a load of international coaches coming in for four years, developing a system they wanted to own, and then leaving again.

But he did want an international coach as a number two. There had to be someone to bring international expertise to a gym that was devoid of it. The choice was simple. It had to be someone from Cuba or a coach from the old Soviet Union, the two superpowers of the sport. Gary looked at the Cuban style and believed that it would never have suited us. It was all about flair, a lot of movement, a lot of high-level skill, all traits way above us. Meanwhile, Russian fighters and those from ex-Soviet states were straight, clean, did the basics very well and he believed we could match that. Plus, with the ex-Soviet states, the technical element is backed up by a very strong physical component. They punch and move at speed so it's technique with strength that makes them very good. We could learn this much quicker than the Cuban style. So Gary targeted a coach from that part of the world.

I'd a feeling he'd go that way all along. Before he started the High Performance, he had brought over a Ukrainian to talk to us. He was a professor of boxing who wrote a book on the anatomical and scientific side of the sport. He had him down for a session with us and the coaches in Limerick and it was interesting stuff. He had one of the lads up at the front, took his foot underneath his arm and was trying to get him to use his hip in terms of throwing a punch. He noticed he wasn't using his back leg to drive his hip through a shot, so by taking the leg away he had to use his hip to get the extra inches.

Not so long before I came to New York, I was talking with Gary about what we had done with the programme and he told me he that he felt a lot of it was destiny, because several pieces dropped right into place, most importantly the discovery of international coach Zaur Antia. There's a Corkman called Dan O'Connell, a very experienced referee both in Ireland and internationally. And he had a friend who is a referee from Georgia, who happened to be the best friend of Zaur. They grew up as kids together, boxed as kids together, and their lives went from childhood to adults with families together.

Gary put out an advert on the web to get a coach to apply but Dan saw this and said, *"I know a guy, he's the head coach in Georgia, one of the best I've ever seen."* Gary insisted he apply and when he found out Zaur couldn't afford to come, he said they'd pay his way. Next problem was his English and he asked for an interpreter and because of the recommendation, he was allowed that too. In the end the job was between him and some coaches from England.

If you knew him, you'd realise Gary is the most methodical man alive and the interviews showed as much. He wanted a process to find the perfect assistant for Billy so he set out a formal questions-and-answers session. He also insisted that each applicant designed a programme they'd implement for a 12-week training cycle and then got them out onto the gym floor with us to put a specific part of that cycle into practice while the interview committee looked on. In Gary's eyes this was tough and it challenged the coach. And Gary's eyes are usually right.

With his English problems the committee was not impressed with Zaur's interview, but his training plan was superb, although some were questioning whether he actually wrote it. But the final part made sure Zaur got the job and changed Irish boxing forever. They put him out onto the floor with me and four other boxers and the committee watched in awe and the chairman of the interview panel Chris Kirwan knew they'd got their man.

The language of boxing is universal and the one thing Zaur had, even more significant than his technical skills, was the ability to laugh and joke and tell stories, even with his language skills in the way. Gary didn't want a strict Soviet disciplinarian. He wanted someone who had the characteristics not just to teach us but to get on with us and those two together could get us somewhere. Zaur also couldn't just target the most talented and leave the rest behind which is what Soviet coaches used to do. They'd zone in on the best and make them world champions, but with our limited numbers that wasn't an option. We couldn't allow that and needed him to be collectively interested. And he was all of those things and more.

His story was a difficult one though because once Gary offered him the job, he had to get him a visa, but he also had to be housed and managed because he was away from his wife and his children. But Billy and Zaur hit it off and a lot of love and care was given to make sure he worked for that programme. Gary had to be sure that he was happy to be part of the Irish set-up, and it wasn't just about flogging him for what he had. Gary had a plan to treat us as humans rather than just boxers and he wanted the same for Zaur. So he sent him home when he could, gave him extended holidays, brought his wife over when it was possible, then his sons, then his daughter. All of that was settling him in and making sure he could become a significant legacy for boxing in Ireland.

I'm fairly sure homesickness was the least of Zaur's worries though when he put us into a ring. He was there at the start, doing the basics like head movements, and hand and foot co-ordination. I'll always remember the look on his face. He was bemused because we were senior champions but to him we were like a bunch of misfits. In his eyes we were novices and it was his job to change that. And everything needed to be changed from body mass to how to throw a shot with increased power to increased accuracy to mobility in both attack and defence. He had to strip away everything we were doing wrong and start again. Just like we were kids, only he didn't have years to hone us.

****

With that my mind returns to this New York bar and I swivel around in my seat, take a look at James Moore and interrupt him. When you've enough drink on board you feel everything that comes into your head needs to be heard by everyone. So I put my arm around his back, start laughing, slur a little and bring the conversation back to boxing.

"You know what Zaur made of you when he first saw you?"

"I'm sure it wasn't just me, whatever you're about to say."

"When we told him at a training session that you'd won a bronze medal in Belfast he nearly choked, he didn't know how."

"Doesn't say much about ye lot then when it was me that did win a medal," is his comeback.

In fairness, part of Zaur did understand how James and Ireland won the occasional medal. When he was with Georgia, and came across any Irish team, he noted that we had good heart but that was where the compliments stopped. There just wasn't much boxing in us. We had a country of four million people, and every two years someone might pop up and win a few fights and a medal and that was it. There was no system. According to him, we didn't even know how to do a proper warm-up. We just went for a run whereas pretty quickly he introduced a warm-up that was technical and had purpose. He said to us that a warm-up had to be very specific for a complicated sport and since we were so far back, we could build our heart rate and work up a sweat while learning.

He started us off with the things he taught children back in Georgia years before and built on it. But his English isn't much better now than when he came. He went to school for a while but I think he gave that up. One day he got in a taxi and asked the driver to bring him to DCU. A little while later he was in the Phoenix Park, looking at lions and tigers and shouting at the driver, *"DCU, not the zoo."* He was disgusted because he had to pay extra and he was never one for spending money. Fair play to him though. He was 100 per cent committed and he was later offered big salaries to go to African countries after Beijing to get them ready for the 2016 Olympics in Rio. But he declined all offers, opting to remain with the Irish team and it was great to hear that.

If Zaur was the technical coach and Billy was a father to that team, Gary was still the brains behind it all. The story goes that when he pulled the team together initially he closed down the gym for three months. It was just the support team, the coaches and us. We didn't know each other too well because it had all been so scattered up to that point, and Gary didn't know too much about trying to put a system in place and trying to build a unit. What he wanted to do was lock down the place and any fall-outs, fights and mistakes that happened would happen behind closed doors. But most importantly he wanted us to learn as much as possible about each other in that time.

While we got to know each other, his role was to develop a system that would consistently stand us on podiums and given where we were at, it would take a lot to achieve it. So he went at it very much from a systematic perspective to ensure whatever he was bringing in, it was the right move at the right time. First up was the obvious alteration. The culture had to change and we were responsible for creating that. He targeted not only how we trained but what we believed in and how we behaved.

He went hard at those areas in that three-month lockdown. He was challenging us in a lot of areas from drinking water to making weights and tackling our diet. He was also determined that the length of our training match the intensity of training, and volume of training required. We challenged him and the coaches to an extent as well and at the end of that period, he settled on a medium and structured the entire programme based on what had happened in that time. From there it was very much on a trial and error basis but at least that was a start. Every corner we turned though, there was another new problem facing us but Gary was always coming up with solutions.

After those three months were up, Gary felt the programme needed to be officially launched to make a statement and a commitment. Not too many people took notice back then and who can blame them? But while the public were indifferent, Gary was excited. He sat us all down and told us that he had set a target for a podium in Beijing 2008, because Athens was too close at that stage. Those Games were just 14 months away and there was no way we could improve so quickly. In fact, even his Beijing target seemed a case of shooting for the stars given what Zaur was viewing downstairs on the gym floor.

We were under huge pressure, but the lesson we learned very quickly was that if we focused on results, we'd take our eyes off what delivers results. There was a huge lack of belief in us as well, growing out of years of mediocrity. While it was all well and good getting to strut around cities in Irish gear after early eliminations, hit bars, sleep with women and think we were superstars, in terms of competing with the best we were absolute nobodies. The boxing world didn't know us and neither did people in our own country and that was a real wake-up call.

We needed to build belief in performance and on the basis of the strengths and attributes we had, however limited. Gary reiterated that again and again, that we needed to stay honourable to that because we could get carried away and start focusing on the result or the failure, as opposed to the performance. He knew that through performance we could grow confidence and through confidence we could grow belief. It was building character while building boxers.

Boxing can be daunting when you look at the scale. At the World Championships in 2007, there were over 100 countries and not many sports can talk about that level of participation. So Gary, Billy and Zaur started looking at just Europe which, because of the break-up of the Soviet Union, was and is by far the strongest continent. On that basis, they reckoned if we could be competitive in the region, we could be competitive on the world and Olympic stage. But to do that we had to travel across Europe and learn everything we could. We had so much to learn as boxers, and they had to learn as coaches and administrators. The job was to build a network and bring everything we could back, and use it in an Irish way because we still wanted our own identity. We never wanted to be Russian or German or Cuban but we could learn from them. That was the approach taken by Gary and that's how we began moving forward.

People wanted results early and so did we, but while you've to learn how to win medals, before that you've to learn how to get to the medal rounds. Before that, clearly you've to learn how to get through the first round of the first fight, then the next one, then the next one. That's the kind of basics we were forced to return to. And it was always a learning process because even when things started going well, we got to a point where we were winning bronze medals and that was enough because we thought the job was done. I and the rest of the team had to change that mindset.

In our first year we did bring performance to another level and started doing things at multi-nations level but championship level was where we were targeting. We needed to select the right path and we needed to select competitions based on where we were at at that time. Gary couldn't just put us into multi-nations that were too hard for us. He had to try and select ones we could compete in, and eventually succeed.

Of course he wanted to take us to the toughest environment but we had to build towards that and the ultimate goal. In that sense, Russia was the end point. Training camps there were the target. But like building our way up in competitions, Gary had to build relationships with other countries to get there since being allowed to train with the Russian team is something very exclusive and we weren't even on their radar at that time.

Initially he looked at Britain but didn't bring us there because he felt a lot of the issues we faced as boxers, Britain was facing too. He visited their system and they let him in, but he could see these great ideas at the top weren't being implemented and weren't getting down as far as the boxers. Process is no good when something else is happening on the ground. Gary knew they were better than us in terms of investment though and at least he'd tried. Even if it wasn't for us, things were beginning to happen while we were training away.

Britain had this belief that we were messing, that we weren't a serious nation and they could let us in alright but we wouldn't learn. They reckoned this new High Performance programme would be full of energy for a year and then disappear and we'd return to our old ways. But if that opened a door there, it closed the door in other countries that we needed to help us improve. On that front, Gary still talks of what happened when he asked France for help.

After he came back from Britain, himself and Billy said they'd look at western European nations that were successful in a pre-dominantly eastern European-dominated sport. They wanted to know why these western nations were successful when we weren't. Take France. It wasn't traditionally known as a boxing nation but it was still a successful boxing nation. Their system was 20 years old and was churning out results, so Gary wrote to the French Director of Boxing. When he never responded, he wrote again and kept emailing and emailing to the point of near-harassment. But Gary's persistence paid off almost four months later, when the French invited us to attend a training camp before the European Union Championships. It wasn't exactly a big event but it was our first step into the world of high-performance preparation with a team that was successful.

They invited us to INCEP in Paris, the institute for sport in France, and they put us up in this accommodation in sweltering heat with no air conditioning. But that didn't matter. Gary pulled us together on the first morning and told us that it had taken a lot to get us to this camp, so there was obviously a serious issue with our international credibility. So we needed to make an impression. We needed to look like professionals, behave like professionals and spar like we were well prepared. We had to be on the gym floor early, leave the gym floor clean and leave our quarters clean. No messing. This was our chance to change perceptions we'd built up over time. In fact, it was our only chance because if we went back to our old ways there, other European teams would close the door on us for good.

Thankfully, we didn't step out of line because had that gone wrong, who knows where we would have ended up. Afterwards the French director took Gary for a cup of coffee, they got talking and Gary asked why it took so long to get a response, never mind an invite. The French guy said they didn't really want to allow the Irish in because we had a bit of a reputation. Gary asked for an example and he had one at the ready. He said he remembered being at an airport coming home from a cham-pionships and he saw a load of us, still in our Irish tracksuits, drunk and falling around and shouting in the departures area. He told Gary there was no way he wanted that culture near his team. He had his own challenges and didn't want to take that risk of us contaminating it. But at the end of it all, there was an upside. *"I took a chance on you this once,"* he said. *"But after this camp, I'd be glad to have your team back again."*

Our journey towards getting to the Russian training camp had begun. Gary quickly built up a relationship with their Director. Billy and Zaur got to know their coaches and studied and learned from them, and we were starting to build confidence in ourselves and our ability. Gary even noted that we had started to respect who we were, that we had started to stand a little taller and to think of ourselves as professional athletes by speaking the terminology. But we were not just talking the talk, we were beginning to walk the walk.

There was of course the odd discipline issue. It didn't all go that perfectly. Five of the team found the new regime too much and walked away. But that was part of growing into the system, we had to live with some failures. Gary kept the rest of us on track, told us that for him it was all about commitment and willingness to apply ourselves over the longer term. He taught us this mindset of continuous improvement, to keep searching for it, to keep coming back looking for it, to keep striving for it.

Gary kept the pressure on as well. After our positive experience in France came an invite to train in Germany. The French director introduced Gary to his counterpart across the border and that was a very different experience. The German culture was new and it was a little harder for the coaches to build friendships there. They had this attitude that if you had a huge pool of fighters, you find superstars and after that you don't need too much around them because superstars will always be superstars.

But from a testing and preparation perspective, Germany had a lot more science whereas the French had a better mindset. But Billy and Zaur still learned what they could out there. And while we improved from sparring with their boxers, what the coaches took home was more important. It was a week of testing ourselves for the boxers, but when we came home they had methods to actually improve us in the longer term. And because of that, every year we were a better team and that was a sign that they had planned their strategy correctly.

From those two countries, we took what we could, and we could always benefit from them in terms of preparation for a major championships. But in terms of building our system, Gary recognised that we needed to learn more. So he kept his sights set firmly on Russia. What was crucial was that right in front of him was Zaur who had worked as part of the Soviet Union team before the break-up and was so well respected. Not only had Gary got himself one of the top technical coaches in the world, he'd got the key to unlock the passage to Moscow.

Zaur had friends in high places and had the language, which was a massive barrier. There was only myself and four other boxers at the time because the team had shrunk but Gary still asked Zaur about the possibility of going there. I don't know what it was like for the rest of them but for me that was a hugely intimidating trip at the tail end of 2003. We all knew we were miles behind the Russians, but we had to see just how far behind we were, if we ever hoped to catch up.

On that flight to Moscow I didn't know what to expect and I don't know if I was ready to experience it all. But I had to. We all had to. It was about seeing what it was like and it was a massive opportunity to kick on to a new level. We knew we were going to experience pain, and the look on Gary's face on the plane suggested he was questioning his choice and his timing, but there was no turning back now.

We arrived in a Moscow airport, collected all the gear that was well packed and organised in terms of food and diet and equipment. We were a professional little team, we just weren't delivering professional results yet and pretty soon we'd be finding out why. We wandered out of the terminal where it must have -30C and there was this guy standing outside with the butt of a fag hanging out of his mouth. He was about 70 and had a military combat uniform on him, and he spotted us before we spotted him because we all had these jet-black tracksuits on.

Those were Gary's idea. He felt our poor results and our behaviour after continued failure was living proof that we had lost respect for the crest and for the Irish jersey. There were too many vests handed out and we hadn't done anything in them and it got to the stage where gear was dirty and creased and was being thrown around the place.

So before Russia he'd asked us for our tracksuits, put them in a black bag and dumped them into the skip. Then he introduced that black tracksuit. We are Irish, we are green, this was sacrilege, but he wanted to play with our minds a little and we got a crest on the shoulder which said 'Member Of The High Performance Team'. It was a statement and that tag was reminding us of what we were expected to become. Then he brought in a sprig of shamrock on the chest. He believed that we'd be going around and people would ask where we were from. It was only going to be temporary but the objective was to say that this is different, this is new, that the old ways were dead and buried. We'd grow to love it because it made us stand out, but this Russian guy was less than impressed as he finally let the fag butt drop from his mouth into the snow and guided us to the minibus.

We went over to it and as we were loading all our cases for this 10-day camp, we realised that the engine was in the middle of the bus. It was right there on the floor, sticking up, covered in these dirty blankets. The journey seemed to last hours and smoke was belching up all around us. My stomach was churning waiting to get there, and I don't know if it was this engine placement or the thought of what was getting closer.

Finally we got there in the evening and settled into the dark environment of our quarters but at least it was warm and dry. Then we were told the first session was at half-six in the morning. Lesson One: these guys train early. So we got up the next day, walked out of this accommodation block and the Russian team were standing in front of us. Sixty odd fighters lined up in the cold like an army regiment. We wandered out, tired and half-asleep, standing in shorts and GAA jerseys.

It was bloody freezing but we tiptoed our way into the line and stood there as their captain stepped out and gave them a talk. Eventually we made it as far as breakfast. A plate landed in front of me and there was this black cow's tongue in the middle of it.

It was only after travelling there several times that we realised their doctor manages the diet and their meals are structured. You are required to eat everything on the plate, and if you don't eat something it's not put on the plate the next time around. It was showing the importance of fuel for performance and that you have to respect food.

But whatever about learning about the protein content of some obscure part of an animal, I and the others learned plenty in the gym. We walked in and there were nine training rings and they were sparring at the intensity with which they competed. It was the same level that these guys fought at when they beat us up at major competitions.

It was hard going and Andy Lee was the only one of us who held his own, and I wasn't alone in coming out of there sore every day. The training we had been doing all our lives was very anaerobic whereas these Russians were all about training aerobically. The change of pace was very difficult but while it was very intimidating, it gave us a great indication of the standard we had to reach if we wanted to be achievers.

They were so much better than us in every way but at least we did get one over them at that camp. Billy knew fairly quickly that he wanted to design sessions that would give us the same intensity as they had in the ring and he had an idea. We had these heart monitors they were amazed by, so Gary through Zaur's interpretation asked if they were interested in having a couple of their fighters hooked up and we'd give them the results and the data. They were delighted with this so we picked out the double Olympic champion Aleksei Tishchenko and double European and world champion Albert Selimov. At the end, we gave them all the heart rate intensities and facts and figures alright, but we kept a copy of them for ourselves as well. They got a little but we got a lot more and when we came back we based our sessions on getting to the same level as their intensity.

Crucially though, while they were way ahead of us in the ring, at least Billy and Gary were getting on with them. Away from the gym they were on the same level and they built up a friendship and spent hours talking about boxing in terms of performance but also an absolute love of history. The Russians spoke about Irish boxing too, of how we are known for having big hearts. Gary explained to them that we wanted to bring our heads to the game, show we were more than just heart and that we were an intelligent people. Sporting performance is about skill at the highest level but also smarts and intelligence. It's about the expression of that skill under pressure in a tough environment. Zaur spent hours translating all this and drinking vodka with these guys, although that was Gary's biggest problem. He doesn't drink and it's an insult out there to turn away a drink, so he was trying to fill his glass up with water all the time and pretend he was just like them.

He got away with it and we got away with just surviving that camp. And that was the origin of the High Performance Unit, a model that could be translated to any sport in Ireland. It showed that we had to be dedicated and brave, but the attributes we needed meant we had to have addictive personalities too. That was good in the gym but not so good in life, and after hours spent in a room filled with people who only had your best interests at heart, it all made the wider world more difficult.

Initially it got me to where I thought I wanted to go. It made me an Olympic medallist, but it introduced me to a life I can't seem to cope with as well. It's daunting looking up at the mountain now and sometimes it's easier to just turn away. So I stare behind the bar, squinting to make out one bottle from the next as I contemplate moving on to a beverage that might provide me with a boost. James and Stephen keep talking, the world flits by while I sit still, but there's one image that sticks in my head and it won't get out.

"Accept your mistakes but learn from them." - Kenneth Egan, Olympic Silver Medallist.

CHAPTER 6

3.01pm

I'm hungry so I drink. I'm tired so I drink. Before all this I used to love my food and my sleep almost as much as I loved my boxing. Nowadays, my new lifestyle is taking away all the things I enjoy most. But only people who have a problem will understand why I keep doing it when I know it's self-destructive. It's hard to explain how you get to a position where you don't want to face what's happening outside the doors of the bar. But it's out there that you always assume the worst, and you learn to dislike people because you think they have it in for you. Instead, it's comfortable here. It's easier here. No one can blame you or exploit you or hurt you here. You're shielding yourself and, in a strange way, it's soothing.

That's just the way the gym was up until Beijing. Soothing. Before my performance allowed the world in to ask questions and take pictures and offer plenty of money. I never wanted any of that. I was always happy when it was just me, some punch bags, a ring, and the rest of the team. It was tough going, more than most people could handle, but it was fun. It was fun even when we slogged away for hours to reach world class levels. Like the time I was sparring Connie Sheehan, the heavyweight from Tipperary, and my left hand that was crucial in the Olympics was coming good. I caught him perfectly and he hit the deck squealing. Next thing Carl Frampton hopped in through the ropes, stood over him, and started laughing. Carl was half his size but Connie was rolling around the canvas moaning until he finally said through gritted teeth, *"When I get up I'm going to kill you Carl."* But he couldn't stand for five minutes so I joined in the laughter.

Billy Walsh took the piss out of Connie the next day when he walked past the two of us sparring, and told him to watch out for that left. *"He's not going to get me with it today, I learned my lesson,"* said Connie, as he strutted out of the corner for the last round. Billy walked back past us a couple of minutes later and Connie was lying flat on his back, once more in agony. *"Told you to watch out for it,"* Billy laughed.

I miss those moments because so much of me was based on making it to an Olympic Games. It's what I dedicated my existence to. Achieving that goal stripped away the majority of me so that now I'm sitting in a New York moment, just filling an empty shell with alcohol in the hope of forgetting there's nothing to look forward to and nothing to aim for. I'm young but I don't feel it because I'm already tired and have ticked too many boxes.

Granted, I'm sure it happens to a lot of sports people because if you are committed enough, good enough and lucky enough to make it, how do you replicate the feeling of utter contentment that I got in Beijing? For a few weeks in China, life seemed to become perfect but having experienced that emotion, it's very hard to have it taken away, to deal with anything but perfection, never mind the mundane.

But it's not just those Olympics that I want back but the path that took me there. I crave for the feeling of just being in the gym, knowing I was throwing punches for a reason long after I'd run out of breath and my arms felt like lead. Now, in the pit of my stomach, I sense the hurt you experience when you lose your first girlfriend, only this pain doesn't subside. I want the whole rush again more than anything but it's gone and rather than accept it, I drink to forget the fact that it's never coming back. It was gone from the moment the country started banging at the gym doors, when they started looking for access and a piece of me. When you are so committed to something for so long, you become attached. But when all you've known starts to change, it's hard to adapt and the end result is that it changes you. In my case the change has been anything but for the better.

We spent so long focusing on the top of the hill in the High Performance Unit that we never planned for coming down the other side. For that I blame the IABA and the Irish Sports Council. They never had anything in place when we returned from Beijing, never advised us on how to cope with media and agents and the entrance to a different life. I think that's because they never expected us to rise so high but when we did, they could at least have told us how to swim with the sharks.

All of that is why it's comfortable here in this bar. That is why it's easier here. That is why another drink with friends is better because no one can blame you or exploit you or hurt you here. Those types of people are all outside the doors, away from me. But it's all gotten so out of hand that I even reflect on the Olympics with a tinge of bitterness. I've lost sight of which is worse — making it at the Olympics and dealing with the after-effects, or missing out on them altogether because of the feeling of failure I suffered in 2004.

And of course it hurt to miss out, like it did at the European Championships in Croatia in 2003, when they acted as an Olympic qualifier. We had a full team over and Andy Lee advanced after getting the bronze, and fair play to him, but I got beaten by a Turk. He was my nemesis — dirty and strong and really aggressive. I knew I wasn't good enough at the time. He took the lead in the first round and once that happened the fight was over because I was negative and didn't fancy the fight at all. He wasn't all that good but neither was I and psychologically he had the better of me. That was a huge disappointment, but at least there were high points to balance it out. Unlike now.

Even in Croatia during that tournament there were moments that can still drag a smile out of my ageing face. Camera phones were just out and if you were on the road boxing, they were a way to pass time. Paulie Hyland and Paul McCloskey were a couple of rooms down from me on that trip and I had this awful habit when we went away of going into the lads' room as if to say hello, but then I'd sneak into their bathroom and go without flushing. My bathroom was always spotless but pretty quickly they copped onto this and in Croatia they started returning the favour. I had to nip that in the bud, told myself I'd fix it once and for all. So I went into their room's toilet, emptied myself, stuck their toothbrushes in it so it was like a sailing boat and took a picture message. When I sent it on to them they hit the roof. I was bored so I had to occupy my time somehow. That's my excuse anyway.

But it was tough on the road. The odd time there'd be a launderette near where we were staying but that was as much of a novelty as it was a luxury. More common, after every training session or bout, we'd wash our gear in the sink and hang it up all over the room to dry. The smell of damp would mix in with the smell of sweat and our quarters would stink. We were like animals, hanging stuff to dry on everything we could find, be it on radiators, a lamp in the corner or on picture frames. Anything would do. And when we were competing we still had to keep an eye on our weight so we'd be training in the corridors and lobbies. We would work with the pads, skip and run down the hall to get warm. There was no glamour. But I still miss it. And I'd trade that for this stool, this bar, this life, any time.

After breakfast in those places was the worst, because when you went back to your room, the stench would hit you hardest. You'd leave a nice air-conditioned space, smelling of healthy food, to come back to the smell of damp and dirt. It was hard to sleep as well because when you got to bed, you'd lie there listening through the night to the whip of the skipping rope. The next night it would be the same as it was someone else's turn, and so it went on. That was our life long before Olympic success but if there was comfort in slumming it, there's none in the padded existence of a supposed high life.

After Croatia, we headed to Bulgaria for the next Olympic qualifier for 2004. It was on in Plovdiv and even though the High Performance was up and running, there was still chaos at times. And that was one of those times.

I was sharing a room with taxi driver Martin Rogan, the super-heavyweight. He was a lovely guy who just recently won a Commonwealth title, beating Matt Skelton. Don't ask me how he did it but I'm delighted because he's a character with some history behind him.

When he was 14, he was playing handball on his way to Mass one evening when a yellow Avenger pulled up outside a nearby house. Distracted, he mishit, the ball flew towards the car and he followed. It was then he saw the silver gun between the seats and tiptoed away, too scared to run. Moments later he heard shots, a wife screaming and went to take a look. What he saw was a man on the ground with steam rising from the bullet holes in his chest.

When he was 16, he and his friends were scaling a wall in west Belfast, hoping to gain access to some green space and some time alone with a football. They had made it to the top when a gunman suddenly opened fire on them. They jumped down and fled as the bricks shattered behind them and somehow escaped. When he was 26 he saw some police terrorising a man at a petrol station. He couldn't stay quiet because that's never been his way and tried to intervene. Instead he was arrested and the police fastened the handcuffs so tight that a doctor came to the station at four in the morning and suggested he be sent to hospital immediately. But he was kept for another five hours before being released without charge. By then his hands had turned purple and required surgery because of the damage to the arteries and veins in his wrists.

But none of that stopped him and these days he tries his best to unite communities through boxing. Not long before I left for here, a man rang a radio show on BBC Ulster, complained about the Tricolour on Rogan's boxing shorts and said he represented the Shankill Road and no one else. Within minutes Rogan called up and did his best to explain that the green, white and orange was for Catholics, Protestants and peace and that's just what he wanted to see around him.

I make him sound sensible but back in Bulgaria in 2004 he was anything but. He had a head like a bag of potatoes, and came to boxing late so was all brawn with little brain. But Billy was improving him and really liked Rogan.

But after he lost his first fight on that trip, he disappeared. The next morning when Billy got up around six to get things ready for weigh-ins, a coach from another country came running up to him. *"Billy, your boxer is downstairs. He's at the bar and he's very bad. Very bad."* And there was Rogan with this Bulgarian local at the counter drinking Bacardi Breezers. This guy didn't speak English, I'm fairly sure Rogan doesn't speak Bulgarian, but the two of them were laughing and hugging and having this great conversation. He was still in his Irish gear, so Billy walked over and said, *"Do us a favour Martin, drink that up and go on to bed."* But Rogan started getting annoyed. *"Why? I'm not making a show of anyone, I'm just here with my friend."*

He'd already put on a show though, as Billy quickly found out from staff. A few hours previously, Rogan had come in, stood on the staircase and taken a piss into the fireplace in the lobby from quite a distance. Billy was a brave man to keep at him but finally got Rogan up the stairs and steered him towards the room where I was still asleep. All I remember was the door getting kicked open, and Rogan standing there in bits, dazed and confused. He tried to fall onto his bed but slipped, missed it, hit his head off the radiator and fell asleep half across my bed. I got up and looked out the door and there was this Bulgarian guy who he'd been out with staring at me. I was due to fight my first round later that day so Billy told me to go and sleep in his room.

Somehow I got the better of Babacar Kamara of Sweden in the first round. Meanwhile, Billy was making arrangements for Martin and one of the coaches to be put on the next flight home. But there was yet more drama. When Billy went to tell the aggrieved coach he was being sent home, he was caught with an uppercut that left him with a black eye. And then between drink and tiredness the coach got emotional and called me into the room. *"Kenny, whatever you do bring back the gold for me. Bring back the gold."* How could I? Winning one fight in that atmosphere was some going but next time out I lost 33-15 to Daugirdas Seiotas from Lithuania. It was all a disaster.

That was an opportunity lost because from there it was off to the last qualifier in Azerbaijan and the scoring in that place was the far side of dodgy. Eastern Bloc countries had it all sewn up and when people used to ask me what it was like, I always used the example of the Eurovision and then they understood. If you come from our part of the world, unless you leave a guy unconscious in hospital out there, you just won't get a decision. And even if you do that sort of damage, there are no guarantees. The judges were just hitting buttons for their own and their near neighbours and the western countries couldn't get a look-in.

Deep down, maybe, I was glad of that and to have it as an excuse. Looking back now, I was afraid to let myself go to the Olympics. I didn't have that extra push and it was almost better to blame something else than to put myself on the line and admit that maybe I wasn't good enough.

But there are better places to lose fights. As well as being biased, Azerbaijan is a kip. Inside the stadium there was a very hostile crowd. And outside it, the whole of Baku isn't much better, and full of Lada cars. After I lost out over there, I was hanging around with Andy Murray a lot. That he was walking, never mind representing Ireland in the ring, was a story in itself. His first coach Brian McKeown often recalled him as a kid *"crawling around the street on his arse, forever pulling bandages off his legs".* After an eternity of what were presumed to be severe growing pains, one day, aged seven, his legs collapsed right out from under him. A trip to Cavan Hospital saw him sent further afield to Navan and a few X-rays later he got the diagnosis. The doctor told his father he had Perthes syndrome, a condition caused by a deformity and subsequent weakening of the hip joint. It was a year before he was out of crutches and a wheelchair.

But he never even mentioned that. He always had his head down and got on with it. I can remember the two of us going to McDonald's out there to cheer ourselves up and replace an Olympic dream with the only edible food in the place. When we finished up, we went to get a taxi back to the hotel and I said to him, *"Watch this."* All the drivers were out, playing a game of draughts on the roof of a car, all standing in their suit jackets and slacks and dodgy pointy shoes in the baking sun with their cars lined up. We were standing at the top of the road where it came into one lane. I raised the hand and roared, *"Taxi!"* Next thing the board got cleaned off the roof, everyone scattered and jumped into the cars, and there were two Ladas rubbing off each other to try and get the fare. Murray couldn't believe it. I got into the car and the guy was sweating and out of breath. And we were only going around the corner.

The hotel was really run-down as well and another day, as we were walking up to it there were two men standing there, arms folded in their suits, looking down at a car. From what we could make out, one guy was telling the other he had gotten new wheels. A Lada with 20-inch sparkling alloys on it. Priceless.

Glad to get out of that place, win or lose, the closest I got to those Olympics in 2004 was a training camp with Andy Lee in France before he headed on. It was just the two of us and Billy Walsh and it was nice to be there with him. Before he left,

I wished him nothing but luck, shook his hand and I really wanted him to do well. But it was hard because he was getting on a plane to Athens and I was getting a plane back to Dublin, disgusted with myself for not making it. But my mind was never really on the job, and full of self-doubt. Mentally I wasn't ready and it just slipped by me.

In fact during those Games, I was out in Crete on my final holiday there and I got wind Andy won his first fight and then he lost to a Cameroon fighter. I was sick for him. The Africans tend to be just strong and energetic, they aren't technically talented whereas Andy was gifted. I don't say that because he was a teammate but because he was one of the best fighters we ever had in the gym. He was really genuine, a good trainer and incredibly focused. I thought he would have hung around after Athens for Beijing because they offered him the top grant, but the professional guys were talking to him and he had good connections in the States. We all wanted him to stay amateur because he was a huge asset to the team and it was a pity he went because he would have been peaking in 2008 and very much in his prime.

By then my mind was completely in a state. I was thinking to myself, 'What am I going to do? Am I going to give up another four years for a shot at the Olympics?' It seemed a long time. But even in those moments where I considered drastic action because of disappointment and underperformance, there was always a serious upside. Now the only positive is that there are still so many hours until last orders and closing time. But back then there was Zaur Antia, and when I got my head down towards the end of 2004, every day in the gym I could see the High Performance Unit coming together and his work was paying off across the whole team.

Zaur had started boxing himself when he was 10 under a very famous coach in Georgia and won cadet and junior titles. Later on he'd be six-time Georgian senior champion but like any top boxer, his dream was to go to the World Championships and ultimately the Olympics. But with the Soviet Union boxing team made up of 15 republics, it was easier said than done because first you had to be Georgian champion, then Caucasus champion and finally Soviet champion just to compete internationally. He won bronze in the latter which was some achievement, and in 1981 became a master of boxing in the Soviet Union. He had a smashing amateur record, was a knockout merchant and could box any way you want. Because of his talent, he'd get annoyed with us in training because he could still do things when nearing 50 that we couldn't do at our peak. And when he'd demonstrate shots, we could still see his speed and his power. But none of that was enough to take him where he wanted to go as a boxer himself.

When he boxed he was superb, but as a coach he knew he could have been an even better one. His own coach was like his father growing up and looked after all of his fighters like a parent and Zaur took that on board. And when he stopped boxing in 1985, he got married, and his old coach brought him into the club he'd grown up in. He found his place and his strength there and started working with children. But he was never selfish and always wanted them to be better than him and to achieve what he couldn't.

In 1984 he had started in the sport institute while coaching at his local club. It took five years of education to be a professional coach, his studies ranging across all the sciences, from physiotherapy to anatomy to physiology to psychology. It was a good combination because while he can't remember how many Georgian champions he ended up with, he trained three Soviet Union gold medals winners, and he had more boxers on the Soviet team than any country outside of Russia.

So he had proven himself from the very basics to the top because he started out with kids, was then working with the Georgian team as a coach, then assistant coach, before he became head coach for three years. He was re-elected to that position shortly before his refereeing friend told him about a job in Ireland, asked would he go for it and Zaur started thinking that maybe it was time he tested his capacity in a new country. Part of that was probably down to what was happening around him during his best years coaching in Georgia.

At the time of the break-up of the Soviet Union, he had two number one boxers and the Russian head coach, who had been his friend, said if they signed a contract and went to Moscow, representing Russia, he'd pay them. He couldn't betray his country and that never came to pass, but before long he was training them in the dark, waiting for miles in bread queues to feed them, trying to find a way out through Turkey to tournaments. Europe couldn't help and he and his country quickly became isolated and poor.

The recent war there has only made things worse. Russia stopped supplying electricity and petrol and there was no transport. But Zaur is always positive and keeps insisting that they are still a young country and some day it will all come good. We just nod and agree when he does.

Not surprisingly, given all that, as much as he settled here, you could always tell that he was so proud of where he comes from. We reckoned for quite a while he was a plant by the Georgian tourist board because he'd never stop talking about the place. We were coming back one year from a tournament abroad and I was looking through the flight magazine and there was this Irish wolfhound in it. I was showing it to Zaur, told him they were the biggest dogs in the world. He was having none of it, was adamant that in Georgia they had bigger. Anything we have, it's better there. They've the best wine and bread, the most beautiful women and even bigger dogs. He'd never stop.

"Kenny, a man in Georgia, if he is to be a real man, needs three things. One, you have to plant something, a tree. Secondly you have to have your home. And then you have to have a son to continue your legacy because it keeps your name. If your son has a son, Egan will continue forever."

"Kenny, Georgia was always rich in food and people had a good heart. Home of hospitality. And we are better than any other former Soviet state because of the people. Very similar to Ireland, a big history, a big culture."

With home meaning so much to him, he was lucky with Gary's methods when he came first because first for Zaur was friendship — everything else came after that, even boxing. He wanted to trust people and when he arrived in Ireland he saw it was fun, there was no in-fighting, we all got on and we had good intellect. He liked that. But he was suffering from homesickness too, and when he left the gym he'd always say *"one month and I go, two months and I go"*. But he hung around and picked up a few more words of English, although most of it was bad language. At first he told us his name and then he'd just wave his hands about and grunt a bit; he was like a caveman around the place. But he had a good humour and a good relationship with us even without the language.

He was very aware that the measure of a coach is his boxers and he must have seen something in us as fighters because after the World Championships in Bangkok he said there was talent with us and it was different from Georgia. We were more open to learning, to listening and to coaching. We had no other problems on the outside so our minds were in the gym and solely on bettering ourselves as boxers.

For two years he stayed without his family, going home every six months but come 2005, the IABA brought over his wife and sons and once they were there he was happy and could properly concentrate on his job. Not that we ever saw him distracted or distant when he was working with us. I admire Zaur because he's done well for his wife Nona and their kids, and they are now well settled out in Bray. One of his sons, David, has taken up boxing and now looks like making it to college. In Ireland we often see the worst in everything, but ask someone like Zaur what we are like and you get a different perspective.

When Zaur came to Ireland the first thing he recognised was

that the standard wasn't as high as it was in Georgia. The second thing was that the facilities weren't as good because there they had more rings, more scales, more weights, all leftovers from the Soviet era. On top of that the pay was different in Ireland and not necessarily better. They don't pay boxers but, for example in the European Championships a bronze medal gets a boxer €10,000, a silver €20,000 and a gold €30,000. On top of that the coaches would get about €8,000 of a bonus for successes and money is given back to the clubs as well.

At least Zaur agreed with Gary about the direction he was taking the programme, following an Eastern Bloc methodology rather than a Cuban way forward. But there was and is more to Zaur than just boxing. With conscription he ended up in the Soviet army for a couple of years. He was in uniform for six months, waking up at five, walking for miles in the snow on security missions, 20 miles from the Turkish border. After that they let him into the army's sport group, where he boxed and played a lot of chess, and from there he played music too, piano and a guitar which he still regularly whips out.

He is very funny though because we got to know his habits. He's some man for eating. He'd sit down and devour a plate of pickles for a snack but then vanity would kick in and he'd get up, go over to the scales and weigh himself. He was always coming into the gym looking for stuff too. *"Kenny, have you any old DVDs?" "Kenny have you any old DVD players?"* Then it'd be iPhones and I was trying to explain that they were only out new on the market so he'd ask, *"Any old laptops then?"* I told him I had one in the house but it was broken and he still took it. But we all love him and I owe him a lot more than worn-out electronics because he was so important in turning me into a world-class boxer.

But aside from Zaur and the coaching, other aspects were being added in to the High Performance Unit after the 2004 Olympics. Gerry Hussey was brought in as a psychologist and one day we came in and the coaches started analysing our performances. From then on, after each fight we'd sit down and we'd get a print-out of how many jabs, back hands, hooks and body shots we threw in each round. The coaching team would look at the time between each attack. A top-class amateur boxer waits three to five seconds but back then it wasn't uncommon for us to sit back in the pocket for eight or nine seconds. We'd attack once and get lazy and let the opponent settle. But to see this in black and white opened our eyes and we knew we had to work on it. The gym was expanded too. We got three rings and extra weights, so we could see it all changing with us. Suddenly the much-improved structure was all around us.

Performances still lagged a little behind that side of it though. Senior titles kept coming for me but they weren't enough. There were good years and bad years in terms of opposition at home. At the start there were guys like Conall Carmichael and Marvin Lee, a good fighter from Galway. Just this year there was Tommy McCarthy who I beat in a tough scrap. But some years you'd wonder, 'What's the point?' In 2007 the only other entry was Willie Mitchell from Tyrone. He was like a 57-kilo boxer in an 81-kilo body. He was about 4'11", fat, and shouldn't have been near that weight. I caught him with a shot and there was a count. I hit him again and his gum shield came out and he kicked it away and kicked the ropes, went a bit mad. The referee stopped the fight and got a tirade of abuse for his troubles. If the fight had gone on I would have hurt him. But when the Irish Championships were like that, I knew I needed to take it to another level abroad. But that was easier said than done.

In 2005 there was the World Championships, my third, and we were back in Russia training to get ready, only this time in the summer heat. With the weather better, we'd run around the track before heading to the gym for afternoon sparring but after that everything else had remained the same. We'd be up early morning to line up with them, there for roll call, and the same cold meats and black tongue were staring up from the breakfast table. We were there in the corner giggling while they were like machines moving from one ring to the next, taking on a different opponent every couple of minutes. And there were endless rings with a thick, spongy canvas that worked your legs even harder.

I recall looking out the windows of the gym one day and there was this playground where they had kids of about eight learning to box. It was staggering. They had perfect technique. They trained like they'd been around for years, textbook hand and foot movement, stuff I learnt at 18. No wonder they are so good when they have all this 10 years before we get near it. When they reach their teens they are already masters of the sport whereas we have guys coming into the gym at 16 or 17 and they don't know the basics. Our senior coaches end up having to teach them from scratch.

But being there was helping. I fought Yevgeniy Makarenko in the Chemistry Cup and got close. It was my best performance yet and because of it, I went to the Philippines for the final training camp ahead of the World Championships in good spirits. That was the nicest camp we ever had. We were up in the mountains outside Manila in an old American air base. But there was a golf course and we had our own caddies, and the food was amazing. It was lovely but the training didn't do us justice.

That realisation would come after the World Championships, but while in the Philippines we were working hard and playing even harder. Three of us grabbed a taxi one evening and went looking for some prostitutes. We even offered to buy the driver one but he declined. There were about 10 compartments with a curtain pulled over them. So I was in the first one and the three of us stuck our heads out as the first girl came down. She wasn't great so I said she wasn't for me and let the lads fight over her. Then the second one came out, same story. Which meant there was only one left, and I'd left myself no choice. That was a bad choice because she had a head like 100 miles of bad road. I'd paid up though so I went ahead and did the dirty deed anyway.

If that was the lasting memory of the Philippines, the lasting memory of the World Championships which followed wasn't any better. They were staged at Mianyang in south-west China. There was an earthquake there shortly afterwards and the place where we were staying was completely flattened. My Dad and some of his mates came over to see me compete, but there wasn't much to see. I was beaten by the Swede Babacar Kamara in the second round. It said a lot about my mindset that over the course of my career we've met eight times and while I've won five, he always got the better of me in the contests that really mattered. That was the mind playing havoc with me, telling me that this next few minutes was important and the event became bigger than the fight.

Every day the food was dire and you'd wake up in the morning to rice and chicken curry for breakfast. My Dad and his mates didn't think much of the cuisine either because they used to get a bucket of chicken and a litre of coke in KFC every day. That was their diet for the entire week they were there. They were staying in a place with rats running around their feet when they were drinking in the hotel bar. They wanted to see what China was like and they found out pretty soon. But I was just concerned about losing that fight. It was even worse that people had travelled halfway across the world to see me fail once again.

It was a disaster. For me, some days I could be the best amateur boxer in the world. Other days I'd end up losing to people who weren't all that good. That was the mental thing and I just couldn't crack the code; there was something wrong. In the High Performance I was in with psychologist Gerry Hussey and was asking him just what my problem was. The self-belief wasn't there to go and get on a podium.

But if sports psychology was the long-term answer, the short-term thinking was the nearest pub. I went drinking with

Eric Donovan in Mianyang, although he was a lot worse than I was. He was a small featherweight from Athy who had a wild side and we became very close after he joined the team in 2004. I liked him from the start because we were up in City-West one day and the Irish rugby team was training away beside us. There were a load of their big lads pumping iron, and many were queuing up to take a turn on the scales to check their weights. Ronan O'Gara was there and he recognised the boxing team, probably because Andy Lee had just qualified for the Olympics. He saw Eric and introduced himself and said to him, *"So you're a boxer, would you be able to knock me out with a good hook?"* Eric just looked up at him and said, *"I'd knock you out with a bad one."* O'Gara went back into his shell fairly quickly.

But that was him all over. Pretty soon after that we were out after a competition having a few. I had a girl on one side and Eric on the other. She had broken English but I got kissing her. Next thing I felt this hand down my jeans. I got turned on and when that happened there was this scramble with the hand trying to escape. I looked down and it was Eric's hand.

However, that night out in China we got separated and I lost him. Later he came back and Billy quickly got word of this. He got up half asleep, and there was Eric sitting outside the lift with this local girl. We had these Chinese minders and if anything happened to us it was their responsibility, so Billy told Eric to get into bed.

"No Billy, this girl came all this way, I want to walk her home now. She's a friend of mine."

Billy told him there wasn't a hope he was leaving the hotel but Eric got up and got in the lift. Billy told him again and again and the minders were getting more and more impatient, so Billy grabbed him and fired Eric's eight-and-a-half stone frame across the hall. He flew through the air and landed on the ground and was looking up. When Billy boxed he had a great left hook and used to knock out a lot of people with it.

So Eric let out this roar, *"All you ever had was a left hook."* Billy told him that if he wasn't careful he would see it but Zaur came charging out and got Eric back to the safety of a room. Gary Keegan wasn't too impressed though and Eric got a fine and a ban after that.

Which makes me now wonder about the ban and punishment I'll receive for doing this runner to New York. Will it overshadow the fact I need help? It also makes me wonder where all this will end up and, more importantly, where it will leave my career. But all those worries are outside the door of the bar right now. Instead, it's comfortable here. It's easier here. No one can blame you, exploit you or hurt you here.

CHAPTER 7

9.00pm

If only the people back home could see me now, sitting on the same stool in Jack Dempsey's that I began the day. I still haven't moved but my body is slowly moving beyond my control and experience tells me my mind will soon follow. It makes me think of the letters that fell through the door in the days and weeks after the Olympics, as if I was somehow different to a man that's good at any other job. A builder or carpenter who builds a nice house or a plumber who cleans a drain doesn't get the same response and they are doing nothing different to me. So why am I deserving of so much goodwill when I'm just pissing my life away?

Hey Kenny,

Congratulations on everything you've achieved. I've been debating this for a while so I just thought I'd send you a letter.

I met you one night in town, you said hello and gave me a smile. My God, your face is infectious. I'm sure you smiled at plenty of people that night but I'm trying to convince myself it was just me. Ha. If you're still with your girlfriend she is a very lucky lady. Oh, PS, if she's anything like you in the ring don't show her this letter, a black eye really wouldn't suit me. I know you probably think this is odd but I just said feck it, it can do no harm and at least it will put a smile on my face. I was going to send my number but don't want to get done for stalking. Ha ha. Anyway all the best in the future.

If I do happen to bump into you in the future, I'll give you a face to put to the name. X.

This person sitting here on the bar stool in New York?

Attractive to a woman?

Dear Kenny,

The letter is very late, and for that I apologise. I would have written sooner but events sort of overtook me. Your timing was so spot on, you wouldn't believe how much receiving the T-shirt and the timing of it meant to me. Thing is, I went to hospital for a back operation, which sort of ends my involvement in contact sports. I was lying in my hospital bed the day after the operation, very sore and full of self pity when my family arrived to visit.

My daughter Lorna, your second biggest fan in the house, was really excited and told me they had a great surprise for me. I faked interest and she landed the parcel on the bed — it had been torn open in the post so they knew what it was. My heart soared. I genuinely forgot where I was for a while and of course, stupidly, tears ran down my face — not the reaction my kids were hoping for...

Me? Inspiring people?

Dear Kenny,

Thank you. Thank you for everything. Thank you for making me forget that I am an out-of-shape, cynical, 45-year-old father with debts and worries. Thank you for reminding me that I was once a wide-eyed, uncomplicated, 12-year-old who dreamt of being an Olympian. Thank you for making me feel like that 12-year-old, sitting on the mat in front of the TV surrounded by my family, watching the Olympics of 1976 in Montreal, overwhelmed by the wonder, the glamour of the Games, wishing, praying desperately for Eamonn Coghlan to sprint past John Walker to win gold...

I know how hard you worked for this — you earned every bit of glory and success. But I hope you know how lucky you are. You reached the mountain top. Have a good look around.

This person sitting here on the bar stool in New York? Lucky?

Hi Kenny,

This is just a short note to say not only 'Well Done' but a big thank you also for your achievements at the Olympic Games. As a mother of three young boys living in the area, it's great to see such a positive role model for them. All they have been doing with their friends is talking about you and wanting to be like you one day...

This person sitting here on the bar stool in New York? A role model?

Then I remember the old me. I can just about make him out. He's the one I want to be like again. Confident, dedicated, strong, forceful, driven. Maybe it's the drink or maybe it's all the other components of this new life, but I'd nearly forgotten the person I was, and by extension how to get him back. That was the person those people were writing to and while it's sad to end up like this, there's a tiny sliver of hope. Here in my lowest moment I begin to think about my highest achievements. The Kenneth Egan all those people look up to began in a humble place too. I think back to that journey to the training camp in Russia to get ready for the 2006 European Championships.

We'd been on bad trips before. In fact all of them started badly because they involved getting on a plane and I hate that, especially the take-off and landing. But this trip to Dagestan in Russia was the worst. During that trip the seats moved around on the airplane. There were cobwebs in the cabin and these flies were going up and down the aisles. I spent that flight much like any other, my hands stuck to the arm rests and the sweat dripping off of me as if these were my last few moments on Earth and we were about to nosedive.

On that trip there was just myself and Darren Sutherland fighting but Billy and Gary realised that after Athens they were not going to be able to build a system with just five or six boxers. They needed to build a pipeline and to invest in that area to make sure more and more youngsters came through. They may have taken in more boxers through the years, but I was still a nervous wreck on airplanes.

Out in Dagestan I was getting battered from pillar to post in sparring. I had a beard and looked dark, and felt even darker. Even then I realised it was in my personality to turn to misery and self-pity very quickly. But it was in my nature to make sure I kept coming back, kept getting into the ring each session to take more and more punishment and I refused to back away. I continuously tried to break out of the blackness but Russia is not a place to have a bad day, never mind a bad camp.

It got so bad I took Gary outside and sat him on a bench and started talking. I was so tired of getting so close and looking at four guys standing on a podium and wondering why I kept getting it wrong. I wanted that so bad yet it never happened despite the fact I was always great in training and multi-nations events. But come the big tournaments I was collapsing. With sparring going so badly and another big tournament just around the corner, I could see it happening all over again.

So he talked about progress, about steps, and about how if you get too far ahead of yourself you've already started to fail before you've even competed. But with me at that time it was all, 'what if it goes wrong?' How could I walk through Neilstown and Clondalkin after almost winning another medal? I'd already mapped out what that would look like. And I talked to Gary about the shame I'd feel if I didn't perform again. It wasn't just about me, though. It was about the club Noel Humpston had built up, it was about my Dad who had travelled to China to see me lose at the World Championships, and it was about the coaches who had worked so hard to give me the chance to win. And winning was something I seemed incapable of when it really mattered.

Gary mentioned how he'd heard GAA players talk of going back into their village after not performing or delivering and the fear they have of such a scenario. I understood where they were coming from. Since then I've heard Katie Taylor say that she doesn't let the expectation get to her because it's something she can't control and that it's always someone else's expectation. But she is clearly more mentally tough than I am because I was truly challenged by this. So Gary talked and talked about one step at a time and literally one punch at a time. About getting into the ring and having 100 per cent attention on that bout and not thinking about the next bout. Every round was a final that I had to win if I ever wanted to achieve.

For a while it worked. Even if I didn't fully understand it and it was a plaster rather than a cure, once we left Russia I was brand new again. I have never been a guy who likes to be serious about things as I like my surroundings to be fun and light-hearted. Some people think that makes me a bit of a clown but that was never the case. It was what worked for me. In the dressing room I always liked Billy to be laughing and joking because when people are too serious it creates anxiety around me and inside of me. Others are different. Darren Sutherland was so serious, always with his earphones in. Paddy Barnes was a mix of both of us. But I lost a lot of energy through nerves so the more my mind was taken off what was about to happen, the better.

But something happened in Bulgaria. Suddenly I started sparring and sparking. My pad work was good, I began talking right and put my shoulders back. I didn't feel worried anymore but it wasn't just that my mind had been cleared, it was the fact it had been emptied of bad thoughts. All that mattered was my time in the ring and if that was where I was at, it would come good. And it did come good.

I fought Robert Woge from Germany first and hurt my thumb, but the programme had built up such a strong network that the French doctor was on hand and he treated our fighters as well. We had a fantastic physio there and a superb doctor at home but we didn't have the resources to have one with us when travelling abroad all the time. So we used the French doctor, he'd ring our guy back home, they would talk and he would treat us. It was a brilliant set-up.

This French guy was going to do the injections into my hand

after that first win but I hate needles almost as much as I hate airplanes. Billy was busy with the rest of the team so Gary went into this room with me. There were two beds, we sat on one and Gary told me to put the injured hand behind me on the other bed. Later he joked that it was like bringing his child in to get a tetanus shot. *"Don't look at it, keep your eyes on me and we'll have a chat about other things,"* he kept reminding me as I winced.

But more came of that than just the numbing of pain. To this day Gary believes that the hand injury helped me go so well in those championships, because it was a positive distraction. I was focused suddenly on keeping my hand safe and wasn't thinking too far ahead. Maybe he was right in his assertion because in the next fight I put Mamadou Diambang of France on his arse and the referee stopped that fight. I was probably in good enough form to get more than the bronze medal I got but Artur Beterbiyev finally put me out in the last four.

He was an absolute fighter, a big puncher, and we'd sparred at that horrible camp before we went to Plovdiv. In fact on the bench that day Gary tried to build my confidence up and told me I'd absorbed everything he could throw at me. No matter what he'd tried he couldn't take me out. *"You are at 30 per cent of what you normally are, but you are still standing there taking his best,"* he'd said. *"When are you going to start believing in yourself? When are you going to take absolute ownership of what you have? It's yours, don't be afraid of it."* But if bronze was good, there was still the problem that I hadn't stepped up a level from that semi-final and that was a worry lingering about the place.

But there and then, that was Gary's concern, not mine. He saw this fighter who'd been around quite a while and who still wasn't delivering on his maximum potential. But I saw my first major medal, a bronze to bring home and show the club, my Dad and the community. A bronze medal to show for all my years of work. The monkey was off my back and it felt so good to be in top company on the podium having my photograph taken and shaking hands. I was part of that elite club after years of working and waiting.

That called for a celebration and a quiet beer. Only it wasn't quiet because there was an American air base near where we were staying. One of the other boxers who'll remain nameless had met this girl the night before who was stationed there. And that night myself, the girl and the bloke were sitting in the hotel, talking about the fight.

"Did you ever have a threesome," he asked her, joking.

"Yeah, why?" came the understated response as the whole table leaned in like dogs around a carcass.

"Well, want another one?"

"Sure, why not."

This was marvellous. My first big medal... and now a threesome. So the other guy said he'd run up and get the room ready, and up we went up shortly afterwards. Eventually, we got down to it, but when I looked over at the other fella he was doing all these poses while staring into space at the end of the bed. I didn't know what was going on. Next thing she slipped and fell on top of him. She was a heavy girl, and he was roaring at her to get off him. That ended all the shenanigans and, after she left the room, he got up and took a camera off a suitcase. He had been posing and staring at his hidden camera which had been recording the three of us all the time. He was delighted with himself. We stuck the DVD on and watched it back and never laughed as much. That DVD is probably floating around somewhere to this day and if me taking a trip to New York made news headlines back home, I hope that disc never resurfaces because it would probably make Prime Time Investigates.

Thankfully Gary never knew about it. Instead he was thinking about what he saw in me at those championships. Despite not getting to the top of the podium there must have been something there, because after that he expressed real belief in me as an individual. To a point I could see it in myself but if a monkey was off my back, winning a major medal, there was an elephant still on there — getting to the Olympics. I guess when it came to the Olympics I was scared to believe because I did everything I could in the training environment to deliver a performance but didn't do everything mentally to prepare.

Deep down I knew there were issues that impacted my performance, mental issues that could be fixed. And if I fixed the last piece there was nothing else I could do. At that point, if I didn't deliver, then my dream was over. Maybe at the time it was only subconscious, but even with one per cent of me not right, it was enough to use as an excuse, to say that was the reason I wasn't going to the Olympics. It wasn't just that I wasn't a good enough boxer. I was clinging to a fault and that was the reason I hadn't performed when it came to those qualifiers in 2004. With the problem still there, the same thing started to happen in the qualifiers for 2008.

The first of those opportunities to qualify was at the World Championships in 2007. If Plovdiv had given me a little belief, those Championships took away all that confidence and then more. Chicago did a great job hosting them because they took the Championships at short notice after Moscow failed to meet certain criteria. There was an opening ceremony and Muhammad Ali was there waving out at us. It was a good start and we were confident because the scoring there is okay and you won't get robbed. Big things were expected of both me and the team but it all fell apart.

I won my first fight against Julius Jackson of the Virgin Islands, and then won my second fight against Julio Castillo of Ecuador. Suddenly I was a win away from making it to the Olympics at the first qualifying attempt, with just Marijo Sivolija of Croatia standing in my way. It shouldn't have been too hard an obstacle to overcome since he'd given me a walkover on my way to the EU gold just a couple of months previous. But yet again I lost in a major bout. He qualified. I didn't. And all the memories of the 2004 qualifiers came flooding back and were drowning me.

But I wasn't the only one treading rapidly rising water. Everyone bar Paddy Barnes failed to qualify and by the end of it Eric Donovan went a bit mad on the gargle. We were in a beer garden early one of the days and I suggested we get showered, head to the stadium and watch some boxing. He said he was okay, so he stayed and I went off. Not long after I saw him again though. The Championships were on during the Halloween period and myself and a few other of our fighters were sitting in our seats in the arena when we heard this wailing from up at the back. We turned around and there was Eric, dressed in this gear he'd taken off the pub wall. There was a mask and cloak and wings out the back of it and he was running around pretending to be a ghost. We were halfway down towards the ring, with Billy and the rest of our coaches a bit ahead nearer the ring. So we ran up and grabbed him and got him out of there, and saved him a lot more trouble in the process.

That summed up those Championships and by the end of it everyone was slating us. Mick Dowling was talking about how Gary Keegan was a waste of money, how the programme was clearly a failure and should be scrapped. Worse still Gary had only wanted to send the top five or six fighters from the programme but Dom O'Rourke stepped in and said other senior champions should go too because the more there, the more we had a chance of qualifying. That Paddy Barnes was one of those others and was the only one to qualify heaped more pressure on Gary and the programme. But Keegan stuck to his game plan and said he wanted five fighters at the next year's Olympics and he was determined to get to that figure. It was important that even with the abuse being aimed at the team, we stuck together. Because as bad as it was, it was only one qualifier and there were two more left.

We had achieved three gold and two silver medals at the EU Championships and the previous year the European Champion-ships had been like a coming of age for the High Performance. But suddenly we were back to a low watermark, the tide had gone out and even if the radical changes suggested by the likes of Mick Dowling were way off, smaller tweaks were needed.

Altering what we had built up over years in a matter of weeks was do-or-die but Chicago had shown us at the highest level we still weren't doing things completely right.

As team captain it's hard to say it, but we were lethargic. It wasn't a physical flatness but it was representing itself as that. The coaches had all the data to show we were in the best shape of our lives. But what we were feeling was impacting how we were acting. Gary needed to find out what was causing this.

The boxers were always debriefed separately to the support team and there was always an independent facilitator so we could say what we wanted. But Gary still gave us a stern telling-off at that time and said, *"If you can see me driving you into the wall, it's your responsibility to tell me to turn. We think we are doing the right thing but you are the vessel. There's no point in telling us what you think we want to know, you have to tell us what we need to know. That is a big test of our High Performance."* And that was a turning point.

Gary saw that we needed to change in terms of the support structure. When he was initially building the system, there were a lot of new elements in terms of the training regime which meant a lot of new knowledge directed at us as boxers. So for a period it had to be heavily instructional and we had to be told what to do. But once we had learned, there needed to be a reverse in the balance of communication from 80 per cent telling to 50 per cent discussing what the best way was. The management team had been so focused on other aspects that they had missed out on that and only after Chicago did the tactics change. And that was hard for Zaur in particular because he was very hands-on.

Up to that point we started a session with a warm-up that was quite technical and the coaches would stop here and there to give more instructions. That shouldn't have been happening so close to the qualification tournaments. On top of that our sparring sessions involved the coaches shouting in as if they were trying to manage the performance themselves, as opposed to allowing us to manage and think for ourselves. Everyone did it for the right reasons and were focused on how we could get to the next level but we had missed out on little elements like that.

For example, if I was in sparring and came to the corner, Billy and Zaur would tell me directly what I was doing wrong. They weren't asking me how it went, what is the next step, how did I feel? Gary saw that as something that had to be reversed across the whole group. We needed to adjust the feedback process and how we communicated. One of the things that happened was when the boxers came to the gym after the World Championships, there was a whiteboard with all our names on it. After the debrief from Chicago it was decided we would choose what we wanted to work on across a given day and we decided what our targets would be for that given day. There could be no more than three, no less than one and the coaches then went and looked at the targets and the only communication would be around those.

From then on the coaches weren't telling us what we needed to work on, we were assuming the responsibility we had earned over the years and they were putting questions to us rather than giving us answers. And if we didn't give the right answer, they'd ask other questions until we evolved towards that right answer. In essence that was handing performance back to the boxers. Had this not been spotted and changed, Beijing would not have worked out the way it did and we would have all failed each other as a team. It was taking ownership with lots more free sparring as opposed to technical sparring which had been very stop-start. We were making mistakes but could work through them ourselves and had time to fix them through our own free expression.

There were other changes too. Training times and locations were altered. Up to this point it had always been training at 10 in the morning and four in the evening every day in the stadium, but then they started to mess with our heads. Gary knew a Donegal man called Eunan Devenney and was interested in a set of external eyes staring at the programme. Eunie is a typical Donegal man, wild and unpredictable in the best possible way. He did a 48-hour marathon of punching bags or something along those lines once. The two of them agreed they would take us out of Dublin and put us in the mountains. So up we went to Donegal and they had us out of bed earlier, forced us in to change, challenged us, hit our heads and our bodies. It was unpredictable.

One morning they drove us up a hill in the dark, opened the doors, told us to get out and do a 10-kilometre run. Billy had said he would go for a run too so Gary told him to get out as well. Billy argued he'd do his own run but Gary insisted and shortly after Billy was vomiting in a Donegal ditch. If Billy occasionally didn't know what was coming, then we never knew what was coming. Sometimes we'd be told to bring headgear, expecting a sparring session and we'd end up in a field. Any semblance of being on autopilot was driven out of us. But it was different and exciting and it motivated us.

For real change to come about so quickly though, that group component was working alongside the individual component. On a personal level, when we came back from Chicago, the language and support the psychologist Gerry Hussey was giving me was the right support. But I wasn't hearing it and taking it on board. The solution was simple but with me there was a huge amount of fear and I was always thinking that it just cannot be that easy. Plus fear added to the pressure I was under as a boxer and as team captain meant I was carrying a serious weight in my mind. There were times when it was scary but you have to be a warrior and try and fight through all that. Mine was just one story but we were all feeling the strain and were dealing with it in different ways.

I dealt with it by retreating to Gary's office. He told the psychologist afterwards what happened and said it was very hard to watch. *"There was no actual noise but the psychological noise was deafening."* I am a good sized light-heavyweight but I looked like a middleweight, not because of my stature but because of my body language. My shoulders had dropped again and Gary was seated and I was pacing from one side of the room to the other. I'd stop to his right and go off on one about how it was only the Olympic Games, it was only sport and it was not the end of the world. Then I'd go to his left and panic about missing out for a second time after all the work and then what? I was going from one world to the other, they were equally as bad and there was no place in between which was exactly where I needed to be.

For me it was never about winning a medal at the Olympic Games, it was about getting there and being an Olympian. That was massive and all I ever wanted. I can't express that enough. It was too big and overwhelmed me at times. What Gary needed to do was near impossible. He had to pull me away from being overwrought, get my feet on the ground, and focus me on where I was, what I had inside and how I could deliver.

He had three months to turn me and the team around and whereas before Chicago there was talk of 'dead certs' for an Olympic spot, suddenly we didn't have any. They were trying to draw everything out of themselves as a support team and everything out of us as boxers in a short time and in a pressured environment. It got very close to breaking point.

Soon there was more pressure because of the second qualifier in Pescara in Italy in February 2008. Again I left Ireland thinking of how badly I wanted to be an Olympian, to own a tracksuit with five rings, to spend the rest of my days being able to tell friends and family I was there. And somewhere inside me was a voice saying I am good enough but I just needed to find my very best and bring it out on the biggest stage. I was asking myself again and again why I was beating some guys easily in some competitions and then losing in bigger championships. What was the difference? I couldn't figure it out. That question would soon chip away at me again.

I got a bye in the first round, beat Emi Krastev of Bulgaria in the second, and just like in Chicago I was just one fight away from my dream spot in the Olympics. This time Ramaza Magamedau of Belarus was in the way. Gary later told me after that when he saw me leaving the dressing room he knew I was gone, long before the bell tolled. My eyes were glazed over and my head wasn't in the stadium. The pressure had beaten me again. I broke my routine, left the hotel early, was in the changing area early, I was sitting there not knowing what to do with myself feeling the occasion getting heavier on my back. The Belarusian was decent, he was rough and liked to pull and drag and get inside. But I still bottled it because he wasn't near my best level.

He didn't even fight the final once he reached it, claimed he had a hand injury but that was rubbish, he just didn't want to go up against this tough Ukrainian called Ismayl Sillakh. I should be too classy for someone who runs away from a fight. Problem was that my class wasn't in the ring, it was back in the hotel room. I couldn't access it, draw from it and when he caught me early with a haymaker I was on the back foot. I couldn't throw a punch, and I felt like I'd forgotten how to box. I could see the shot, but my brain wouldn't tell my arm to move. It was like one of those dreams when you need to run away but your legs won't move fast enough and the frustration and fear mounts, until you wake up.

After that, I had to learn to box again with the train coming down the tracks. By then I was five weeks from the last chance saloon. I couldn't handle the pressure even though there was a safety net. Now there wasn't even that, just a fall from grace and into obscurity and a life of what ifs. It was an injury like any other that had to be resolved. But we had to see it like that. It wasn't a weakness, it was just an injury and a factor we weren't fixing and focusing on in the right way. And most importantly I wasn't taking responsibility for it.

Worried I wouldn't be able to fix it, I even thought about back-up plans, so low was the confidence I had in myself. My brother Willie was in the Army still but was thinking about other ways of making money and there was a course in town where you pay €150 and they teach you how to pass the taxi licence exam. This is what I had in my head before the last qualifier. I was telling myself I would miss out, I'd go in and get myself a taxi plate and that would be my future, my life. At the time you'd hear all the stories of drivers pulling in €1,500 a week and this was already my consolation for losing in the ring.

You could even look at the idea of going to that course in two ways. Either I was thinking I'm not good enough or maybe I was being sensible, trying to get a job and having a back-up plan. Myself and Willie did the course and were delighted with ourselves afterwards. Besides, how could I not think like that? John Joe Nevin qualified in Pescara joining Barnes. He'd won the seniors that year and came from nowhere to qualify. Fair play to him but here was me around forever with one last chance. There were kids getting over the finishing line while I was going grey and going nowhere.

But we were still together as a unit and a team in the build-up to the final qualifier in Athens. Even others came in and tried to help. Jimmy Magee got in contact with Gary Keegan and recommended I go and speak to Ireland's No.1 golfer Pádraig Harrington. I rang him, went out to his house, and I was really nervous because this guy was a superstar and didn't really know what I was going to say to him. He came out to the door in his bare feet with a tracksuit on. There was a driving range with a big net in his house, a putting course in the garden, but as a person he was normal. He put on a cup of tea, was eating a scrambled egg and started yapping away.

He's a great man for talking but a lovely person. I was asking him how he prepared for big occasions and how he would get his head right and keep mentally strong. The one thing that stuck with me was his ideas on preparation. He kept talking about it and how if you prepare right you won't have any negative thoughts eating away at you, telling you that you should have done this and that. He mentioned Miguel Angel Jimenez, how he doesn't over-think, how relaxed he is and how he's this really cheeky character. Whether he missed a putt or nailed a shot, he smiled, moved on and made the most of the next shot.

It was funny actually because at the end of the year, we were both at the sports awards out in CityWest. There was talk I might win the main prize but it went to him in the end. They called all the boxers up on stage that night though, as we won the Best Team. As team captain I talked about how it was a great achievement. Then I said I was out in Pádraig's house one day before a qualifier and that we sat there for two hours. Cheekily I said that I gave him a few tips and he went on to win the British Open. But in fairness I took on board everything he said and kept revisiting the mental side of my performance.

Partly because of that I got into a very interesting relationship with Gerry Hussey and another psychologist Gary brought in to work alongside him at that time called Phil Moran. After Italy, Gary had sat down with the two of them and they said, *"Gary, I think we can fix this. If we can just get him to take ownership we can fix this. It's not a huge problem but it's causing a huge deficit in terms of his performance."* So the deal was that I'd work with the psychologists and then I needed to come and see Gary after every day's work so he could get a sense of what side of the room I was on. I could lie to the psychologists but he'd know if I was bluffing because he'd gotten to know me so well.

Not long into this new regime, Gary got a phone call from Gerry Hussey who said they'd a problem. I was feeling the pressure and looking for excuses again, looking for a way out and a fault to blame in case the last qualifier went wrong. So I'd called up and said there was a problem with my car, I had to go to the garage and I wouldn't make it. Suddenly my phone rang and it was like getting a call from your boss when you've skipped work. On the other end was Gary.

"How are you doing Kenneth?"

"Oh, hi Gary, what's up?"

"Remember I said I'd check in with you every day? Well I just want to wish you luck for your meeting this morning."

"Eh yeah, I'm on my way now."

"Great stuff, come in and speak to me after."

It took a little push but it kept me on the right path. The guys were confident of finding a solution but again I wanted an escape, so metaphorically I ran away from the problem and didn't want to face it. That was effectively what I had been doing for years in boxing. But what I solved in the ring seems to have transferred over to my life. The very thing that affected me as a performer is now hurting me most as an ordinary human being. Coming home, in terms of being a household name, was another massive challenge, only this time I didn't have a team to keep me on the right path. So I've stumbled down the road that led to this American city, this bar, this stool, this pint.

I wonder will there be an awakening in me, a realisation and a will to change like there was back then. Because all it took to bring me to the next level in the ring was the smallest oddity. In the lead-up to the final qualifier, I came in one day to meet the psychologists and told them I'd cracked it. I read somewhere in a Paul McKenna book about living in the moment. Looking back now it's funny because there were these two world-class psychologists thinking, 'Holy God, this is what it took to get him to understand?' But in truth they didn't care if I read it on a cereal box, they were under their own pressure to get me to understand the concept and adapt to it. And that was the last piece of the jigsaw. The two lads simply helped me work through it.

But Gary's attention to detail meant he wasn't happy with just that. Everyone was under pressure to deliver support or a contribution and he needed to make sure the psychologists weren't just trying to get him off their back. So to validate this he called me into his office a couple of days later and I told him how simple it was, that I just needed to live in the moment. But he asked me to explain further.

"Well Gary, I've been coming here to this gym for five years and I don't remember one journey, I don't know how I got here."

"We've all had those days but what's different now?"

"I get up in the morning and I have breakfast with my Ma, and I enjoy breakfast. We read the paper. And we have a yap and that's what I'm doing, spending time with my Ma."

"What next?"

"I pack my bag for training, put all my gear in and I'm focused on that."

"Then?"

"I get my CDs and I prepare for what music I want to listen to in the car when I'm driving to training. That's what I'm doing. Then I start to look at the journey, pick out things I see, take things in. I press the clutch, I feel the car go into gear."

Gary started smiling because to him this was progress and I'd finally got it. As obscure as it might seem, this was what could take me from being a hard luck story to a winner. It was the first time in my life that I wasn't just talking performance, but also understanding it. It became a natural process. I got away with it being something I had to force into my head at the Europeans in Bulgaria but suddenly it came to me as naturally as breathing. All that work in the gym had been held back by just this but now I was free.

Once I'd got it, it was more comfortable boxing in that space because I saw the performance I now owned. I also saw what I could deliver. Plus I had a smile on my face because I'd got the two things I'd wanted most. To laugh and to perform. Show me a happy under-performer and I'll show you someone that'll never be a champion. I'd worked it out after all these years, so I kept talking to Gary.

"When I get to the gym, I turn off the car, take a moment and ask myself, 'What's next?' First session warm-up. I do the best warm-up I can. When it's over I ask, 'What's the next session?' Bags. I give that everything I can and I'm not past that. Then pads. Then sparring. I'm not thinking about the qualifier, just a small part of the session. That's all and I'm doing it the best I can."

Hearing all this Gary saw a clear connection with something he witnessed years earlier. He was laughing one day because I was eating with my head down and couldn't focus. The soup would be gone and I'd be on the main course before I took time to enjoy it. I was rushing through things, rather than tasting it, enjoying it, one spoonful at a time. I'd be eating my main course, but my mind was on the dessert. And the meal was a metaphor for where I was at in life. So for Gary my change of mindset was an example of control of performance in a preparation space. And after that the challenge was whether I could hold onto that in a pressure environment. We'd all get the answer at the final qualifier in Athens.

Before we went there, I'd heard Sillakh had failed a drug test and Turkey's Bahram Muzaffer, who he had beaten, was put through in his place so he wouldn't be at the last qualifier. On top of that, another fancied Greek was gone too, so I wouldn't have to overcome any home-town decisions. But the way I was feeling, even had they been there it wouldn't have stopped me reaching my dream. My mind was no longer holding my body back.

When I went to Athens I was being challenged to slip back to my old ways at every turn. It was a thin line between returning to what caused me to be defeated and staying with what was causing me to win. One of the psychologists was saying to Gary as he watched me in the ring that my body language was actually changing from round to round and between rounds. I was shifting from a body language of protection to one that was going forward and it was almost as if I was fighting the mental battle in each fight with myself, while at the same time fighting the opposition. But now I was winning both.

After all this work and all these years, we were finally heading up towards the venue on these side roads for 30 or 40 minutes and my head kept talking to me saying, 'This is it, this is it, this is it'. The stadium was the same as for the 2004 Olympics and there were two rings going at the same time. That can be a little disconcerting. You don't know if you've scored or not, because a cheer could be for the other ring. You need to get back to your corner to find out how you are doing, and you just hope for the best news between bells.

My first fight was against an Italian called Allessandro Sinacore and after the first round I was a few down. But in the place I'd finally reached, I didn't panic. I knew I was better than him, that he wasn't of a high standard. He had a good round but the pay-off was that I had him worked out, knew what was coming, and went on to beat him by nine points. That was a good sign because after the first round, everyone in my corner was wondering how I'd react and what would happen next.

I came back so strongly that after the fight Gerry Hussey asked me what I was looking at during the bout and what made it work for me. I told him I was looking at the movement the guy was making. It wasn't about his arms moving but the shape of his torso. That told me what was coming and I'd react to that in plenty of time. Gary had always said I was very elusive and hard to hit and he understood then. *"He sees things before others and that's a champion attribute, an innate skill,"* was his description. *"He looks slow but he's fooling the opposition and you say 'how did he catch up?' but he saw the shape of the body, coming into a set position, rather than going out of it. You've to set before you can unset and if you get him in that time, the punch doesn't have to be fast."*

It was that which got me through my second fight as well, against Daniel Kooij from the Netherlands. He's a pleasant guy who I'd beaten a year before in a round-robin in Germany. He knew he couldn't beat me. I just knew by looking at him, he had too much respect. In fact the previous time we'd met, it was after I'd lost to a local guy in my first bout and after that I didn't want to be there. But I had another fight against him, it was level after the first round and Billy was like a demon. He said if I didn't get my head out of my arse, he was throwing in the towel. And then he roared at me to get off the stool and to start boxing. It was the first time he did it to me. I got up and beat up Kooij and little things like that matter. If I had lost that fight, it could have affected me in the qualifier. But as it happened I won both comfortably.

And then there was the German, Gottlieb Weiss. Two fights out of the way, and suddenly this was it. One fight away from qualifying. Again. Weiss was a big lad, in superb nick, really well conditioned. And he was staring me down in the biggest fight of my career. I'd sparred him at training camps around the place and he was good. I'd never left a ring after fighting him thinking he was a better boxer than I was but I'd never thought I was better than him either. It was only the semi-final technically, but it was my entire career wrapped into one contest. Just win this fight and I would be going to Beijing. Once again I stared at the final hurdle. Push on or fall over?

This was what it was all about. I was thinking that morning that if I win I am an Olympian, lose and I go back home to Dublin and be remembered as an eight times senior champion who has a taxi plate and rambles on to customers from the front seat about how 'I could've been a contender'. Maybe I shouldn't have been thinking like that, but while part of me suggested I'd failed here so many times before, I was able to really convince myself there was a big difference this time. I had that belief in my preparation that Padraig Harrington had talked about and my mind went into autopilot when it came to breaking things down to their smallest. It wasn't this fight, or even these rounds. It was the next punch.

John Joe Joyce had qualified just before me and Darren Sutherland had been brilliant and qualified too. That was four qualified, and who was left? The old dog.

We kept it nice and relaxed in the dressing room where there was a big Irish flag hanging on the wall. I don't know if this happens to all boxers but there's a point in the warm-up, no matter how big the fight, when I think to myself, 'What am I doing here?' It's been happening since I was 11 years of age and I say to myself that I must be mad because at its most basic this is a fight, he's going to punch me in the face as hard as he can and it's going to hurt. But I tried to get rid of that thought and replaced it with how I'd box Weiss, what I'd start with, how I'd go from there, how was my hydration. Ticking boxes, just making sure everything was good to go.

Then I got dressed in reverse order, like always. Finally I put on a T-shirt for the pad work because it gets wet and you don't want your vest making you cold come fight time. You do this about an hour before you are due into the ring. With 20 minutes to take-off I wrap my own hands. I have always wrapped my own hands. I start a slow warm-up, take my time, get the heart beating, break a little sweat. Then I do a minute of fast stuff on the pads. When you are around long enough you know your opponent, how to score against him and you work on those shots. Then you speed up the pad work even more with a round to go in the fight before you. That's it then. Face Vaselined up to avoid cuts, you head out into the unknown.

I came out of the dressing room before that fight, Billy and Zaur behind me. *"Take your time, one punch at a time,"* they kept saying. *"The here and now, don't think about the result,"* I kept saying. The referee checked my head guard. I punched Billy's hand as I always do. And then ding ding. My life on the line.

I was moving, feinting, picking the shots. We clashed. Then another clash. No matter how big the crowd is you only hear select voices. There is muffle from everyone but I always hear Billy and Zaur. *"Left hand. Go to the body. Double jab."* It's not on top of everything else because the rest comes naturally. If I'm moving, I'm doing what I'm trained to do. But when they call the shot that means an immediate instruction because they can see the opening. Then I'd nail him. But I'm around long enough to know the shot. Besides, the coach isn't supposed to talk much. Zaur got warned once during a fight of mine. He was screaming and shouting and the referee had a talk. Next thing Billy was shouting, the referee came over again, Billy pointed at Zaur and he got sent away. He was F-ing and blinding his way down to a seat at the back while Billy was trying to keep a straight face.

In Athens, the bell went at the end of the first round and it was all-square. Billy was telling me to keep doing the same. A good coach will only tell you one or two things because you are only there for 45 seconds. You don't want lists of instructions, just simple advice, a drop of water and then back out again.

At the start of the second there was this little devil in my head, creating negative thoughts that were creeping in. They were about the other qualifiers, falling flat on my face at final hurdles. But halfway through the second round I took a step back, told myself it was time to take this fight. It was just me and him in this ring, nothing else mattered. Suddenly I got into a zone where I was close enough to score my points. You have to get into that danger zone where you can throw shots, there's no point in being out too far, and lunging and missing. It's like fencing. But in there I'm busy and you have to be able to avoid his shots and then score. It's very hard to stay there and work all the time but you have to if you want to win against quality.

Next thing I started scoring points and he was missing, I get ahead by one, two, three, four, five, six. I got back to the corner

Standing full of hope alongside tragic Darren Sutherland (right) and John Joe Joyce after we qualified for the Olympics. Darren was a good friend and he is sadly missed. BELOW: With Minister for Sport Martin Cullen before heading to Beijing with the rest of the Irish team

Dad and my brother celebrate after my first fight outside the Beijing Workers Gym, and (below) mayhem inside my family home in Clondalkin

Smashing Tony Jeffries in the Olympic semi-final ...

... and getting in a big shot into China's Xiaoping Zhang in the final

Photos by: LORRAINE O'SULLIVAN/INPHO

I drop to my knees after losing out to China's Xiaoping Zhang in the final

A consoling hug from Billy as Zaur looks on. It was the end of the dream, but still my biggest moment in boxing, and one that changed my life

The Irish fans were unreal in Beijing, and even though I was disappointed with the result, I couldn't help but have a sneaky kiss of Xiaoping Zhang's gold medal

Myself, Darren Sutherland and Paddy Barnes pose with our medals after landing back at Dublin Airport, and (below) with Mam at the homecoming

Photo by: MICK O'NEILL/ALLPIX

A day to remember as I took home the Olympic silver medal to my native Clondalkin

Photo by: PA WIRE

Photo by: PAUL NICHOLLS/ALLPIX

A proud moment for Mam and Dad as we were invited to the Aras to meet President Mary McAleese and her husband Martin, and (below) with my good pal Gary Keegan who presented me with the Irish Sports Council's 2009 Boxer of the Year award

Photo by: JIM WALPOLE

before the fourth and final round, Billy was telling me to calm, Zaur was getting excited with a big smile on his face. This guy was a bit of a puncher but the fight had changed, he had to come after me. I could counter-punch, pick him off, get the scores and that's how I like to box. I went further ahead, 21-11 and then the final bell went. I dropped to my knees. It was 11 April, 2007, the happiest day of my life. Forget about the medals that came later, this was what I'd always wanted. Kenneth Egan, the Olympian.

I came out of the ring and Billy told me that out of everyone in the gym he wanted me in Beijing most, because I'd been around so long, struggling away. But it wasn't just about me or the five of us that qualified. It was a validation of all the struggle and pain everyone went through. It says on the tin it's an individual sport but that's not the case at all. And for so many people that supported me, that moment meant something different.

Back in Dublin, Mam was hearing the news from her kitchen. John had just come in from work and at four o'clock she heard on the radio Kenneth Egan was in the ring, so she turned it off and waited. A few moments later, my coach Gerry Fleming's wife Suzanne rang the house from Athens to say I'd made it and my Mam turned to John.

"There's someone on the phone saying he's qualified."

"Who is it?" asked John.

"I've no idea. Did I hear it right? Did I hear it right?"

Next thing it came on the news. So she rang Dad who was working in the hotel. The night before she insisted that if I came out on top that he would go to China again, and when he answered the phone she never even said I'd won. She simply shouted *"You're going to Beijing!"*

I went on to the final and boxed Kennedy Katende from Sweden. I won 15-10 but that didn't matter. We had both qualified and we gave each other a big hug at the end. By then Gary was out on his feet. We took three gold medals in the end and when it was over his phone rang. He then found a quiet alcove in the stadium but his legs just buckled. He had been drained of all his energy. On the other end of the phone was Sharon Madigan who was the nutritionist and she had the phone in one hand, pans rattling in the other, two babies screaming and she was crying tears of joy. The Olympics was going to be easier for sure because we had earned our stripes, gone through war, knew what it was like and didn't fear it anymore.

That's what that journey was about for Sharon. That's what it was about for Gary. That's what it was about for Mam. We all had different paths and different stories.

****

But if getting to Beijing was, for me, one tough battle, another one is coming at me fast because of what awaits after New York and awaits me as I consider dealing with my drinking. But between then and now awaits another night and another morning. And feeling this drunk at just nine o'clock leaves me wondering what will wake me in the morning.

A spear of light breaking through a gap in the curtains and bringing me back to the reality of day, a reality that I keep trying to run from but can never escape? The difficulty of trying to swallow down a throat that's dry and scorched from shot, after short, after beer? The realisation in the middle of the night that there's a cloaked, faceless figure standing high at the end of the bed, casting a black shadow over me, before I pull the duvet over my head, pull myself together and remember that it's just the alcohol that's making this happen? Or knowing this lifestyle can't go on forever, I can't keep running and just like in Athens I'm going to have to stand up and face my fear?

PART 2

"People forgot that Kenneth Egan was just a normal lad who worked his arse off to get to that position and deserved to be celebrated. But because of alcohol, we never really got to see the champion he was. Look at Brian O'Driscoll or Padraig Harrington and how they are regarded. It hurts that Kenneth will never get that admiration, but it was his own fault because he was almost like a man who hadn't lived out his teenage life in a natural way. But while a teenager can be forgiven for his mistakes, Kenneth couldn't be forgiven and he wasn't handling it very well because his drink problem was experienced in this goldfish bowl of fame. But the bottom line is we cannot avoid the fact he has a problem with the potential to destroy him. It could take one alcoholic 20 years to destroy himself, it could take Kenneth a much shorter time."

Gary Keegan, Director, Irish Institute of Sport

CHAPTER 1

Wednesday, August 24, 2011, Dublin

8.30am

It's strange the things that wake you up from the deep caverns of a sober sleep. There are times when it's still unpleasant because of what went before. And occasionally there's the short, sharp shock of a flashback that causes you to sit up in the middle of the night and try to draw breath through a twisted tangle of panic. It happened a while ago after I'd been in a pub in Kilkenny with my Mam and aunt for a few hours but had enough of drinking orange juice and went to bed early. Next thing I imagined I was waking up with a throat that was dry and scorched. There was the heaviness of my head, the pain in my temple, the horrible clamminess of my body on sheets that were damp from yet another night of drink that had been trying to escape through every pore. But I pulled myself out of what turned out to be nothing more than a nightmare and remembered I don't drink anymore. I won't drink anymore. I can't drink anymore. It's been over a year since I touched alcohol and I'm determined to keep it that way.

This morning, there's none of that. Instead it's the simplicity of a refreshing brush of cool air on my skin that feels alive and no longer dies and peels away from my scalp. I open my eyes to the soothing morning light, I open my ears to the conversation coming from the kitchen. I open my nostrils to the smell of breakfast wafting its way up the stairs. They are all sensations that seem enhanced when there isn't alcohol distorting my body.

I look around my bedroom in my parents' house in

Clondalkin and the recent past puts the present into perspective. I glance over at the clock which strikes eight and remember what it used to be like to wake up at this time when I was still drinking. It wasn't just the sickening feeling of your body rejecting what you'd put in it the night before that hurt, it was the time until the doors of the bar opened again. There were occasions when, before I went to sleep, I'd pray that I didn't wake up before 10.30. And when I did come around a few hours later, before I checked the time, I'd pray once more. If it was 10.15 I could handle it, if it was 9am I'd start to get agitated. If it was the time it is now, just after eight o'clock, I could break down. I'd get angry and nervous and scared all at once and I always noticed that on those hungover mornings time passed by so very slowly. I was counting the seconds in my head and there was a ticking in my mind.

In the corner of the room now, my clothes are neatly folded. It wasn't like that before. I used to piss myself a lot when I was drinking heavily and I often went out the next day in the same jeans. It got to the stage where I knew it wasn't just sweat just by the feeling, and I had to get out of the house in case Mam saw me and judged me. And of course, tried to stop me. Back on the beer then for the day, in tatters and after the first two pints you were tired but artificially raring to go. And then I wouldn't remember. People would say I went to Coppers, a nightclub in town, and I'd just fall around with two vodka and whites in my hands and I'd have to take them on their word. In fact, just before I went to New York, myself and Paul Burgess, the son of Rory who owns Boomers, were in one of the pubs on Camden Street. We came out onto the road and I was about to vomit so he pulled me up a side alley so no one would see. Up and out it came creating space for more and more drink. Normal people would say that's gone way past the time to stop, but I'd say that the tank was then empty and I was now ready for a refill.

The next morning you'd hope you didn't wake too early and you'd go again. Groundhog Day. A goldfish bowl. Misery. You'd go down to the pub at 10.30 and it'd be all old lads nursing a pint of Guinness for hours and talking about the good old days. The Monday club got a bit of a crowd in but the rest of the weekdays were depressingly empty. But I still couldn't leave. If I got tired, I'd often sleep in the lounge for a couple of hours because it had a nice couch. I can't say they should have sent me home, it wasn't their job. It was my job but I was incapable of doing it.

****

Back in my bedroom and the voices rise and fall with the swell of the conversation downstairs. There's the noise of knives and forks against plates occasionally cutting through the laughter. Before, those were sounds that kept me here in this room until I saw a chance to get away without anyone noticing. I was constantly paranoid. But now those same sounds tempt me to get up because I want the company, I want to be part of their banter and laughter, and now that I have stopped drinking and making a fool of myself, they want to include me as well. *"Will you get out of that bed, Kenneth,"* someone roars up.

When I was growing up Mam told us that as brothers we all had to look out for each other. There were five of us and she told us to care for one another and never make a show of one another. We were pretty good at it too. There was a time Willie had a Seat Ibiza and Tony took it without permission and wrote it off. Willie was on the sofa when a garda came to the door and the first thing Willie asked was if Tony was hurt. The garda wondered aloud did he want to press charges but he clearly didn't know our family. By that evening I was with the two of them and our Dad having a post-mortem over pints in Boomers and talking about how to fix the car. But there was no blame or anger. We were that close and we knew what was most important.

But when it came to me, they saw the changes after Beijing, and they didn't want to be part of my new world. My brothers wouldn't go for a pint with me because by the time they'd head out for a quiet one at an acceptable hour, I'd have been hitting it hard since 10.30 that morning. Then at night when I finally did come home they'd sit me down and lecture me. Mam would tell them to wait until the next day but there were too many next days. When I woke up knowing there was a stern talking-to awaiting I always had an escape plan. I'd go out the door with the gear bag, say I was going to the stadium, but there was no training and I wouldn't come back for three or four days. I'd do anything to avoid that conversation in the kitchen and the noise of knives and forks, people and life.

My brothers would lie to me too just to keep their distance. Once I asked them if they were going out and they told me they'd prefer a quiet night in the house. A few hours later I saw them all in a pub. They just didn't want to be near me and looking back now I don't blame them. At one stage in Boomers I fell clean off a high stool in the lounge. If that happened to someone else, people would just ask if I was okay but by then the same people had started to look at me and shake their heads. A couple of days later I was in a pub and someone said *"Alright Paul McGrath?"* That struck a chord. That's the road I was going down. I was a mess.

Nothing would stop me though. For most, money is a barrier but I didn't care about cash. I was living at home and there was money coming in from the sports grant and from sponsorship. John told me to cut up my Banklink card and I even did that a few times, drunk, of my own accord. When I'd come home feeling miserable, I'd take a scissors to my bank cards hoping that it would stop me. But then I'd wake up sober and get a new one, even though deep down I didn't want it. And while I was waiting for the new card I'd go into Boomers bar and say, *"Give us a loan of €200 quid and I'll give it back to you Wednesday."* They were happy enough because if I got it early it was going straight back over the bar. And if it was later on, I'd hit them for another €200 because I'd want to go to a nightclub to prolong the night and avoid coming back to this room, my own company and that shivering misery and loneliness.

Forcing my brothers to push me away was one thing. Managing to do the same to my Mam was another.

Imagine driving your own mother to a point where she is close to disowning you? I don't remember it but she tells me I came back to the house one night, and all she heard was this thump. I fell into the bath tub while trying to take a piss and whacked my head off the tiles. She was sure I'd killed myself such was the bang. She was trying to pull me out of the tub and the next thing noticed all this blood running down my face. She kept trying to get me up but she's a little woman and I was close to 13 stone of unconscious, but not quite dead, weight. Finally she panicked and called her friend Bernie and between them they rolled me onto the floor and dragged me into bed.

But Mam was so worried about the bleeding she spent the entire night at my bedside making sure I was still breathing. When I did come around I asked where I was. There was all this cotton wool in my ear and for months she didn't tell me what had happened. She thought she'd be better off leaving it because she saw I had become so self-righteous that giving out would only make me worse. No one cared though outside of my mother's house. To the rest of the world I was a great lad, everyone wanted a piece of me. But the nice, polite guy who didn't offend anyone was gone. I was turning into someone even my own mother didn't like. Dad even suggested she throw me out after that bathtub episode but she said she couldn't because I'd have been worse than ever. Dad wasn't happy.

But they are now downstairs in the kitchen and despite everything they are calling me. They've forgiven so much, so quickly. There's a cup of tea poured and a place set and they shout up as I lie here enjoying waking up, feeling alive, looking forward to the day and getting ready to embrace it rather than kill it dead. And I look forward to getting down there and enjoying their company. I've never said it to them but I admire how they've stuck by me after I tested them so often.

They've told me since that the first six months after the Olympics were grand but they could see me losing my way, day by day. Mam cursed that medal even more than I did. Whatever people might say about me, I was never rude before, and suddenly I acquired this obnoxious attitude and it all came from that medal. Quite simply, I put them through hell. More hell than I was ever experiencing. More hell than I was living through in *Jack Dempsey's*, and *Seven*, and the twin room in the Chelsea Hotel on West 23rd Street.

I still can't work out why I did it and can't recognise the person that was there in those places; the person that by the end of that Sunday night in New York ended up with Lauren, but was far too drunk to appreciate it. In fact, when Lauren came to the hotel reception, I had to tell Stephen to send her up because I couldn't physically stand to go down and meet her. She made it up to the room and I'd say she was shocked because I was lying on the bed twitching and she kept asking was I alright. She didn't know about the Olympics so I took out my iPhone and was bragging, showing her some pictures. There was quite a difference between the person in Beijing and the person shaking there in the room. I passed it off as just a little bit of a bender and because we were together, Stephen couldn't get back into the room. Later that night he opened the next door down, found a laundry closet and slept there for the rest of the night.

But it was a bender that ended suddenly. On the Monday night, myself and Stephen went to the cinema. We had enough drink and saw some horror movie. I only read recently that the actor Jonathan Rhys Myers has some reaction where his legs twitch because of the drink. I had that reaction in the cinema again. I was sitting there, eating bits of popcorn, twitching for the whole night. I don't know how it works but I couldn't stop it.

That should have been the last night in America but when we went to the airport that Tuesday we were told we'd missed our flight by a day. It wasn't our fault though, we had expressed the dates we wanted in Dublin Airport and it was the airline who messed up. So after a bit of pleading they agreed to put us onto the flight the next day. That actually worked out well though. The media had got wind that we were coming back on Tuesday and were there waiting for me. By Wednesday they were gone.

But just in case, in the airport in New York I bought sun glasses to cover my eye and called Billy Walsh and Gary Keegan. They knew a guy working in airport security in Dublin who used to box and he was able to usher me out a side door.

I feel so guilty for all of that because of what those caring people downstairs went through when all they'd ever done was support me. But I still have never understood the reaction of the press. I missed an international. *So what?* There are Irish soccer players pulling out of internationals right, left and centre and there isn't a whole lot said about their commitment. It's the way I approached it which was wrong but the way the press approached me was every bit as wrong. It was so bad that when I did get in touch with Gary before we left for home, he said it was best I didn't go back to Clondalkin. Instead he suggested I meet him in the Irish Institute of Sport in Abbotstown, where he was working.

Billy was there with him and since I've dried out they've mentioned the previous international trip to Poland and believe the first signs of a problem occurred out there. So they knew there was a background but they never had a bad experience with me in all the years that followed. A couple of times I'd gone AWOL but it's normal to lose it for a short while when you've spent nine months working and then don't deliver. It's an acceptable pain and sometimes a person has to retreat and heal themselves.

Both Billy and Gary had personally known alcoholics, and knew that it could be hidden well. But whatever I was doing with the other 10 per cent of my life, 90 per cent of the time I was a professional so who were they to complain? But both of them knew that after Beijing, they were on the back foot in terms of the challenges they were facing when it came to me. But the strength of the relationship and the caring they had for me as a boxer made it hard to make the tough decisions I needed. After Beijing I was given too long of a soft landing and that hurt me. People were always trying to cover for me but I'd taken an inch, then a yard, and New York was the 3,000 miles that pushed it all too far.

I guess they could see that I was running. It was weird the way it was probably the same person Gary had in front of him after the World Championships in Chicago in 2007 who was pacing from one side of the room to the other, lost. The same guy who was running scared because he couldn't handle it all. More than most people, it takes a lot of time for me to trust someone and a lot of new faces had come into my sphere of influence after the Olympics. They had things they wanted to achieve with me, or around 'Kenny', and I was someone that people could make money from, or a name off. A lot of people tried to do that and I think through all of it Gary and Billy learned that we may have trained like machines, but the boxers in the gym were normal people with flaws. At the end of the day, we were just regular men: dads, husbands, ordinary guys who could do some things and couldn't do others.

There was a lot I couldn't do and people were learning that fast. But before Beijing, Gary and Billy never saw me as a big ego. Even though I was struggling at times with my own perfor-mance in the ring, I was team captain and always the guy Billy could turn to. I never upset anyone in the gym, I always gave my all and was open. They cared about me so much that before the plane landed from New York, Billy actually cried. Gary had put on the motivation piece I used on my iPod at the Olympics and it made him think of what I was like then and what I had done to myself and it brought him to tears. I guess I meant so much to them and now they saw me suddenly in the gutter.

I had hurt them but, strangely, they weren't angry at all. They just didn't know where they were going to find me and if they could put me back on the right track because what we do as boxers is very addictive. We train every day. If you don't, you feel guilty, because you are always in routines. And this drinking had become my new routine. Billy and Gary both said that I had a giving nature which put me at risk because when I became a name, I wasn't streetwise. I might look like the tough guy boxing out of Neilstown but that was just a tag. A lot of people didn't have my best interests at heart but I never suspected that. I'd grown up in the gym where everyone only wanted the best for me. Gary and Billy always cared and they wanted to get me right again after New York.

But if I didn't want help, no matter how much they wanted to help it wouldn't matter. They'd be wasting their time. And I still wasn't sure if I wanted to get back on sober feet even though Gary had calls from my Mam crying down the phone when I was in New York. She probably had it worse than anyone. She didn't fully realise how bad things had become when she got the call from the air hostess as we were leaving Dublin. All she thought about was that I was supposed to be boxing the next night. Then the phone started ringing off the hook. Billy was wondering where I was but she had no answer for him. Another man rang the house demanding the money back for his tickets even though the international went ahead with a replacement filling in for me. And she still didn't know where I was. That was the worst part for her. Had she known I had boarded a flight and was away drinking it would have made her angry, but that emotion is an awful lot better than fear and worry.

That entire weekend she was left wondering. It wasn't until the Monday that Willie came in and said he knew where I was. *"Where,"* she asked? *"New York."* It clicked then, lined up nicely with the seven hours the air hostess mentioned she'd be looking after me.

The journalists didn't care about her feelings though. Outside the house a media frenzy was building up. A reporter asked Dad if I'd be coming back here to his house and my bedroom and he said that I wouldn't. The next day there was a story suggesting off the back of this that *'Kenny's father has thrown him out'.* That wasn't what he meant at all and they knew it. They had microphones taped on the windowsill and were listening to private conversations inside the house. It seemed like there were no boundaries.

In my mind it was the first time the media in Ireland really attacked an athlete outside a sport in that kind of way. For instance, one day my father was there, sitting at the bar in

Boomers, reading the paper with his Guinness parked in front of him. This female journalist came in, and asked for directions to the toilet as a way of breaking the ice. *"The toilet is down there, go have your piss and when you're finished fuck off out of here,"* he said. And he's the calmest man you could meet. They'd never ask directly, they'd be really sly, and then throw in after a while, *"Have you seen Kenny Egan about."* The barman told another reporter, *"He was here this morning, but went to Johnnie Fox's."* Off up the mountains this reporter went while I was a couple of doors down.

But I was caught up in my own little world. Feeling sorry for myself. Thinking about myself. Worrying about myself. No one else mattered, they didn't even register. By the early darkness of that Wednesday morning after New York I was out in the institute and Gary told me I looked like a ghost. I hadn't shaved and had this cut on my face and he thought I had been in a row. But I'd got myself into this dark place and Gary and Billy were there to get me out of it. First up we agreed to issue an apology to the people that paid to watch me box alongside my teammates. So we gave a formal apology. Then Gary told me to go to his house and stay there so after a long talk I left the institute with him. His place is out on the north side of Dublin, and the media were all still outside my house. There, the entire saga was finding ways to reach new lows.

My brother John and a friend, Alan O'Reilly, were driving around having a ball because the media thought John was me and they were following him everywhere. They started playing games, changing cars, thinking they were in *'The General'.* Everyone wanted the first picture so some sections of the media were chasing around the estate after family and friends just in case they were going to meet me. They even offered my brother Tony money to set it up. He was going to work one morning at 7.30 but when it happened, he rang Mam straight away and told her to be careful. It wasn't just affecting us either. Later that day, Pat Foley who lives across the road came over and told them to get their cars off the street because he couldn't get out to work.

We'd never seen anything like this.

In fact, when Mam and Willie were coming to see me at Gary's house they had a car trailing them too. Being in the Army, Willie knew this game and he could see what was happening straight away. So when they passed the toll bridge they swung in and stopped and this other car had to keep going. They watched it fly by and headed off down along the back roads.

By this stage, poor Stephen was in town collecting my car, which cost a fortune to get out of the car park, and he was heading to the Quays too, hoping that silver medal was still sitting behind the bar. But he'd gotten dragged into it too. One newspaper wrote about him being a *hanger-on* and were blaming him as if I was this innocent pillar of society. There were stories that he was just using me. But the truth is that I was using him. Anything that he was, then so was I. The two of us were as bad as each other.

Thankfully the medal was still in Temple Bar, and while he was getting that, Mam finally made it out to see me. She was so mad with all this, but relieved too as we hugged. She kept asking if I was okay, and I kept telling her that I was fine. Some papers had even suggested she was going to give me two black eyes. I knew she'd never do that but I didn't know what to expect. To be honest, all I saw in her was relief. When I'd left, I didn't think it'd be that bad missing an international but moment by moment, the reactions of people closest to me were telling a very different story.

I hadn't slept properly in a long time and didn't sleep right in the few days I was in Gary's house either. I used to joke when I was drinking about getting insomnia. But it wasn't that. It was alcohol that kept me awake and some nights the bed would start to vibrate like something out of 'The Exorcist'. Then every now and again I'd just hear a bang in my ear. The loudest bang you'd ever heard. I'd laugh about it when I told the lads but it was scary. But it was very good of Gary to let me stay there, sleep or no sleep. He essentially brought me to live with him and he and Billy spoke to some friends in the media, asking them to try and step away and talk to their colleagues and get them to back off because it was not nice to witness. There were things I did that everyone knew and they weren't all that serious. But people weren't focused on the most serious thing in all this — I was destroying myself. I was upsetting my family and parents but wasn't really hurting anyone else. I was the one who'd be paying the biggest price.

At that point in Gary's house I had a little bit of clarity and spent time with his kids. Gary's youngest daughter was 16 and son was 20 and I watched movies with them and talked to them. Seemingly they liked the fact they had an Olympic medal winner in the house and I was just sitting there talking to them like an ordinary person. But I wasn't the ordinary person I'd trained myself to be over many years. A good bender would go for a week and I'd go from 83 kilos right down to 79. I wasn't eating, just picking at food, and all the muscle I did have was turning to fat. I'd notice the skin on my arms wasn't tight. Others wouldn't notice it, but I could. I could even see it in my face as my chin and cheekbones drooped.

****

But right now I don't pick at my food. I eat. I'm strong. I'm 83 kilos and there's little fat. So I jump out of bed, and feel energetic as I walk to the bathroom, I throw some cold water on my face and it makes me feel like the last three years have just been a nightmare. I can believe in Beijing because I worked so hard for that. But all of the rest is hard to comprehend and I sometimes think I'll just walk into my mother's kitchen, take my place for breakfast, and none of it will ever have happened. Nothing aches, and I feel alive. So much so that my stomach rumbles with the smell of food and I'm glad I'm up so early because there's so much to look forward to. The good seems so much better when you've come face to face with the bad.

It's a million miles away from Gary's house and the days I spent there. Fair play to him, he looked after me and when he went to work, I hung around. Both him and Billy had told me to forget boxing. They were worried about my health. With that, I started drinking water, and it was needed because my skin was flaky. Mentally I was starting to come around but I felt that I was in somebody else's body. Before that I'd look in the mirror and, seeing the ultimate fighting machine, healthy, on the weight, good skin, I was so positive. Suddenly I was a coward lying in a bed shaking, cold sweat running down my back, my hair didn't even feel like it belonged to me. People who have been there understand. There are cramps all over your body, pains in your kidneys and stomach because you are dehydrated and haven't eaten properly in days. The smell of sweat was disgusting. I was showering a couple of times a day because I was vile. And I felt sorry for myself, wondering why I was doing all this but could not stop. I didn't even think I had a problem with drink. I thought I'd get back to training and everything would be okay again. I never thought I'd be in AA and off drink. I'd travelled miles on that path and still didn't even know what direction I was going.

Finally I decided I needed to restart some sort of a normal life. There was a team heading to Belfast and I wanted to go. Billy and Gary asked if I was ready for that but I told them I needed to get out of there and just do something I was familiar with that didn't involve a pub. Back in my house Mam had told my brother John that I needed gear for this so they were getting the suitcase up over the back wall so those waiting outside couldn't see. Stephen's brother Alan came over. He's a big man of about 30 stone and I'd have loved to have seen him and John trying to lug this case into a neighbour's garden and into a car. Worse still, Mam had to pack this suitcase for a week's training in Belfast. I didn't know what was going to be in it but she did well in fairness.

When I did get hold of some training gear I went out to the beach beside Gary's home and tried to run. I got about 200 metres and stopped. I wasn't fit. I was thinking to myself, *'how could I ever get back to where I once was?'* All the negative stuff was getting into my mind, I was wondering, *'how I was ever going to get out of this rut? How was I going to explain myself to all the people I'd let down?'* I was embarrassed. So I stopped running, went back to the house sweating and got into the shower. Then I just went back to bed again with a barrage of thoughts running through my head. Stupid stuff. Random stuff. *'What I was I going to tell people, and how could the Olympics be so good but lead to all this?'*

But every day I was improving. I'd eat a little more. It was like I'd been sick and was on the mend in hospital. I was holding down food and started to feel good about things. So I went to Belfast. I was with Gary and on the way he took my phone and there was every sort of number in it. Within the space of six months I'd built up a network of people in my life that had never been in it up to then. Half the time I didn't know who I was talking to. I'd give a number to a journalist thinking they worked in a sports department when actually they wrote gossip columns. And I kept losing phones and just adding more and more numbers. In Billy's phone he had Kenneth Egan 1, Kenneth Egan 2, Kenneth Egan 3, Kenneth Egan 4 and Kenneth Egan 5.

So Gary took out the SIM card, folded it until it snapped and threw it out the window. He told me to close the Twitter account as well because this wasn't Kenneth Egan; this was a human being in a state of intoxication, out of his head and trying to handle this pressure and success. It was a bad combination.

With all that done, we went on to the camp and I was tipping away. The coaches asked me to stand up and say a few words to the team so I did. I told them I was back, that I was sorry that I'd let them down for the international against America. I said that I was out of order as I was supposed to be the captain of this team and everyone else was leading me by their example when it should have been the opposite. That was it. They accepted me back in.

We were training in the Ulster University in Jordanstown and on the second day I was coming across the car park and looked towards the far end of it, just gauging my surroundings.

There was this guy with a long-lens camera staring at me. He was like a sniper over the bonnet of his car. But I managed to duck inside and he didn't get the picture. But when I got inside there was another crowd from Dublin asking if they could get a photograph of the team. At a training camp? *Bullshit.* The coaches said no problem, stuck me into another room and brought everyone else out for a few shots. I could hear them asking after a few minutes, *"Any sign of Kenny Egan?"* and Billy replying, *"Ah no, he's not part of this camp."*

But finally the newspapers got the photo they wanted and it was all very Irish the way it came about. The bus in which we travelled was an Irish Olympic Council transit van, with a big logo on the side of it. We came out of the university one day, got in this thing and the lights must have been left on because the engine wouldn't start. So we all got out and were pushing it up the road and that was the picture that was snapped. The next day, the captions in the papers read 'Kenny EgAAn'. They obviously meant it as in the Automobile Association, but they missed the real meaning which was that I did actually need AA of a very different kind. Or maybe they didn't.

I sparred well up there. I know that I am gifted but it still scares me to this day that I nearly wasted it all. Once I started eating healthily again, was regaining my muscle and got back into a routine, I was telling myself that I was healed and all was well in the world. And, at least, that is the way it seemed.

That day in the institute after we talked about all the other problems, the idea of me still fighting Zhang Xiaoping, the Chinese guy that had gotten the decision over me in the Olympic final, came up. I was due to fight Xiaoping as part of the undercard for Bernard Dunne's world title fight, and I was telling Gary and Billy that I'd be ready to take him on. They were looking at me, asking if I was sure. I was there nodding with a big scab on my face, weak as a kitten and light for the weight. The Chinese camp wanted to fight at 84 kilos and he was a big man. But the fight was a pipe dream and it's my only real regret from that time.

That it was even a possibility was all thanks to Gerry Fleming, my coach. At the start they had me on the bill and the promoter Brian Peters just wanted me to fight anyone. But Gerry said we'd try to go big and knew a Chinese girl that spoke English and managed to get in touch with their association. Peters said, *"If you can get the Chinese guy, we'll look after you."* Katie Taylor was on that undercard as well and I don't know what she received, but I was to get €20,000. And that was just to fight four two-minute rounds. I was going to give Gerry four grand for organising it and we agreed to it with Peters. I did the photo shoot with Dunne and Cordoba, and Dom O'Rourke and the IABA didn't mind because the association was getting a few quid out of it.

I was thinking in New York that I'd come back and do it, but then I changed my mind and axed it. Luckily enough I didn't sign a contract because Peters could have sued me, but on the small print of the poster it said it was the title fight that was guaranteed but that the rest of the card could change, so Peters was covered. In the end I watched that fight between Dunne and Cordoba in a hotel room in Cork. I had gone down to visit a friend, and I was kicking myself while watching it. The atmosphere was incredible, the title fight was epic, and I could have been a part of it. Missing that fight is the one moment I struggle to get over in my career.

Peters was pissed off with me as well, and rightly so. I haven't really spoken to him since and he's another person in a long list I have to apologise to. I will do it too. He puts on the best show in the country and it would have been great to have been part of that. If I had of been in top shape it would have been a nice little earner and some small bit of revenge as well. Drink cost me all of that.

But it's not going to cost me anything this morning, or this day or any other day in my life. I assure myself of that as I walk across the landing, enter my room and look at the clock. It's 8.32 and standing in this airy room surrounded by the memorabilia of my proudest moments in the ring, I tell myself the best part of the day now opens out long and wide in front of me.

CHAPTER 2

8.33am

I head out the bedroom door, down the stairs, across the hall and into the kitchen. The warmth of family life wraps around me. I take my seat at the table, grab my cup of tea, and tear into my breakfast, making conversation through a stuffed mouth. We talk about the distant past, the present and the future. But no one mentions recent events. It's a no-go area because while I'd like to say that life automatically returned to this kind of existence after New York, it didn't. That trip should have been a wake-up call but for quite a while I kept hitting the snooze button. So while that trip to America was a shuddering bump on the road, there were many more that didn't make the headlines but were every bit as bad. I'm ashamed to admit that some were even worse when it comes to the anguish I put the people here at the family table through.

Dad sits quietly as always, listening to us interrupt each other because we all have opinions we think matter most and we all have a story that we think is funnier than the previous one. He flitters through the pages of the newspaper and takes in what we say as my Mam and my brothers join me in talking about almost everything. Stories from when we were kids. Boxing. The Olympics. But the one glaring omission causes me to retreat from what's happening at the table. Ignoring the days and months after Beijing is so obvious and so artificial that I cannot avoid it in my head. So I take a small swig of tea, lean against the hard back of the chair and drift away into the past, as the rest of the family go on laughing and arguing.

****

My great fear in life, aside from airplanes, used to be getting knocked out in the ring. I guess that was proof I didn't know my own weakness because it wasn't someone else I needed to worry about. The biggest danger was staring right back at me every time I looked in the mirror. For years I was never put on my arse, even in sparring in the High Performance Unit. I was always thinking that was inevitable at some stage and it was always in the back of my head. I saw other guys going down so I said it to Gary Keegan one day, told him I'd this silly fear that I was going to be floored. The worst thing about it was not knowing what it was like. I was a middleweight when I first mentioned it and Gary was going to arrange to come into the stadium on a day off and get Alan Reynolds, who was heavyweight, in with me and let him knock my lights out. That would be it out of the way but it never came to pass.

Finally in 2006, at the European Championships in Latvia, I was fighting this small Russian and eventual winner Artur Beterbiyev, in the semi-final. He caught me with a hook and I hit the canvas. When I got up and looked at Billy, he smiled as if to say: that's it out of the way now. I went back at it and got nailed with the same punch. Back down again. That was the end of the second round but I kept on going and only lost on points. Zaur was there at the end, *"My God Kenny, you have some heart."* But forget about heart, experiencing it was most important because it's an odd sensation and not what I was expecting. Your legs just disappear. It wasn't sore, even afterwards. It's just if you get hit by someone properly, and it doesn't have to be hard, no matter how much muscle you have, you are going down. That's why it's so important to have hands up, elbows in, chin down.

I sparred last Christmas with Darren O'Neill and he hit me with a hook and it happened once more. He creased me. *"That's payback,"* he said because when we were coming through the ranks, I'd done it to him many a time and he was always in my shadow. He was 81 kilos and came down to 75 and used to lose to Darren Sutherland quite a bit. He'd an awful bad habit of locking up when you attacked him. He couldn't hit you and the opponent could do what they wanted. But now he's up taller so you don't know where he's going to throw a punch from. He never gave up though. He could have easily turned away when he was losing finals and been happy being a teacher. But he kept coming back.

I was coming off the beer at that stage though and it's the hardest shot I'd ever been hit with. I got up and boxed on, but it was supposed to be five rounds of three minutes but Billy called it after just three rounds because we were killing each other. But at that stage having experienced both a knockdown and alcoholism I knew well which one to worry about more. There was no competition. While my family will joke about me being flattened as we finish the remainder of the food that's out on the table, they won't even mention the alcohol.

When it came to the alcoholism, the biggest problem for me was slipping out of one routine and getting dragged down by another one. I have it in me to go crazy on drink if I don't have something else to focus my mind on. Boxing was that something else for a long time because all of it is so regimental. Take our training. It's Tuesday to Friday and at 11 o'clock you have to be on the line in the gym while the coaches come in and explain what's happening. There'd be a running session of high intensity. We'd have lunch then, go back in at four, do the warm up and then four rounds here and three rounds there.

Wednesday would be weights in the morning, strength and conditioning with John Cleary. He's a real timid guy but so passionate about it and he'd have a programme of a month or two months and he'd be analysing all this. He'd design stuff with medicine balls and we'd have a med ball circuit with 10 different stations. At one would be the punch pass, throwing it off the wall and using your opposite hand to catch it — it's all explosive. Side passes, working your core. Med ball slams onto the ground. Med ball sit-ups. That stuff would be good closer to competitions because you are doing strength work but also working the cardio, getting a sweat up and keeping your weight down. That evening there would be bag work. And so the week would continue until you have Saturday off, a light Sunday, and you could do a bit by yourself on Monday.

There was a diet routine as well. I'd eat four or five times a day. Weetabix for breakfast, salad for lunch, cereal in the afternoon. But I'm not killing myself to make weight. I'm only 84 kilos normally, and you'd lose three after a good sweat session. I'd normally take the weight down to a kilo and a half over when I was approaching a bout, and I'd be hydrated at that point. Then I'd lose a kilo by sweating it out the day before and then I'd dry out over night. I have it off to about 0.7 of a kilo over the limit the night before and when I wake I do 20 minutes on the treadmill, shower but don't drink water, and then I'm on the mark. Granted it can be a long night with a dry mouth. You can't wait to get on the scales because the minute you are off them and cleared to fight, you have your Lucozade powder, your breakfast and then go back into bed.

You wear boxers on the scales and that can be 0.1 of a kilo and there are times when they won't let you take them off. There is a test scales, you check that, and if you are over you bang on the sweat gear again. Or if you are lucky enough to have a bath in the hotel, you boil it out of you for 10 minutes and lose it like that. Darren Sutherland used to love it when there was a bath because he was always so tight on the weight. But flunking the scales is a schoolboy error, you are supposed to make your weight and there should be no excuse.

You have to be clean-shaven as well. Some doctors won't even let you away with a day of stubble growth, they are so strict. They'd send you back up to your room to shave and you'd be dehydrated and desperate to get on the scales but this holds you up even more. These are just the rules because if you get a cut they can't work on it with hair in the way.

It might seem over the top but I need all that. I need the army-like lifestyle because when I don't have it, I lose myself. Some people just get down without knowing what they are doing day to day, slip into a rut and potter about. But I always needed to find the replacement, another routine which made me forget about my life. And as I look around the table I look at all the other routines facing me. My father the chef. My mother at home. My brothers working regular jobs with no extreme highs or lows. Just the steadiness of a normal life. I'm back to a place in my own life where I love being a boxer but I still wonder what if I had been just like them. Would it be easier and better for someone with an alcohol problem?

Before I stopped drinking, I'd get depressed and would often have wished I'd got a trade. I told myself I should have become a carpenter so I wouldn't have been totally reliant on boxing and that might have eased the pressure in my head quite a bit. A few months ago I was on iTalkSport on Setanta and Eanna Falvey was on the panel as well. He was a super-heavyweight in the World Championships in Belfast back in 2001 but packed it in and got studying. It took him 10 years but now he's an established doctor and works with the Irish rugby team. I'm not saying I would have been able for that, but I could have been more than just what I am.

And if you offered me the chance to be in his shoes, I'd consider it. But I'd have taken your arm off to have a life like his back in 2009 because it would have given me the responsibility I needed. Instead, a few months after New York I was losing it again. You'd think I'd have learned my lesson because everywhere there were reminders. There's a big poster of me in my local boozer, Boomers, standing in the ring in Beijing with a smiling face and 'Welcome Home Kenny' written underneath. Of course it changed when I came back from my missing days in New York. It now reads, 'Welcome Home Kenny... Again.' But regardless of everything else, my next escape followed such a similar pattern.

It was myself and a good pal Owen McMahon this time, and

I fell into something random and stupid. I had a week off from training and was I sitting in Boomers on a Tuesday, having a few pints. No one was annoying me there and I didn't feel safe going to town at the time because of what I'd done before. But Dad wasn't well and my Mam came into the pub and told me to put the pint down. That was it. I couldn't take anyone hassling me or telling me what to do. She went to the toilet and I did a runner, went home and took the passport and left her looking after her husband who was taken to hospital. She went home that day distraught and John and Tony who were now sat at this very same kitchen table had seen enough of my behaviour and decided to wash their hands of me. They didn't know who I had become. I was supposed to take my Dad to the hospital but that was left to my mate Alan O'Reilly.

Think about it. I was the guy that wouldn't even bring his own father to the hospital. That was the selfish person I had become and I still haven't apologised to Dad for that either, but I will. I look at him reading his paper and consider apologising now, but the timing isn't right. Over breakfast with the others around won't do. I'll pick a moment and do it properly because it will have to be heartfelt. What I did was appalling and he needs to know that it hurts me and I haven't just forgotten about that entire episode. I want to make amends.

My poor Mam hated me because of all that. The brothers were trying to hold down jobs, I was the guy with a bit of time but where was I? Busy thinking of being in front of a pint, and slobbering over women. But that was more important to me at the time so I got a lift from a friend to the airport that day and decided to get out of town. Neither myself or Owen had any baggage, just some money in our pockets. We took a look at the screen and decided we wanted somewhere warm. Malaga.

But the girl at the desk must have alerted security or something because two guys with no gear going to the coast of Spain doesn't look too good. We were only settled down in the airport bar having a beer when three policemen walked up to us. *"How are you lads, is everything OK?"* But then one of them recognised me and as I tried to play it cool and sober and asked where I was off to. *"To Malaga for a week,"* I told them. *"You jammy bastards,"* was the response. They may have been in uniform but they were just another group of people letting me off because of the name I had. I could do what I wanted and no one even questioned me or pulled me up for my actions, least of all me.

So off we went, drinking on the plane after drinking most of the morning. We were drinking away in Malaga too, but when I get very bad I always find somewhere comfortable to sleep. On this occasion it was a bus shelter. We still didn't have any accommodation booked, that was well down the list of priorities, so Owen went off looking for a taxi. He couldn't wake me up and left me there for a little while but when he came back I was gone and I hadn't turned my phone back on after we landed so he couldn't get me. It was like that film, *'The Hangover'.* Only it's not as funny in real life.

I woke up the next morning and didn't know where I was. I remembered little of the previous day and after a quick glance around I realised I was on a deck chair on the beach with my jeans and shirt on me, sweating like a pig. There was no sign of Owen and he had my wallet and passport because he didn't want to leave them on me as I slept on the side of the road. I looked at my watch and it was 8.30, the sun was up and some old women were getting into the water. I turned on my phone and it went dead before I could make a call. Good start to the day. So I took off the boots, jeans, left the boxers on and went for a swim to clear the head.

I tried the phone again but there was no life in it and I didn't know Owen's number off by heart. So I walked up and down the boardwalk a couple of times and it was starting to get hotter and hotter as the sun rose higher and higher. The clothes were sticking and I was stinking. By chance I looked over and saw a bar called The Irish Times, just off the square in Malaga. There was a guy called Simon behind the bar and I asked could I borrow his laptop. I went on Facebook, left a few messages asking Owen if he came online to give the bar a shout. People were beginning to ask whether I was okay but I didn't reply. I had bigger worries.

So I started up a tab behind the bar even though I'd no money. I had the shakes and as the hours passed I was starting to panic because Simon, who knew who I was, assumed I had a pocket full of 50s and just kept serving up the beers. Little did he realise I was sitting there without a bob in my pocket. Eventually I tried my phone one last time and for some reason it came on. I rang Owen quick. *"Irish Times pub, Irish Times pub."* Dead again. About five o'clock that evening he walked in. The relief was unreal.

"Have you the passports?"

"Yeah."

"Money?

"Yeah."

With that we hugged like I've rarely hugged before. All was well in the world. We had no clothes so we went to a shop, bought matching T-shirts and shorts and flip-flops so we were like twins sitting in the pub. We got chatting more and more to Simon, who organised a cheap hostel for us just around the corner. It was basic enough stuff with just two beds and a television but it was perfect for what we had planned and we went mad for the weekend. We were lying in the hostel one day about 12.30, I woke up and looked over at Owen and he was glued to the telly watching this programme in Spanish. There was some guy in a big heavy leather jacket and Owen looks over at me and says, *"See that guy, he is this guy's son and he's doing this..."* He was loving it, telling me the whole story, even though he didn't have a clue what they were saying.

But I really didn't care because every morning I'd get up and be dry-heaving because the phlegm would build up in my throat. We were a disaster. I used to just skip the shower, because it was wasting time. My body was telling me to stop for one day, to relax for just 24 hours. But I couldn't. I needed to get back down to the pub.

The last night will explain how bad we were. We missed the

flight and I had to get onto Willie to book another. He was going mad at me down the phone. He was worried about my wellbeing but I told him I was fine except for the fact there was another night to get through. We could have gone back to the hostel but we met these two English women in their 40s from Liverpool. The two of us were sitting with them for the night, sipping orange Bacardi Breezers, anything just to have the craic because we couldn't handle any more beer.

I told them our story about missing the flight, not having anywhere to stay and I told them all about the Olympics. They said if we wanted to come back to their apartment, that it wouldn't be a problem. Fair enough I thought, I'll sleep on the floor. So we went up to their place, got a load of cans and sat on the balcony drinking for the rest of the night.

They were very nice to us. Overly nice as it turns out. One of them came out of her room in just a bathrobe and started flashing at Owen. I looked over with raised the eyebrows and said, *"What's going on here?"* and she turned and did the same to me. It was like looking at a big bag of tripe. I looked over making faces at him. *"Owen don't just look at it, eat it"*, I suggested.

Finally he made his move and he was out on the couch giving this woman the good news for half the night. I just wanted to sleep but the noise of her squealing didn't exactly allow me to drift off. On top of that I was lying beside this other one in a single bed. She wasn't great. I was exhausted and I genuinely didn't want anything from her but I got bored and ended up giving her a lash anyway. *"See this thing down here? It's not going to suck itself"* I said to her. I had heard one of the boys saying that on an away trip, and said I'd store it up and use it. She broke down laughing and started rolling around. I fell off the bed but got back to my feet and went hard at it shortly afterwards.

Next morning we got out of there early, left whatever we bought behind and made our way home. There was no media hassle or much talk from anyone else this time because it was just a holiday and no boxing event had been missed. But there were signs the drink was taking over, because you don't just jump on a plane to a different country and end up sleeping rough on a beach.

The worst part of it all was the selfishness though. I was there in Spain after I said I'd bring my Dad to hospital. When he came back from following me at the Olympics my Mam knew that he wasn't well. He is a stubborn man so in January 2009 she made an appointment, said she was after paying the money, and he'd have to go for a check-up. The weight was falling off him, and my Mam thought he had diabetes. In the end it took him until June 22 to go to the doctor for blood tests, by June 30 he was in Tallaght Hospital and by July 7 he had a triple bypass. Up to that point he was still driving and the doctors said he was lucky he hadn't killed himself or someone else in the car. It was so bad he was in hospital recovering for three weeks.

He was the opposite of me though. All I could think of was myself, but all he could think of was my career. The World Championships were in Milan that September, and when he came out of the theatre the first thing he said to my Mam was, *"Are we going?"* He had planned it after I had won the seniors again because he always wanted to go to Italy. But by then he didn't know where he was. After I came back, I finally went into the hospital and he was grand and happy to see me in his understated way. But back at the house, my bags were packed, my presses were empty and all my stuff was in bin liners. I was being shown the door and I had to beg to be allowed continue to live there.

I didn't even understand why Mam would want to throw me out because it was all me, me, me. That's what I cared about at the time and I couldn't see it all from anyone else's perspective. I got back training for a couple of weeks after that trip. I got myself together. From one routine to the next, from drink back to boxing, always giving whichever one I was focused on my all. I used to go up for a sauna and a steam room to pump myself out after those crazy trips abroad and drink loads of water. It was like a detox. The first three or four days are hell but you never really lose much fitness when you are at that peak. I learned that and it gave me one less barrier to drinking. Or so I thought. I might have been able to get it out of the system and catch up in training, but come the major championships it held me back.

At my best at those 2009 World Championships I could have won a gold medal and should have gone home with some sort of medal. Instead, after winning my first couple of fights, I got beaten by Abdelkader Bouhenia of France in the quarter-finals, a guy I'd beaten before and should really be beating handily every time we meet. I was disgusted with myself because I had a solid first round and was level but got tired and mentally my head wasn't there. It was purely because I didn't have the conditioning even though I put in a good four weeks training. Six weeks of proper training would have got me to the final but I couldn't make sufficient time to be the best boxer I could be anymore. In fact, after that first round he beat me up easily. That was my chance to win gold at the Worlds and I blew it.

What came next was a real eye-opener to everyone though. That loss was seen as a big upset but people wouldn't have thought that if they knew the life I was leading and anyone hanging around our hotel that night would have been given a glimpse of it.

Annoyed with losing and even more annoyed with my life, I ended up on the piss with Eric Donovan. I just got plastered. I don't know what happened, but I was beyond drunk and it's scary to think how little control I had over my own actions and my own body. Just the night before, Billy had a talk with us after a couple of our guys went out of the championships and he told them they'd been brilliant ambassadors, had behaved and performed well, and to keep it that way and to keep it clean. But 24 hours later he was sitting in the lobby by the fireplace when the Brazilian doctor came running in and said I was outside in a terrible way. Billy looked out and saw me leaning against the wall to stay upright. I had to be carried into the hotel, with my two legs dragging behind me, by a referee and that Brazilian doctor who had been very good to our team. I'd beaten one of his fighters in the Olympics a year previously and he couldn't believe what I'd become since. That night Billy had to stay with me in case I got sick and choked, just as my mother had had to do upstairs in my family home.

I had never ever let myself down like that on a boxing trip before. Even the Polish problem was a minor tremor beside this earthquake. As Billy said, he'd never seen anyone as drunk at any time in his life and he was sure I was on drugs or had my drink spiked because essentially I was a zombie. And while that's bad any time, this was while representing my country, wearing Irish gear. I was embarrassing the nation and I ended up with a €5,000 fine when I came back. I deserved every cent of it.

The next morning the IABA president Dom O'Rourke came into my room and all I could mutter was that I'd talk to him when my head was right. I was dying all day and wasn't even around to congratulate John Joe Nevin on winning a brilliant bronze. I was captain and I let down the team again. But that was just another marker along the way in 2009 because when I came home from Milan I just kept on drinking, despite the shame I was inflicting on myself and the squad.

Next up was the Oktoberfest in Munich. It was a weekend of pure madness. There were tents with 5,000 people packed into them, with a band announcing when you had to down a certain drink. Crazy stuff. I bought a chicken hat and the pictures ended up in the Irish newspapers, taken from my Facebook account which I hadn't even bothered to limit access to. When I came back I explained to Billy that I was just on my holidays and he said it wasn't a problem, just to avoid putting stuff on the internet for everyone to see. He was right.

There were seven of us over there from the Irish team. Most of us didn't make it down to the actual festival the first night but Willie McLoughlin did and came back with two black eyes. He explained that he had been out drinking and ended up fighting in a boxing ring. We thought he just had way too much booze and had got confused but it turned out he was telling the truth. There was a place you could get into a ring and fight for cash so we all thought, 'I'll have a piece of that'.

The idea was that anyone can pay €15 and you get in and fight these Polish guys. These Polish lads were in really good nick and there was me, Willie, big Connie Sheehan, Eric Donovan, and Conor Ahern looking at each other wondering if we should give it a lash. It was inevitable. No one knew we were boxers so I said I'd have a go first. I was half cut at about two in the day but hopped up and they paired me off with a guy who was roughly my size.

I walked through this door at the back of the ring and the public can all watch. You have five rounds with five guys and if you win you get €200. I had three-quarter length jeans on me with a T-shirt and flip flops, not exactly top-notch boxing gear. I stood there shadow boxing like I never threw a punch in my life. People were laughing at me thinking I wouldn't last long. Finally I put on the gloves. There were no bandages, no head guard, no gum shield. Round One. I charged at this guy, missed and slipped like a drunken cowboy. But pretty quickly he knew there was something about me because I stood back and started picking shots off him. I was cutting off the ring, feinting, dancing. If the IABA had seen me Christ knows what they would have said.

Not surprisingly I won the fight but I didn't hang around because I had better things to be doing. Connie Sheehan hung back and took his turn though. Seemingly he was chasing a guy around the ring, opened him up and there was blood everywhere. He couldn't get enough of this. The round was only a minute long but the Polish guy wanted to get out after half of that and they had to drag Connie off of him. We were at the bar at that stage and Connie came over to us with the T-shirt all red and went back on the beer for the day.

The madness didn't even end there though, because there was one more trip to come in 2009. I headed off to Tenerife for a week in late October. This time I packed the suitcase and went with two friends but it ended up just like all the other holidays. When we landed there was a bus waiting outside, because it was an all-inclusive trip. There was no driver and we were looking at the clock thinking of drinking time. *"Come on,"* one of the lads said, *"we'll get a taxi."* Then the busman got on and started the engine and everyone was laughing at us getting up and sitting back down. Ten minutes later we were still sitting on the bus and finally decided we'd get a taxi. Anything to avoid wasting a couple of minutes when we could have been sitting at a bar.

I got slaughtered one night over there, and coming back home I lost the boys. I didn't know where I was going and was walking down the street trying to remember where the hotel was. I never thought of taking out the room card but instead was just wandering around looking at buildings even though I didn't know what the hotel even looked like. The police must have passed me stumbling around a few times, because they eventually stopped and asked if I was alright. I told them I'd lost the hotel so they told me to get in the back of their patrol car. I was wondering what they were doing, started panicking after a few minutes of them driving around and said, *"Oh there it is there."* I didn't know where I was at all but I was paranoid and wanted to get out of the police car as quickly as possible and away from them. Any figure of authority used to scare me when I was in that state.

So I jumped out and there were these steps behind a few palm trees, into a shopping centre. I walked down there, hiding until the cop car drove away. But I gave up trying to find my way back to the hotel. I just lay down with my head on my jacket and slept rough until the sun came up the next morning. I recognised our place pretty quickly the next day but the lads were hardly worried about my whereabouts. They were joking that I'd clicked with some girl when, in truth, I was a sad state of a human by then. I knew nothing about anything but getting so drunk that I got depressed. I couldn't even consider doing anything else because that day when they went to an aqua park, I sat at the bar on my own with my Facebook open because I couldn't stand being sober.

Only then did I remember that I'd helped organise a white-collar boxing charity event back home and the first night's training was on while I was away. I had hired the High Performance gym but hadn't even paid for it. So I had to sort it out over the phone. But the lads back home were having real trouble gaining access to the gym and the event was going to be axed. I had to ring Don Stewart and plead with him to let them use the gym and assured him that I'd pay when I got back. The lads were taking the flak for this because I couldn't even look after myself and the little things I had organised.

****

"Isn't that right Kenneth," Mam says as I'm forced out of my daydream and try to tune back into what's happening at the kitchen table.

I look a little lost and there is laughter and I don't know why so my brothers explain that they were just saying that I must be the only Olympic medallist still living in his parents' house. I can't think of anything in reply so I fill my mouth with another swig of tea and sit there slightly embarrassed. My Mam comes to my defence but while they're only joking, they may be right. After the Olympics I had the chance to move out and move on and move up. I could have been a contender. I could have been somebody. But in truth for a long time I felt like a complete nobody.

Finally I gulp down the tea and blame Willie, suggest it was him that couldn't afford to move out, even if he saved me from a bad investment given what's happened since. He's having none of it and says as much. He's right too because when I did get back from Beijing the two of us were going to buy a place in Clane that we were planning to rent out and the builder wanted €370,000. But then the market collapsed. I went up a second time on my own, the builder was in the area, so he said, *"I'll give it to you for €350,000."* I shook his hand. The final time we met he had driven down from the north in a big Range Rover. I was with Willie who said we'd have to think about it and the builder started going on about how I shook his hand and was getting really angry. Willie just looked at him. *"I don't care what he shook, we aren't taking it for that price."* A few days later, his last offer was €230,000 and we still didn't take it. Thank God, because that would have been another weight on my shoulders and there was already plenty there to push me down towards the gutter.

Even so, it wasn't so much the money that stopped me buying a house and starting a normal existence for someone my age. It was the lifestyle. I didn't have the mindset to make responsible decisions. I was getting invited everywhere, the phone was hopping and everyone wanted a piece of me. I believed that I was suddenly a star celebrity and I was burning the candle at both ends. I had to go down to Cork to open a restaurant. I was on the piss the night before and I got to the airport stinking of drink. I had to meet a load of kids and I was told by an organiser to eat chewing gum because it was unacceptable stuff. That was happening regularly. I was opening shops, going to schools but always going on the beer afterwards. It was manic and it was a rush that shielded me from what I was doing because I was engulfed in the next rush before I could analyse the previous one.

I had gone to Turkey with my girlfriend at the time, Karen, just after the Olympics. In fact the night before, myself, Paddy Barnes and Darren Sutherland were asked to go on The Late Late Show. It was on in the new opera house in Wexford. And when I came back from that getaway, a guy called Donal Scannell approached me to make a DVD. I said I might as well, as it would keep me busy. It was about me, where I came from, my family, what it took to get to the Games and the aftermath. It was a fly-on-the-wall type documentary and a film crew followed me around for two weeks which I didn't mind because I'd nothing else to occupy my head. They interviewed my parents, went to Neilstown Boxing Club and had me in the Ryston club in Newbridge where I trained a few kids with a gut full of booze from the night before. Then they recorded me opening the odd shop and brought Jimmy Magee in for it as well. The two of us had two stools in the ring and were talking about the pro game. He was saying, *"Kenneth, if you are thinking like that, remember it's a cruel sport."* But all I remember is sitting there, dying from drink with my eyes half open. It was embarrassing but I was falling asleep on camera. I'd just say, 'yeah, yeah' now and again as much to try and stay awake as to look interested. I must have broken Donal's heart during it because I was coming in every day with a hangover.

I had to go around the country promoting the DVD when it was released so myself and my mate Stephen O'Reilly travelled around together, just going into different shops for an hour. It started in Dublin and went from there. We ended up down in Cork doing a signing and he had a cousin living there so we were able to stay the night. We did the gig and went to a 21st of a friend of Michael Roche, who boxed in the 2000 Olympics. I was sorry I went to it because everyone there was all over me getting pictures and the guy whose birthday it was didn't get a look-in. I made a bit of a speech and all, along the lines of 'congratulations to whoever's birthday it is'. Utter crap and quite embarrassing looking back.

That night I ended up back in the housing estate but couldn't find Stephen's cousin's place. I was wandering around, knocking on windows, ringing door bells. People were coming down to their door steps in dressing gowns and telling me to go home. I couldn't get in touch with Stephen so I finally rang his brother Alan back in Dublin, he got on to his cousin's house and told them to go out around the estate to find me. Eventually they did find me by walking around shouting my name, so I followed the sound, got back and went to bed straight away. The next morning though Stephen was all excited. *"You wouldn't believe what happened!"*

It turned out that he lost me in a nightclub somewhere, got a taxi back to the house but had no money to pay the driver. So he was brought to the Garda station where he spent quite a while telling them he was down with his friend Kenny Egan doing a signing and he thought he had more money on him but then lost me. They were sure he was off his head as he kept rambling on. They refused to believe him but he said the medal was in the house so four gardaí eventually accompanied him back. When they go to the house, Stephen got the medal out of a drawer and the gardaí were fighting over it to get photos. They all took turns posing for a picture and then let him away with the fare in the end.

From there we went to Limerick and then on to Thurles, but I've never been anywhere like it. I was standing like an eejit outside a supermarket in this shopping centre. People would pay for their shopping, come out and see me, or at least that was the idea. I was sitting there and there were locals walking past, staring with these bushy eyebrows and beady eyes which would stay focused on me until they'd walked out of sight. A couple of minutes later the same person would come back and stare again. It was creepy.

We did the signing there for an hour and hit the road as quick as we could. We were heading out of Thurles when we stopped into this garage with a house and a bar and a shop stuck onto the side of it. This old man behind the counter was staring at me and asked was there any chance of a photo. So I went behind the counter and got the picture taken with the family and took off. We had to come back that way later on though, and when we pulled in a second time he had it printed, had me sign it, and took the marriage picture off the fireplace and put my picture up in its place.

All this madness was happening but I still hadn't had the time to draw breath since the Olympics or get my feet on the ground and take stock of it all. Instead I was being dragged this way and that and didn't know who I was anymore. Anyone sitting around this table here now in my mother's house will tell you as much. I had started to believe the hype and my family had to endure someone who thought he was untouchable and better than everyone else.

I did an ad for the Mace supermarket chain where I was orange with all this fake tan, like the guy out of the Tango advert. I was 'punching' their prices and to make matters worse, they gave me this stupid haircut and I got some awful stick after that. Lads at traffic light would roll down the window, *"Any Coke there Kenneth, two bottles for two euro?"* I got a car off Toyota as well, a Corolla with my name on the side. I was thinking it'd be for four years but I got a call a year later and they wanted it back. There's a dent in the back of it after Tony reversed it into something, but they still wanted it back quickly which came as a little bit of a surprise to me.

But the most detrimental part of that time was that everywhere I went I was getting too much attention for my own good. My head was growing by the day. It got to the stage where I was on the ropes with my girlfriend Karen. We needed time for our relationship but the invitations kept on coming, and I was attending the lot. I was in Krystle one night, and there were gorgeous women everywhere, walking up and looking for numbers. One girl I met called me afterwards and I brought her to the Morgan Hotel in Temple Bar. She worked as an Irish dancer in a bar in town and I said I was moving to America to box and she could go there with me and dance her way to the big time. I was filling her full of crap and she was making big plans, whereas I only had one plan and that was to get her into bed. I went to her sister's house near the Phoenix Park one night and another time I brought her back to my mother's house.

But the next morning Stephen was trying to call my mobile, and when he couldn't get me, he called the house. Mam answered and said I was in bed and she'd go up and get me. She walked up the stairs to be greeted by the sight of a pair of green shoes and a purple thong. Mam walked into the room and asked what was happening? I looked at the girl and said to Mam, 'this is so and so, she's sound, even into the Irish dancing... blah, blah'. But Mam was in no mood for polite conversation. *"Well I don't care, she can get down those stairs and do the Highland Fling out of here."* She was disgusted looking at this girl beside me with her face covered in mascara.

I was meeting the same girl in town another night and I texted her, telling her to 'wear something tight'. Of course she had all these texts in her phone and went to a newspaper. Some female reporter took her to a coffee shop, sat her down outside and had someone taking pictures of them in conversation from a car. The next day my phone was hopping. The girl I had slept with was saying she was all over the papers when it was supposed to be about me. I told her that she got caught trying to make money off me, to shag off and never to ring my phone again. I was trying to work things out with my girlfriend Karen at that stage but there was murder over this and there were reporters camped outside her house. I didn't know what I wanted and I realise now I was looking in the wrong places for happiness. I could have just sat down like I am now, supped on a cup of tea, talked to my family and I'd have been satisfied. But I couldn't work out that much in all the turmoil.

But say what you will about me, the women are not the completely innocent parties in all this. They were worse than me. I got my name and my medal through hours of dedication. They wanted a name by just sleeping around. I couldn't even take a drink without photos. I was having a few pints in the Quays Bar one day and it's only natural that people would recognise me so soon after the Games and would often stop and ask for a photograph. But someone was taking photos of me with my hand around these girls. Three different girls asked for pictures at different stages of the evening but all with the same photographer. In a newspaper the next day there was a headline 'Egan out on the prowl' with three different pictures of me standing beside three different girls, as if I was trying to bed all of them. I wasn't doing anything wrong but everyone was getting the wrong idea and it was adding to my stress. One of the women even rang my mother to apologise, said nothing was going on and that she just wanted the photograph because she thought it would make her son proud. That was what I was living through. Granted, it's still no excuse to jump on a plane and run as far away as you can from responsibility either.

The more I tried with Karen, the worse it got. It just couldn't work after Beijing and sometimes it wasn't even my fault. I was in the nightclub Club Diva at one stage and got talking to a young one, only 18, who lives across the road from Karen. But word got back to Karen that I was doing more than just talking which wasn't true at all. Karen hit the roof, ran up the stairs in my parents' house, kicked open the door of my bedroom and was screaming and shouting. I threw her out of the house and I know now that I wasn't showing her the respect she deserved — I'll take the blame for it — but it was hard when everyone was coming up with stories.

I was regularly on the beer in Copper Face Jacks in the city centre as well. These were the type of places where I wouldn't normally go but I was loving the craic and thinking the attention made me better than other people. I was like a spoiled brat. Myself and Paul Burgess came back to my Mam's house and I told him to jump into the bed beside me. I was in the bed fully clothed with the boots hanging out the end, fast asleep, when the next morning the door got kicked in again. Karen saw the second lump in the bed and was roaring. She pulled the duvet clean off the bed expecting to see some girl. Instead, Paul turned around to me and said, *"Oh Kenny, my arse is very sore."*

I broke down laughing, but that was it, the show was over with Karen. She stormed out and I told her that was the end as far as we were concerned. I was drinking too much, dragging her through all this shit. Whatever about it being hard on me, to take someone with you on that journey just isn't right. But I didn't care. I couldn't look back because I was going forward at such a speed that I couldn't control it. I was signed up with the Assets modeling agency and I got invited out to Charlestown shopping centre. It was a handy gig, €3,000 to stroll down a catwalk. All the models were there and I just went in a pair of boots, jeans and a shirt. The kids were screaming and it lasted just 20 minutes but it was the hours afterwards that were really hurting me. Chantelle Houghton from TV show Big Brother was there at the gig as well and afterwards I ended up in Zanzibar on the quays with her and the photographer. There was free beer in this sectioned off area and she ended up sitting beside me and I ended up snogging the face off her. He took pictures but in fairness he didn't publish them. They were harmless enough. I didn't sleep with her, but not for the lack of trying and so began another all-night bender, all from 20 minutes of a gig.

I was starting to think I was famous. Before the Olympics I used to go to Club Diva with my friends and we used to stand right beside the women's toilets, so you could see what was coming in and out. It was like fish in a barrel. But after the Olympics it all changed in terms of the location and the company. I'd keep getting invited back to Krystle and remember looking at two lads I know standing around a table with a bottle of champagne. I stood there in my sandals and asked for a pint of Coors. Another night I went into Lillie's Bordello after doing an appearance on the TV show, The Panel. Charlie Bird was sitting beside me telling me I'm very big. *"Thanks Charlie,"* was all I could think to say. This wasn't my scene at all, but rather than reject it, I changed to embrace it.

I didn't get a minute's peace no matter where I went but then I was always too drunk to care. There must be photos of me out there with my tongue hanging out and my eyes freezing over. And it catches up with you. There was a time I got into the ring and I was sparring John Joe Joyce who was just 64 kilos at the time. But I was weak as a kitten. Off we went for the first round and I was in bits, and by the second round I had to get out of the ring because he was giving me a hiding. Zaur was looking at me wondering what was wrong. Pretty quickly it clicked with him, and he pulled me aside.

"You can destroy your life forever by drinking, Kenny. Just one drink can ruin everything. You have to be patient, keep training. After an Olympic Games there's a lot of stress but you don't take many punches, you can hang around longer than a lot of boxers and win more. There is another Olympics, more medals if you want them or you can lose everything very quickly."

But I never listened and the few lads I'd be close to on the team never said anything. Maybe they didn't have the guts, with me being the captain and one of the oldest in the gym. But they surely knew because of the state I was in at training. For instance, I went there to do a weights session after being out on a mad session that no one knew about. There were hurdle hops where you had to jump four of them to get explosive power in the legs. I could see the hurdles but my eyes started going and I got dizzy and I was missing them, falling into them, making a show of myself. I knew the boys were looking at me and I felt terrible. My equilibrium was gone, I'd no balance, no sense of distance between them. I was bluffing it and not training properly. But the person I was really cheating was myself.

As this went on, Billy was trying to look at the whole team as a unit and he knew that if I was to get away with it, others might start thinking they could too and it could rot the whole programme. He came into training one day at the beginning of 2010 and said, *"Kenny, get your gear and fuck off out of here."* I was messing around in training and it was affecting everyone there. I told Billy he was a fucking bastard as he threw me out. It was the shock. I was disgusted with myself. But it was the right thing for Billy to do. He needed to set me right and set an example at the same time. And he needed to treat everyone the same.

In the midst of all this, I was trying to consider my future in boxing as well. I could remain amateur or take one of the many offers to turn pro. It started just a month after the Olympics when a cousin of mine called Tommy Egan gave my number to the promoter Shelly Finkel and he contacted me. I rang my coach Gerry Fleming straight away because he had a level head, and of all the times in my life I needed someone like that it was now. The two of us ended up going out to Los Angeles shortly after the Olympics and we met Richard Schaefer, and were brought into his office which had Oscar De La Hoya's gear all over the place. He welcomed me to Golden Boy Promotions and Finkel was giving it all the talk. We stayed there for a few days, made a weekend of it, and they tried to make the sell the only way boxing promoters know how.

They got me and Gerry a car and driver and showed us around LA, saying I could live in this place or that place, and from there we went on to Malibu Beach where Baywatch was made. They stopped at the Playboy mansion and I got out but it was all locked up. The driver was telling us who lives in what house, and they were all the size of the National Stadium. But little things turned me off it. We were in Freddie Roach's gym and there was this open area for everyone but there is a closed room out the back just for his main boxer Manny Pacquiao when he's there. I got talking to a Crumlin boxer called Dean Byrne, a light welterweight, and he turned pro out there but he only got paid when he fought and on the side he was working as a personal trainer to make a living. I was aware that could happen me too.

We were even given tickets to the Shane Mosley-Ricardo Mayorga light-middleweight title fight. But there were more warnings signs when we went to that. Finkel was there ringside with us, WBA super middleweight champion Andre Ward was a few seats up and Don King was opposite us with his little flags. In hindsight being placed within these famous circles of self-importance was all done for a reason. They thought it would tempt me over but Craig McEwan was on the undercard that night and the crowd was booing him because he was Scottish and I realised that the west coast crowd was very pro-Latin American. If I was going to go pro this wasn't the place. I'd have rather been on the east coast.

But the contract was there on the last day. They came up to the hotel with it and there was a signing-on fee of $75,000 and then $5,000 a win after that for the first six fights. It was poor money but Finkel wanted it signed there and then. It was for five years and if I was inside the Top 10 in the rankings within two years they'd add another 12 months. If I won a world title they'd add another two years. That's a long time and if it goes wrong early they still have you, they could end up using you as a journeyman for some up-and-coming kids to punch around. As well as that, there was no guarantee that the main man, Freddie

Roach, would be training me. It all depended on who was in the camp at the time. Because of all this, Gerry said we had to bring the contract back to people in Ireland.

"Why, it's good to go, you won't get a better offer than that," argued Finkel and he was more than a bit pissed off. He thought he was slick with all his tricks and it annoyed him that we didn't fall for it and sign away my life.

Besides, there were better offers and not long after that myself, Gerry and Willie went to New York, a few months before my lost weekend there on the piss. It was on that trip I met Michelle for the first time and discovered the bar Seven but the real reason for us being there was to talk business with a guy called Joey Winters. He was showing interest in me and while he had no history in boxing promotion, he had fought before, had Irish parents and wanted to turn an Irish fighter into a superstar. He had a waste management company, sold it for millions of dollars and was living the high life. We saw it first hand when he brought us to his house for dinner. He even showed us another house that was under construction with a cinema at the bottom.

I was thinking at the time that he seemed genuine enough and he was passionate about what he wanted to do. My only worry was that I was going to sign for someone with no history of promoting and while I don't know the ins and outs because I never had a huge interest in professional boxing, it still seemed a risk. *"Who will promote my bouts?"* I asked him. He just said, *"It'll be fine, you're Irish so the crowds will come."* On top of that, Brian Peters was looking into the Irish side of that deal and promoting fights I'd have back here. He even looked at the contract for me and thought it was a great deal.

While we were there my cousin Tommy who'd initially arranged talks with Finkel had contact with some Italian called Lou DiBella. It goes to show how little I really do know about the pro game that I'd never heard of one of the most famous promoters out there. When I was finished talking to Winters without a deal being finalised, I told him about the DiBella interest because I felt bad after him flying us over and paying for accommodation. Fair play to him though, he still had no problem with this. He reckoned he was still the right man for the job and I was thinking the same after we spoke to DiBella ourselves.

There was just me, him, Gerry and Willie and he offered me $200,000 with none of the installment stuff either. He said he'd pay me up front and he must have had money coming out of his ears because he didn't even seem to have any great interest in me. He just wanted my signature and I felt like some sort of plaything. His idea was to have me fighting everywhere so I could have been sent off to Russia, Mexico, Brazil or Thailand and you don't want to be going to these places when you are starting off. You want to be based somewhere, call it home and win 15 fights. Then you can start going abroad. He was saying he got a phone call off Darren Sutherland too but that Darren came across as being really arrogant and that it wouldn't work.

It wouldn't have worked with me either though so it was a now a choice of going with Joey Winters or staying amateur. I was over in the Irish Sports Council with John Treacy as well, talking to him about staying on until 2012. He said, *"Look, myself and everyone here wants you to stay amateur, we'll offer you the top funding to keep you here."* I didn't know what to do and said I'd think about it. All the drinking didn't help because I couldn't make a proper decision. I wasn't myself, didn't know who to turn to, didn't know where to get the right advice. Winters even came to Ireland that November and I was very close to agreeing a deal with him.

I ended up meeting him in Merrion Square and he handed me a contract. I took time to go through it and after Winters returned to the States I had a Skype call with him, talking about parts of the contract that had to be changed. Eventually I just decided this isn't for me. I didn't feel comfortable leaving my country and turning professional given the way I was. I was in a state, mentally and physically. I wasn't well and I wasn't happy with life. My head was wrecked. I was in a world of hurt even if I kept smiling on the outside but starting a new career in the midst of that just couldn't have happened.

Eventually I went over to Gerry Fleming in Cherry Orchard Hospital where he worked and told him I couldn't do it. He said, *"That's fine but here's the phone, you better ring Joey and explain to him yourself."* So I rang him in the office, told him the news and thanked him but I didn't want to waste any more of his time and didn't want him investing money in me when my heart wasn't in it. *"I'm not the right man for you."* He said fair play for being honest, because I could have led him up the garden path but didn't. And he asked if there was any young Irish talent on the radar, to keep in contact and to let him know.

I think Gerry was the one that was most disgusted, even though I was expecting Winters to be angry. He took time off to go to LA and New York and put a lot of personal time into trying to get me the best deal. He is a great man for talking. He works in the painters' union so he has the gift of the gab. I let him down but at the end of the day it was me that was getting into the ring and who was taking digs. You have to be 100 per cent and I wasn't like Darren Sutherland who wanted to go pro and didn't care what was in his way. I didn't know what I wanted because I was waking up every day with a hangover and couldn't manage myself, never mind a new life. I was a walking disaster, not someone ready to box in the pro ranks. But for months I wondered if I'd regret the decision.

It wasn't until I lived out the rest of 2009 in such a crazy and wild manner that I was completely sure I'd done the right thing. Ending up as a washed-up pro abroad would have been far worse than everything that happened because at least I was at home and I had help all around me from the same people that are all around me now.

But as my mind wanders back to the people in front of me at my mother's kitchen table I decide to keep all of those bad memories to myself because I feel it's better that everyone basks in the present rather than resents my past. So I join back in their conversation and look around again. Dad sits quietly as always, listening to us interrupt each other because we all have opinions we think matter most and we all have a story we think is funnier than the previous one. He flitters through the pages of the newspaper and takes in what we say as Mam and my brothers join me in talking about almost everything. But for now some things are better left unsaid.

CHAPTER 3

8.40am

Dad puts down the newspapers and heads upstairs to get ready for a later-than-usual start to his working day in the Green Isle Hotel, but on his way out the kitchen door he glances at me. He knows what goes through my head when I fall silent, as I've done for the last few minutes. My brothers feel there's work to be done closer to the sink as the breakfast plates are cleared so they head for the sanctuary of the living room, but on their way out they too glance in my direction. They know as well. Mam clears the leftovers into the bin, begins to fill the dishwasher but catches my eye as she looks over at the table. She knows too.

I stay put as the room empties and finally, another meal taken care of, Mam comes over and sits across from me. *"How long's it been now Kenneth?"* She doesn't need to be any more specific because I am only too aware of what she means. *"Well over a year now, Ma," I reply.*

It was April, 2010 when I went to Alcoholics Anonymous for the first time. A little while after I finished with Karen I started dating a girl called Sharon, and one day I could take no more, came clean with myself and said out loud for the very first time what had been bouncing around my head.

"I think I need help."

It had all built up and life had not only caught up with me but passed me out. And I felt so bad because I was getting nowhere and Sharon had seen me in some awful states back in her house. She lives just up the road from me at Newland's Cross and I'd lie to her because she wasn't even my number one priority in life.

I'd wake up when she was leaving for work and I'd tell her I was just going to get an hour's sleep and then be off to the gym or the stadium. For quite a while she even believed me but I'd brush my teeth, put some gel in my hair and I'd go off drinking. She went into more pubs around Dublin and Kildare trying to find me after that. Too many to mention. So maybe she knew those words were coming.

"I think I need help," I repeated.

She put me in contact with a friend of hers called Conor. I met him in town and he was off the drink 10 years, and was telling me about AA meetings and the idea was to go to one and keep coming back as often as possible. It went from there. There is a neighbour of mine whose son is in AA as well, but I hadn't known. I went around to him and said *"I think I've a problem".* He just said, *"That's fair enough, I've a meeting tonight in Lucan, do you want to come?"*

It seemed so sudden. I was ashamed at the start because I imagined a load of people in a circle, rocking back and forth, like a mad house. But it turns out that they are some of the nicest, most educated people you'd meet. They just have a problem with alcohol. I've been going to meetings nearly every day since. Even when I'm abroad training I try to find one just to make sure I never turn back. It's become a part of my life.

I didn't speak that first day in AA, I just listened to all these stories I could relate to. Especially the men who spoke of being consumed by it all and being selfish and letting people down. The story that came into my head as they spoke was of a charity run for James's Hospital I was asked to take part in the year previously. I went to the photo shoot for it but a month later where was I for the run? On the piss somewhere. I still haven't said sorry to the woman that organised it but I will when I get the chance. She's just another one on the list that I will contact when the time is right.

When I first told Mam I was going to AA, she shot me a funny look because she didn't really understand it. She couldn't quite grasp why I couldn't go drinking for just one day and then leave it and I was trying to tell her if I did that I could never stop. As for Dad, he was very quiet and didn't really say anything. At one stage I got the handbook with all the locations and times of the meetings. I left it on the coffee table in the living room but while he saw it, he never opened his mouth. He never does. Mam does all the talking and I kept telling her I can't drink anymore and she said just to keep my head down until after the Olympics in London. Eventually she realised the truth about the depths of my problem and she was one of the reasons I stopped for good.

It was August 2010 when I had my last drink but I still get urges at the strangest times. It could be on Wednesday morning on my way to the gym and all these mad thoughts come into my head. But for me now it's about keeping busy because when you are bored you are thinking, 'how will I kill time?' I always think what it'd be like to give it one more go because drinking gave me some serious craic but I just need to remember the Hell on Earth it created in the aftermath. I glance up at Mam and she is much happier in herself because she doesn't have to worry about me anymore. I keep that thought with me just in case, because I still have all those temptations.

Just because I go to AA doesn't mean I'll never want alcohol. I've said as much in meetings. From time to time, you hear the devil again, saying I've been off it for over 12 months now, what harm would a single night out be? But people come back in those meetings and say that happens to us all, that's the vice. They tell me I have to be strong because if I do have the first drink, the devil in me has won, and it'll be day one of another bender. I don't have it in me to stop once I start.

I genuinely miss a lot of it because I haven't laughed the way I used to since I stopped. I still have fun but never like before. I miss the slagging but I've decided it's for the best that I try to stay away from pubs as much as possible. At the end of it all, some of my old friends are still there for me. The others? I don't care about them. Some guys have a go at me about not keeping in touch, guys who would only ever talk to me in a bar. I told lads I was going to AA and they just laughed and said that I liked drinking the same as the rest of the bar and that was all it was.

But the ones who were saying that aren't the ones who have to get up in the morning to go training. They drink from Friday to Sunday, work during the week and then do it all again. That's their lives. But I just keep going. I'm a fighter. I used to tell myself that the hangover wasn't going to beat me. I'd tell myself that I'm going to get a serious bender out of this and drive it on through the week and I'd be excited by the prospect. It was like a challenge. But now my real friends know not to be annoying me with texts on a Friday.

Besides, I'm after taking up golf now and I'm doing different things to keep away from it all and I'm determined to never slip. Everyone is different in the way they go about staying off of it. There was a film with Tommy Lee Jones in it and at the start he'd always have a whiskey on the rocks. He'd order it, the barman sticks it down on the counter but he never drank it. That's just what he did. And he hangs around for 10 minutes without taking a sip and says he is off. It's a daily thing. A routine. People deal with it in different ways but everyone needs some sort of a routine.

As for me, rather than thinking of the positives like the enjoyment I got out of the odd night, I keep thinking of the negatives that were a by-product. There are plenty of those and in a way I'm lucky I caused as much chaos because not only did it help me realise my problem, it's also left me with a reservoir of bad memories to fall back on and that will help me keep refusing alcohol in the future. If I close my eyes for just a second, it's like turning on a tap. A torrent of incidents come gushing forward that make me ashamed. And the first always involves Darren Sutherland.

Me and Darren only ever shared a room together once in all the years we knew each other and that was enough. We were in Dagestan before the World Championships in Chicago in 2007 and because so few of us travelled I was stuck sharing a room with him. There was only a bedroom and a little sitting room. Darren was a terrible man for talking, he'd go for hours and it was all about boxing and fitness. No craic ever, just always focused on training and bouts.

I woke up one morning to the sound of a skipping rope going at 4.30am. I thought I was dreaming but it kept on going and finally I got up and he was skipping away with his earphones in. He slept for four hours a night and then he'd come in and make loads of noise making his porridge. He'd bring all his own food because he was always on a strict diet. His body composition was so much muscle and so little fat that he'd always struggle to make the middleweight division, so he was meticulous regarding what he ate. But I was deadly serious when I told the coaches that never again was I to be put in a room with him. I couldn't handle all that.

He was very tight with money too and he used to admit as much. He'd tell us how he wouldn't buy crap because he wanted to own a house outright. We used to slag him when he'd take his chewing gums out of his pocket one by one. He'd have managed it with a boxing glove on. That was just the way he was. In fact after that competition in Dagestan, we got prize money of about €100 in some local currency they have there. The physio at the time was Orla Sampson and he asked her coming through the airport if she'd any change for a bottle of water. He had all this money and she pulled him up on it. He said he'd change it into euro when he got home so he didn't want to break into his notes but she wouldn't give him the money to teach him a lesson. He was terrible like that and it must be karma because when he brought it back to Dublin the banks wouldn't take it since it wasn't proper Russian money. He nearly dropped to his knees in front of the cashier.

But he knew what he wanted in life and he spoke about the professional game all the time. We were a stepping stone, and while he worked for an Olympic medal, he craved to be a world champion in the pro ranks. And he could have been. He was made for the pro game. He was a hard puncher, had a great work rate, good defence and loads of style. He looked the part too. On top of that, he put so much work into getting his life ready for the future. Consider all the things he went through. He was over with Brendan Ingle in England, came back and considered quitting boxing; spent a while dancing half naked in a cage hanging from the roof of Time nightclub in Naas to make some money; went back to do his Leaving Cert at 20 years of age and had to wear the uniform each day; and got a bad eye injury that nearly ended his career. But he always kept coming back, never gave up and finally beat Darren O'Neill in the Irish Senior Championships and got to the Olympics.

Darren wasn't used to friends though. He wasn't used to sharing as a team. For him boxing was an individual sport. But Gary told me later that for some reason Darren had idolised me. I never noticed but seemingly whatever I said, he did. And he was smart and educated and even when I was losing at tournaments and he was doing the business, he still listened.

After I refused to room with him again, Gary Keegan put him in with John Joe Nevin and Ross Hickey in Pescara at the second 2008 Olympic qualifier. Darren was teaching them how to wash out their clothes, telling them not to just hang up their sweats, to clean them properly and to rinse them under the shower. Then he was telling them that this is the best way to eat, these are the times to sleep, this is how much you should drink. They looked up to him because he was a big puncher and a tough, hard, classy fighter. When he spoke he was like an academic and they didn't get that but when he got into the ring they changed their tune. They respected the boxer in him.

But like me, Darren didn't qualify for the Olympics at those Championships. He went way behind in a fight, came right back and got beaten with almost the last punch before the final bell. After that, he was lying on the ground of the dressing room in floods of tears. Gary Keegan was telling him it wasn't over yet, that the result didn't matter and it was the performance that counted and that was much improved on the Worlds. And it said a lot about Darren's strength of character because the next morning when Gary went to see if he was alright, he was shocked at what he saw.

Darren was standing on his bed giving a pep talk to John Joe Nevin, John Joe Joyce and David Oliver Joyce. He was talking about how he had missed out but there were still chances for all of them and they could all make it. Gary listened to him as he peeked in, said he was brilliantly articulate, and he just closed the door and let him continue.

Less than two years later he was dead. Everyone heard the news in different places. Gary was on the M1 motorway driving home, 20 minutes after it happened, and he nearly crashed his car. He was on the phone and pulled over onto the hard shoulder, devastated. After all, he was probably closer to him that anyone since Darren had joined Gary's St Saviour's club at 14. And Gary felt desperately guilty over it all because a friend had rung Gary during the first month of the High Performance Programme and asked what he was trying to achieve.

"Independent boxers," was Gary's answer.

"Do you think that's dangerous, are you sure that's what you should want?" came the response.

"What should I achieve?" he asked.

"Maybe not independent but, instead, interdependent. Maybe that is better. Independence as much as they need but when they run into a problem they have to have the ability to seek help because they recognise they can't fix it on their own."

The night Darren died, Gary thought of the trouble that I was in as well. *"One is dead, the other is ruining his life,"* he kept saying and wondered had he set something up that just prepared us to win medals and not be able to handle life? Did he wrap too much support around us so that we couldn't take on reality? How could this have happened in a period of seven or eight months when we had travelled on our journey, been in awful places and come through it with medals to show? All in all, he wondered did the programme he ran contribute to what happened to me and Darren because outside the system we both imploded, albeit to very different and incomparable degrees.

But I think Gary knows in his heart that he and Billy and Zaur treated us as all as real people because they were aware of our separate life challenges. From Roy Sheehan becoming a father and needing extra time off, to Eric Donovan sometimes going wild, to myself *constantly* going wild after the Olympics. Besides, it should have been me questioning myself, especially after my reaction to Darren's death. And it was how I acted upon hearing the news that means Darren is at the forefront of my mind when I think of the worst that drink brings out in me.

I had spoken to him on Facebook about six weeks before he committed suicide and he said he was enjoying the training but it was lonely enough being a professional boxer. He wanted more fights, he wasn't getting them regularly, but he never mentioned being upset or being down on life. Neither did I. Then one day I got the awful news through a phone call from his girlfriend when I was in the middle of another day of drinking, this time in Oliver St John Gogarty's in Temple Bar. I couldn't believe it. Then I got more phone calls and next thing it was up on Sky News. I just felt empty, cold, hollow. I kept drinking to try and forget it and to try and understand it.

But the following day the news settled in so I went back to a bar. In a sad way I was using it as an excuse to go drinking. I was telling myself that if I go out now, no one will mind because it's a funeral, a sad occasion. I can tell people I'm grieving and they will think it's understandable. That's as low as it gets after everything I'd been through with Darren.

Billy Walsh knew I was drinking for days after the news broke because he said it to me after I showed up at the funeral with these red eyes and a smell of booze coming from me. It was so sad but I was numb from the night before. There was a little altar at the edge of the grave for anyone who wanted to say a few words. His father Tony spoke first but not one person from the IABA got up and said a thing. I was going to go up but it wasn't my place and kept waiting and waiting for someone from the association or the High Performance Unit to do the decent thing and remember him. But they never budged, never opened their mouths. He was part of our amateur boxing family and the coaches were like parents and I was angry with them for never remembering a huge part of his life that day.

At the end of it I walked up to his father Tony and he gave me a big hug. The first words out of his mouth while he was squeezing me were, *"Don't ever go professional Kenneth."*

It was heartbreaking and I was still shook from the drink. He said we'd have a chat soon after but the next time we met was a benefit night in 2010. It was an auction and a lot of boxers gave different pieces. I had a good chat with Tony that night. He was saying Darren was in and around 80 kilos and had hanged himself from a radiator that goes up along the wall, it was only an inch or two taller than him and he asked, *"Do you think if he was kicking and screaming, he wouldn't have pulled it off the wall?"* He also said that his hands were tied yet there were no marks from the ties. Tony was also saying he thought there was a third party involved. He said the police called it suicide straight away and never had a proper look at the body. No one will ever know though.

Some people say it's selfish, which it is to an extent, but there must have been something seriously wrong with him to take that step. And it's amazing because just like I hid my drink problem, Darren never gave us a glimpse of the turmoil he must have been in. This summer a girl around the corner from my family home here killed herself — she was a drug addict with a six-year-old son. So was that selfish or was it down to the kind of world she was being forced to live in? Besides, who am I to talk about selfishness when I used the death of one of the best human beings I've ever met as an excuse to order another few pints.

That is my private shame but as I keep thinking about the badness that alcohol brings out in me. I have plenty of recollections of times when I was a dislikable person in public too. For instance I was on Ryan Tubridy's New Year's Eve gig with Katie Taylor. I was standing there for this countdown to 2009 and I wasn't feeling well for the same reason I didn't feel well most of the time. I was hungover, and itching to get back to a bar. I was in this suit shaking like a leaf, the cold sweat running down my back and I hardly said a word. Tubridy came over to me and asked how I was doing and I could barely answer him. Katie, meanwhile, was this picture of health and was smiling away but I just wanted to get out of there. It was the same with Christmas the last couple of years. My Dad, being a chef, would cook five courses and I'd sit down and pick away at it. When it came to an occasion that was genuinely worth celebrating with a few drinks, I was already drank out, couldn't take any more and missed out on the times people live to enjoy.

It was always the same story. I did Podge and Rodge a couple of times and I was very wary because I just didn't know what those lads would slag me about. We were in RTE's Green Room and Bianca Gascoigne was in the corner, horsing the vodka out of it. I had to have a few too because without drink I felt naked and besides, I knew I'd be grilled. I kept telling myself that a few drinks would make it easier. I went out and all I saw were these two muppets staring at me and I didn't know where to look because they just have these big beads for eyes. So off they went and I was looking at their hair, their mouths, the rest of the set, and they started slagging, talking about women, the Olympics and it was all a bit of craic.

But that was never enough. The thrill of being on the programme was all too brief. I needed to keep the rush going. After the show Gascoigne and her agent were talking about going to the Dylan Hotel so I landed out there and was drinking away with them. I was sitting opposite her in the chair and she started playing footsie. Her agent kept going to get her these colourful cocktails, but by then they were alcohol-free yet Bianca was so hammered she couldn't even tell the difference. I went to the toilet, and heard the heels coming and was thinking to myself that if I exited the toilet at the right time I could get stuck into her. But I was deluding myself. I'd had my fun on the show and should have been sitting at home pleased that I was even on television. Instead I was chasing celebrities like I too was famous.

I discovered that thinking of myself in such a high regard brought out a lot of sleaze in me. I'll hold my hands up and say I always liked the chase and getting women but after the Olympics they only served to make my ego worse because they came so easy. They wouldn't care if I already had a girlfriend or not. They wanted sex and when I couldn't get to a club to get to them, there was always Facebook.

I'd say about 90 per cent of my Facebook friends were women. That made things worse with my long-term girlfriend Karen before we broke up. And when we split I'd just go on Facebook, and check out what different girls looked like. If one was good-looking, I'd add her. I didn't care if they were single, engaged, married, I was half cut at the best of times and it was just add, add, add. Then came the usual lines. *"How are ya love?"* followed by countless one-night stands.

Even when I was representing Ireland at international training camps, I was on Facebook, arranging to meet women when I came back. I had them boxed off for Tuesday, Wednesday, Thursday. I was driving out to them, going to the flicks and making a move. I used to say stupid stuff just to amuse myself. They'd be lying there on webcam in a bathing suit with a watch and I'd compliment the watch. But I was direct after that. We'd talk, I'd throw in some filth and ask straight out were they up for sex or not. I hadn't got time to mess around because there was always another woman the next night and the night after that. It was hectic and if I ever felt guilty I'd tell myself I'd worked hard to get here in life and this was the time to spoil myself. I almost put up as my introduction on Facebook: *No time wasters, I want action.*

When I went off my drinking binges for a day or two, here and there, I would sit at home and be the sleaze ball. I was addicted to Facebook just like I was addicted to alcohol. I remember a girl called Sinead who said she had a boyfriend but wasn't in a happy relationship. There was one night when I couldn't sleep from the drink and we talked through the night until 9.30 the next morning. I can't even remember if we ever met though because

I was meeting so many women in person that I'd made contact with online. I was even getting their names wrong because I couldn't keep track of which was which. *"How are ya Barbara? I mean Sandra."* It was terrible stuff that I'm not proud of. That went on for a while and I closed my Facebook account down because it was too much hassle. But even without Facebook I was getting bored. I didn't like to sleep with the same woman more than once. It was like these rappers you see on television and they only wear a pair of runners once. I was a complete asshole and there were times when even regular women weren't enough.

I was completely addicted to porn too. I'd wake up and go for the laptop and be watching stuff for hours. I was in a terrible way. It was just a mad phase: porn and me. Maybe that comes with the drink because lads in AA would talk about when they were on drink binges they were also sex addicts. Maybe it's a *'Two for One Deal'* or something. Like when guys drink, they just think of women. I'd be waking up at half eight in the morning and if I'd two hours to kill before the pubs opened, I knew how to do it. I'd go online. It's a rut I got in to.

I was talking to my brother Willie recently and he was saying Mickey Rourke is very funny on Twitter. Rourke would be at parties and he didn't know how he got there and he'd wake up in a thong. All sorts. He's still at it and I don't know how he keeps doing it at his age. Thinking of me carrying on like that, at that age, makes me glad I nipped it in the bud because there's no doubt that was the journey I was embarking on. All the memories make me glad that I'm dry now as well because they keep coming, one after another.

Aside from women and porn, and aside from Darren's tragedy, there were other troubles too. One night I went into Dublin's city centre and ended up in Iskanders, a kebab shop on Dame Street. Some guy recognised me and wanted a row. I wouldn't hit anyone on the street, never did. I'm trained to use my fists so if I ever used them in that scenario I could lose my career. You get the odd arsehole but they only come along late at night and I was at a stage in my life when I should have been at home relaxing.

Another night I was up at the darts in CityWest and some newspapers reported I was thrown out of the place. That wasn't what happened at all. I was there with some friends, sitting on the benches and watching Phil Taylor play. All these kids were coming up with the little boards asking for autographs and I was sitting with my back to the room. "*Go on Egan, you're only a wanker,*" someone roared and I looked around. "*Yeah, you, Egan, you're a fucking wanker.*" I sat down and said to a mate who could see him to keep an eye out just in case he did more than roar abuse but eventually we decided it was best to just leave. The next day there was a picture in the newspaper of me half jarred with a pint in my hand, and said that I had been thrown out. Of course the papers were wrong but that's what happens when you live in that world and I did everything I could to make myself a part of it.

I went up to the darts the following night and security stopped me. I asked why and they said they just couldn't let me in. So I went back to the main part of the CityWest Hotel, and I bumped into the owner's son, Jim Mansfield jnr. When he heard they wouldn't let me in, he wanted to bring me over and get me in personally. "*I own the place,*" he kept shouting. But I was okay, I really didn't want to create a scene. So, instead, I ended up drinking for free with him and he went and got a key to a suite for me. That was far better than the darts.

I'm not sure if it was my newfound celebrity status or my drink problem but there were so many crazy situations like that. There was a time when myself and Stephen went to an auction in the Radisson Hotel in Athlone for the Build for Bosnia Foundation. I ended up buying a pair of Muhammad Ali's shorts because I was drunk. Bidding started going from €1,000 to €2,000 and the higher the price, the more I wanted them. Some guy beside me went to €5,000 but I had got it into my head that I wouldn't back down and in the end they cost me €6,000. Thankfully the guy who organised the auction decided that I only had to pay

€3,000 and do a shop opening for him, although that never happened. The arse fell out of his company, so I still owe him one, although that's one of the few things that I did while drunk that I still deem to have been worth it.

They are a pair of Ali's white shorts, signed and in the frame is a picture of the 1966 Olympic team where you can see his head at the back. I'll hang them up in my own place one day but for now the frame is somewhere in my room upstairs in Mam's house.

There were times when I just stared at that picture and those shorts and wondered how good I could have been. I did it quite a bit when I was throwing my own career away. After beating Tommy McCarthy 9-5 in the final of the 2009 seniors, Marty Morrissey interviewed me and I said to him, *"Tommy needs to stop thinking he's Chuck Norris."* Marty then asked if I was going out to celebrate. *"No Marty, I'm going home to bed. On my own."* But when I came back to Boomers with the cup, some of the boys brought me from there to town and I ended up in Copper Face Jacks until six o'clock in the morning. I left the cup there too.

But after that interview I got booed getting out of the ring. I was thinking that it was rough because I came back from Beijing a hero. It did bother me a little bit because I'd never experienced anything like that before. I thought about it for a while and was thinking that people were quick enough to cheer me when it suited them. I was trying to find someone to blame but only now looking back can I understand why I wasn't liked. Some stories about me weren't true but there's no smoke without fire and I had become like a comic book villain to the public.

But I kept burning the candle at both ends and after a crazy year in 2009, the Irish Senior Championships in 2010 crept up. I even drank in January which I normally don't do. In fact 11 days before the seniors I was on the piss because it was seeded, and the big danger, McCarthy, was on the other side of the draw. I thought the early rounds would be easy and I wouldn't meet Tommy until two weeks after the start date. So I drank away, but Eunan Devenney called me and asked what I was doing. I told him I was on the beer and he said I needed to get my head out of my ass and get up here and do some work. He even said if I didn't show up in Donegal the next day, he'd drive down to Dublin and pull me out of the pub. So I jumped in the car and it was the longest drive of my life.

Up there, I briefly found peace in my head. I brought his kids to school and did normal things and was my normal self, not a big ego. It was part of trying to learn how to carry my success. I will always be proud of what I achieved, but I needed to do that in a more down-to-earth way.

Eunan arranged for me to get into the ring with John Sweeney, a local heavyweight and a really busy fighter. I did two rounds, thanked him and said that was enough. The next day I did three. That was my build-up for those 2010 seniors and after 10 days up in Donegal I came back to Dublin for the weigh-in. Somehow I won the title for the 10th year in a row, but I think it was just experience that was getting me through, not fitness. I was slowing fights down, using my strength because I wouldn't have been fit enough to get into a scrap. I'm not proud to say I still managed to win though and over the years, after each win when I brought the cup back to Boomers, the crowd got smaller and smaller. Some of that was down to familiarity. But last year a lot of it was because of the way I was behaving outside the ring.

Gary and Billy never raised the alcohol issue even then but it was in the back of their heads. But they were among the first people I told about AA. We separated a little during my heaviest drinking days, because it became difficult to be around the people who I knew only had my best interest at heart. Out of everyone, I didn't want them judging me or pulling me up on it because I'd have been forced to listen. Plus, there's a shame in it all. But when I told them I had sought help they were so relieved because, while they knew the journey from openly admitting I had a problem to staying off it could be very long one, this was at least a start.

In those early days of AA, I kept telling myself to keep

busy. But admitting my problem gave me a pillar of support. Having people around who understood what I was going through was another pillar. And, besides, we were getting ready for the European Championships last summer and I wanted to give them a lash because of slipping up at the worlds. But I didn't fully make amends.

In the lead-up we had a good camp in the Ukraine. It was a nice complex with a good gym, clean accommodation, even the internet. I was boxing better than I had in a while but I didn't look or feel like I did in Beijing. There was a bit of doubt there and it cost me. I made it to the last four but Abdelkader Bouhenia from Milan beat me again. I still wasn't 100 per cent fit and mentally I wasn't strong. Part of my head was telling me that all the nights of drinking would have an effect, another part was telling me I wasn't the same person and therefore couldn't be the same fighter without the drink.

At least it was a bronze medal and the team were superb as we came second only to the Russians in the medal table with a total of five. At the end of it all we were asked to the Irish embassy for a dinner and some of the lads were going to go for a few drinks and hit the nightclubs. I had to politely decline on the basis I was avoiding drink and clubs.

But I couldn't keep avoiding them and finally I did slip. I'd arranged to go to Uganda with the AtoZ children's charity run by a guy called Brian Iredele. He bumped into me at a white-collar boxing show and asked me if I would be interested. That was in 2009 and I forgot about it because everyone was asking for something. But a couple of weeks after the Europeans he asked again. It was a rush job and initially I was worried because I never thought I'd be away from AA for so long and I thought it would have an adverse effect. By then I'd been off drink for three months, the longest I could ever remember. But this trip would be three weeks in an alien environment without any of the pillars I'd come to rely on. I didn't know what to expect in terms of how I'd cope but also in terms of life out there.

We got there and they brought us to these little bungalows

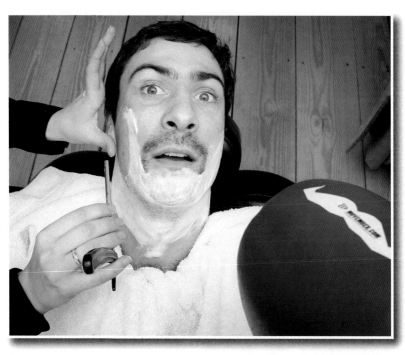

Taking a close shave for the Movember charity at Dublin's Grooming Rooms

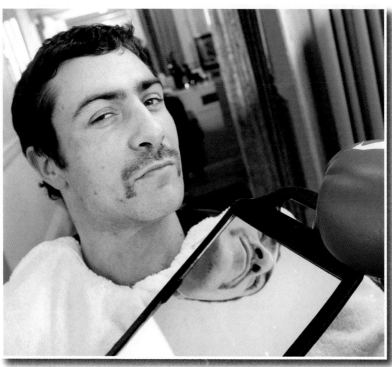

Being honoured alongside my old friend Bernard Dunne at
the 2008 *Irish Daily Star/ TV3* Best of Irish Awards

Suddenly I was in demand to appear on TV. The time on The Podge and Rodge Show was a great laugh, but it was a much different experience when I appeared on Brendan O'Connor's Saturday Night Show just a year later

There were plenty of wild nights. Here I am after a night on the tiles with Chantelle Houghton from Big Brother and, (right) Bianca Gascoigne

'Playing Chicken' while
well sozzled at the
Munich Oktoberfest with
mate Eric Donovan ..
these pictures got us into
a bit of trouble

Training with the High Performance Unit at the National Stadium under the guidance of Zaur... it can be seriously tough

Photo by: GARY ASHE/ALLPIX

where we were staying. They've guards there from six in the evening to six in the morning with guns, just to be on the safe side. There were about nine of us in that complex and we got our schedule the next day. I was slagging because they were good eight hour days and this was no holiday. But it was great to be kept busy. The first few days we were visiting these houses up in the sticks on the back of bikes and there were no rules on the road, just beeping. The problem is that the hospital in Kampala has the necessary drugs and they are free but Brian tries to look after people living high up in the mountains. So he supplies busses to bring kids down to get checked out and then brings the drugs to people in those remote communities as well.

After that we were in at the start of building this big clinic and also houses for poor families. There was a well about 500 metres away from the building site, downhill and we'd go take 20-litre barrels in each hand and carry them back up. We'd have to do that three or four times each morning before we started work so there was enough to do you for the few hours of working. We mixed the bricks, the mud went hard in the sun, and we put in the foundations. You could see how quickly the houses went up. In four or five days the frame was in place and after three or four more days they were putting on the roof. There was a mother and a kid going into the one I was building but the problem is that after you give them the new house they rent it out and go back to stay in their own place. In essence they just get money but still live in poverty.

But it's just a different world. When we were getting the water each morning there were kids just three or four with small canisters getting water too. And the older they get the more they have to haul up the hill. They were lovely kids too. We went to their school and were singing songs. They have a horrible life but they were always smiling. There was a small playground in the school and I started playing the game that I used to play when I was their age, called 'What time is it Mr Wolf'. You line up all the kids five metres away and they shout, "what time is it?", and I'd say two o'clock so they'd have to take two steps towards me. They kept getting closer and closer and at the end they ask again, and I'd shout, *"dinner time!"* and I was running around chasing them.

People here in Ireland think they have it hard and I guess I did for a while too. But everyone should see what those people have to go through. I was drinking away my life, blowing 100 quid and vomiting it down some lane off Wexford Street. These kids are going around barefoot without a cent and living with AIDS because their mother and father had it. To be honest, now I have worked on my addiction and abandoned my own self-pity, I would love to try and get back there again some day.

We did have some time off in Uganda and even with the poverty, it's a beautiful country. There were certain excursions we could choose. You could pay €700 and go on an 11-hour trip to visit the silverback gorillas and you got to spend 15 minutes with them. I didn't do that one, maybe another time, but instead I went on safari and then white-water rafting down the Nile. That was amazing. We were in a big raft with three on one side, three on the other and the instructor on the back. It was myself and a lovely woman from Limerick called Mary who was also working with AtoZ, and all the rest were Yanks.

Half way through it, Mary asked the instructor if we could pull over to an island because she needed to go to the toilet. I told her to jump into the water and go. *"No, no, there are crocodiles in there,"* she said. *"We have all been in, jump in,"* I told her again, but she was quite rightly having none of it.

The World Cup was on while I was out there too and I went to the bars and watched the games with a 7-Up in front of me. The nurses and teachers were drinking but that didn't bother me because there was always some work to do the next day, be it visiting orphanages and schools or delivering medicine. That kept my mind away from my problem right until the end but then I messed up. I was going home so they decided to have a going-away party for me. I was lying in my bed with the mosquito net over me and I was debating whether to go because I knew myself it would be a huge test. But finally I said I'd go down for an hour and be polite.

It was on in this three-bedroom house, with 30 or 40 people in it, all the staff, teachers, nurses, the lot. I was sitting with two of the guys having a glass of coke and everyone was drinking. I was looking at this Smirnoff bottle of vodka on the table and I swear it was looking back at me. It just kept staring over and I couldn't get it out of my mind. I was telling myself if I can get through this I'll be fine, I can get back to Dublin, get back to AA, get back to being an alcoholic who's off the booze. But everyone got drunker, the laughter got louder, and next thing there was a guitar out and there was singing. It was my first time in that situation since I went to AA.

I should have just said, *"Look I'm out of here, thanks, have a great night."* No one would have cared because they were all having their own fun. But instead I kept looking at the bottle of vodka and the devil was getting bigger and stronger in me, saying to have one and it'd be okay. The angel was fading fast. *"Give me that bottle of vodka there till I have a drop,"* I said, finally giving in and this cheer went up. After all, no one there knew anything about AA and me.

I felt great, was working hard, had a bit of a tan, was eating well and there was no drink in the system. And taking a swig in that situation felt so good. I could feel the gorgeous warmth of the vodka going down my neck. I felt it in my veins and it was so, so nice. But after that, the bottle didn't leave my sight for the next hour and a half. I didn't even bring drink there because I wasn't planning to drink myself. But 90 minutes later I was a mess.

I was drinking fast. Another one down the hatch. And another. And another. All of a sudden, I stumbled over to the corner where all these female teachers and nurses were congregated. *"See all you women? I'd ride you all on the one horn."* They thought I was joking but only half of me was. Shortly after, I was ushered out of the house. Elaine, one of the organisers, had to carry me and shortly afterwards I was down for the count.

That was the second last day but I didn't go to work on the last day. Instead I had all my bags packed and was thinking I'd go into Kampala, stay there for a few hours on the beer, and then go to the airport. So I asked Elaine could she organise the case to go with her and I could meet her later. Meanwhile, I went on the piss with a guy from Cork and two girls. Back binge drinking, more of the same old game.

Elaine eventually put a stop to the session to get me to the airport but we got stuck in a traffic jam on this dirt road and the entire way out we were looking at each other saying, 'We aren't going to make this'. Finally we got to the airport though, and your man at the counter looked at us and said sorry, I was late. I was thinking I would stay to catch a later flight but something in my mind was saying, 'I need to get out of here, I need to get out of here'. So the guy let me through eventually, and when I went to the gate I was sitting there and I don't know why I did it because I had my nice few pints and was looking forward to a good sleep, but I ordered a gin and tonic at the airport bar. I started drinking and wanted more and more and ended up as the last person to board the plane. That was the sign that I'll always be an alcoholic and I can never escape that.

There were other signs too, signs that oddly involved avoiding drink. We stopped off in Amsterdam on the way back but there was a 10-hour wait. I went to this Irish bar in the airport, was having a cup of tea and I met this Dubliner who worked on an oil rig. He was on the vodka and whites, we got chatting and he asked if I wanted a drink. But I was like a child not wanting to get home and be caught so I declined. I was telling myself that if I came home with a clear head it would give me some small bit of leeway. Sharon picked me up from the airport and asked me had I been drinking. I denied it but that was just another part of my relapse. Drink. Then lie.

This was nine in the morning, and I told her I was asked down to Wexford because some of the lads were going fishing. So I went home, changed my clothes and went straight down. When I got there the boys had finished up fishing, were back in a bar and I was sitting staring at them, almost able to hear a clock ticking in my head. I ended up having a pint and that was it. And so started another night of drinking. And when I went back to Dublin I started another bender. But back in the house my Mam was seeing all the old signs of the son she didn't want.

I got up one morning dying with a hangover and my Ma said, *"Kenneth, I need a lift"*. I was giving out, said I was feeling shite, but she was adamant. So I got up out of bed, into the car, got up the road and asked her where she was going. She just said, *"Keep driving."* My head was banging. Take a left there, right here. Next thing we were on the Belgard Road heading towards Tallaght. She wouldn't look at me, just kept giving directions and had this anger etched into her face. Next thing I knew we were going to the graveyard where she buried her two sons. I presumed she just wanted to clean up the graves and that would be that. We used to do that now and again.

My eldest brother Willie had a twin who died as an infant. James was his name and he had died from meningitis. Then poor Mam had to bury my brother Keith, who was born before me but passed away in his cot, as well. If he hadn't died I probably wouldn't be here. The two of them are in the same grave along with my granddad so I parked the car and walked in and my Mam was down on her knees pulling the weeds out of the ground and she started crying.

"I have two down there," she roared, pointing at the grave. *"They are the two words in my life. If only. If only I could dig them up and have them come home from Club Diva or Copper Face Jacks. Look at you though. You've everything. You're spoiled by the boxing, the trainers, everyone covering for you. You're running away from yourself. You think you are better than everyone. You're an athlete, you're not famous. How dare you look down on your brother John doing gardening or William in the Army. You're better than no one. You are getting paid to do a job and the buck stops here. I'll dig my way into this grave because I can't listen to you feeling sorry for yourself anymore."*

I felt so bad. My poor Mam was there looking up at me. It was the first time she cried at that grave and it was because they had no chance and here was me, with the best life anyone could ask for and giving it all away. It was so bad that later that same day I rang Billy when I thought I couldn't take anymore. He was in the office and said he could meet me there but I didn't want to go near the stadium. So he drove down to the park in Sundrive and we walked around in the lashing rain and I told him I needed help. I was in shock after what had happened with Mam and we strolled around for an hour and hugged and cried. Just like with the decision I made to win in the last Olympic qualifier though, I was close to making another hard decision that would change my life as well.

My last drink was taken on 12 August, 2010. My Mam and my girlfriend Sharon were out looking for me and you might laugh but my Mam has great faith in butterflies. She thinks they are the two boys she buried coming back to help her, like guardian angels. She didn't know where I was that day but saw some butterflies flying a certain direction and told Sharon which way to go. That brought them to Naas in Kildare, where I thought I'd be safe.

Sharon knew me so well that when she and Mam got there, she walked into the first bar she saw and said to the barman, *"Excuse me, where would I find the nicest pint of Guinness in a quiet pub?"* The barman told her to go across the road and when she got there I was sitting at the bar with a friend from Athy. My friend was looking at the TV which had all the stock market prices on. He turned around and said to Sharon, *"The Dow Jones is having a bad day."* She had great patience but stared him down, said *"fuck the Dow Jones"* and hauled me out.

The drive back was awkward. Sharon was fighting with me and Mam was still pissed off with me after the trip to the grave. *"I don't know what you can do, Kenneth, but my fear for you is that one day soon you'll be sitting in a corner drunk and alone, down and out, and say, 'if only'. If only I stopped drinking or turned my life around."*

She had enough of all the talk, and all the lies. Sitting in the back of the car I knew that was the end of drink for me. I said I'd knock it on the head and rang the same neighbour who had first brought me to AA and told him I was after slipping. *"Right, come on, there's a meeting tonight, are you going?"* I was after letting people down at home but also the people in AA but when I went there I talked to people who lapse all the time. I said I felt so guilty and wanted to apologise to them but they told me that some people have come in on their knees drunk and they put them on a seat. At least they know that person is there, rather than in a bar.

Maybe some things are meant to be because when I finished up drinking I was due to be out in Miami that November for the World Series of Boxing, a competition the AIBA organised where different cities across the world sign up teams and box away. I was questioning if I'd be fit enough or good enough to do it but if I had backed out I think I'd be still drinking. I needed to get away from this country, the rut I was in, the people I was around. It was a blessing in disguise to get away to somewhere with no drinking culture, where no one even spoke about bars. Instead of dark and dreary pubs, there was lovely weather, everyone was out jogging or walking their dogs. We were out running with the team at six o'clock in the morning and even at that hour there was loads out and about keeping fit. Here people would be coming home at that hour and I'd have been amongst them.

I was approached at the start of 2010 by Don Steward, the Director of the IABA about going out there. I'd no massive interest because you didn't wear headguards or vest, and besides, if I wanted to go pro I would have. But Don asked me more about it, said the Miami Gallos team were interested in me and they'd transfer $10,000 over to my account if I agreed. So I signed up and forgot about it but coming closer to the start of the season I spoke to Dom O'Rourke and said I wouldn't go, that I needed to get my head right, and asked would he contact them and I'd transfer all the money back because I hadn't touched it. But rather than just accepting that, he was very good to me and brought me down to Enfield, to this place to dry out. Maybe Dom saw it as a last chance but I was in with a few drug addicts from the estate that I knew and Liam, the counsellor there, was great for me. By the end of it I got thinking again about Miami and Mam said it mightn't do me any harm to get away.

So they flew me out on 3 November. I was the first from this new team to arrive, and this girl brought me up to these amazing apartments where I would be staying. I ended up sharing with a guy called Trent Rawlins, a lovely fella from Australia that used to play rugby professionally, but got injured and took up boxing. There's a bit of craic out of him but the others, well I'm not going to slate them but Yanks are Yanks, they think there is nothing else in the world outside of America. But Trent hadn't landed at that stage, so I picked the en-suite with the walk-in wardrobe. The whole deal with the contract was the accommodation would be paid for but they were hitting us for $125 a month for bills — internet, television, electricity, the lot. That was nothing so I handed it over but Trent went mad, saying that it was not part of his deal.

There were fifteen boxers on a team — five weights, three at each weight. We'd 11 or 12 all the time but were bringing in guys and then some left and others would come. It was the first year so everyone was learning and that included the coaches. I didn't really know what to make of the training because it was all, *"Give me eight laps", "I want six more laps", "It'll be one mile today"*. I never ran so much in my life and was in bits but I kept at it. In the gym the warm-up would be just skipping for 20 minutes. It wasn't constructive. They'd have you doing all these weird bag drills and they weren't even looking at you.

The lighter guys were from Latin America and they are top class, but too small for me to spar because my shadow would be heavier than them. So I was stuck with some heavyweights that weren't even national champions and then you'd get some pros coming in looking for a few rounds and I'd punch holes in them too. It wasn't doing me much good and I didn't want to lose too much of what I learned at home. There it was about aggression because there's different conferences across the world with the winners getting to the finals but the scoring in America is under the power of the commission. The judges and referees in Europe and Asia are amateur but not in America and they don't score like amateur judges either.

There were other flaws too. At the end of the season we sat down with the director, Mike Sophia, and he wanted suggestions as to what he could change from the first season. I told him I thought we needed to get one or two top-class coaches. I talked about the accommodation too. It was lovely but I asked him would he not look for a local sports college with a running track and it'd be cheaper for him. He kept on saying it was trial and error but with something as big as that, there shouldn't be messing about. They should have had us training down on South Beach to generate some publicity, because if they don't get crowds it won't last, and they weren't getting crowds.

The AIBA are pumping money into it but in the States there are so many sports. I was talking to David Oliver Joyce recently; he's with a team in Turkey called Istanbulls and said the stadiums are packed. But we were fighting in the American Airlines Arena where the Miami Heat play. They were clearly thinking too big, too early. Only 1,000 turned up the first night but the rent was $75,000. We had three or four fights in there with about 500 people before we changed to smaller venues, which is how we should have started.

They tried to promote it but I'm not sure how much of a difference it made. Myself and Trent went on the local NBC network, to one of these morning chat shows. There was this huge studio — in one corner there was a cookery segment, then some guy selling some accessories for dogs travelling on planes. Finally we were on. I was yapping away, talking about getting the Miami people to support the team. I was talking for about 30 seconds when the presenter cut in and said she didn't really know what I was saying because of my accent. And with that she went over to Trent for the rest of the interview and he was dropping sponsors' names in every sentence. I'm not sure it made much of a difference though judging by the crowds they got in.

On the first fight night of the season I didn't know what to expect. I always take my gear out from the bottom up — boots, socks, shorts, jockstrap, vest, head guard, gum shield. I was rooting through and I realised my head guard was still in the apartment. Then it dawned on me — we don't have them in the World Series, and that was weird. They put serious wrapping on your hands too, make them like concrete. It felt like a professional fight. We didn't have the robes ready so I was walking out with no top on and I was almost trying to hide myself.

Then came round one of my fight against a guy from the Los Angeles team. I got into a tussle and the heads were rubbing together. I was thinking this is rough stuff, there was a clash and I looked at the ref and he just said *"fight"*. Coming to the end of the third round, there was another clash of heads and I opened up over the eye and there was blood all down my face. But they wouldn't stop it so I went back to the corner and they put the adrenaline into the cut with Vaseline over it. Out I went again, and just coming to the end of the fifth, I caught him with a right hook and he was all over the place.

I'd won but I went to the doctor, got five stitches outside the cut, six inside and was told it'd be a 45-day suspension. That made a mess of my season because for me there were so few fights. I finally got back and fought a Ukrainian they called 'The Pain Train' and he got the decision. Then I fought again back in Miami on Paddy's Day and stopped a Brazilian in the second round. After those fights I'd get guys handing me a card, hoping to get me to turn pro. One guy was in the transport business and did some promoting on the side but I'm not an idiot. That didn't happen much because I'd so few fights and because of the injury I never really got into it. Financially that made a difference too because it was $5,000 a win on top of a $60,000 annual salary.

But in spite of all that I'm actually looking forward to it again, this time as a boxer. Last year it was more important than boxing. It helped me stay dry and it made me more comfortable with the person I was after Beijing. I was fine being me again, albeit a more well-known me and I am starting to understand the people I should trust and the company I should keep. In fact I was so comfortable with the new me that when I went on Brendan O'Connor's Saturday night show last February to talk about the whole Miami experience I found myself opening up when I'd never planned it. It just came out and even he was taken aback.

"I was drinking too much. I was in a bad place," I told him. *"Ever since I got back from the Games I just went mad on it and didn't stop. I'd start with my mates and then the next day I'd go with someone else and then the last day of the week I'd be sitting with an old man in a corner, giving him high fives, having great craic. At the end of it I'd say, 'What am I at here?' I'd go home then, get into bed, feel all sorry for myself, sweats, nightmares, the whole lot. I broke my mother's heart."*

She was there in the crowd and was shocked when I said it. But she was so proud of me and was stuck to her chair. I said that she was up in the crowd, after getting her make-up done, and the camera was on her for a few seconds and she was mortified. But it was a serious night to admit that to everyone because it meant I had learned to live with myself and now I was able to live with everyone else knowing. Backstage afterwards O'Connor told me he wasn't expecting it but I explained to him that 12 months earlier, if I'd agreed to do the interview, I wouldn't have even shown up and he'd have been talking to himself. Granted, he'd probably be well able for that too.

That had me back in the limelight and the Monday after it, a guy came across the road and my Mam told him to take his hand out of his pocket because by then she'd had enough experience to know he had a tape recorder hidden. TV3 wanted me on Ireland AM next but what was I going to say there that I didn't say already? But there were very few negatives to come out of that and so many positives. The amount of phone calls I got looking for help afterwards. I knew blokes all my life I didn't know were going to AA. They'd admit it once I did. Mam met a woman who said she was only in the early stages, but broke down listening to me because she could see herself in my story. And Mam told me I could use it to help people.

Looking at her now she has another question. *"You won't go back on it, will you Kenneth?"* I pause and I think. But whereas before I would have blurted out an answer to protect myself and my habits, now I refuse to lie to either of us. So instead I sit there in silence, and an answer never comes.

CHAPTER 4

8.52am

The house has now emptied and the silence persists, following on awkwardly from Mam's question.

"You won't go back on it, will you Kenneth?"

Those words echo around my mind but finally the suspense is broken, not by an answer that has failed to come charging to the forefront of my mind, but by the gurgle of tea filling a cup. Mam is still holding the pot when she reminds me that three years ago, this very room and this house were full of people and no one could move. It's a fitting link to my life that if the exact start time of my Olympic final was mayhem, now there's some comfort in the quiet.

"If you do make it to the London Olympics," she tells me, *"you'll be able to find me on Achill Island."*

With everyone else now gone to work, there's just the two of us left here and rather than force a response to her question, she goes over to a drawer in the corner, takes out a box and brings it to the table. Inside is my Olympic medal. Three years ago — not just to the day, but almost to the minute — the bell rang and the final started but now we sit here staring at the polished silver and think of everything that it brought. The media, the drink and the pain. The tears and the ego and the chaos. But there is joy too, because now all those things are in the past and I can truly appreciate what was achieved in 2008. I can look back and smile rather than shudder, although Mam pipes up and says she is *"still getting over the effects of those few weeks, never mind what came afterwards".*

I remind her of how she couldn't hide her pride, even before I left for China. A week before I got on board an east-bound 747 she had a banner made up with the words, *'Good Luck Kenneth in Beijing'*. After she placed the order she got a call from the guy in the shop because he didn't know how to spell *'Beijing'* and it was just as well he rang, because he had a 'y' in the original. Dad thought she was losing the plot. He went outside to see what it was that was draped right across the road, from chimney to chimney, and didn't know what to make of it. But soon all the neighbours were putting up bunting and a frenzy was building.

Dad went to China with his friends in the end but Mam was left here at home, with only her friend Bernie to help her through the madness. Neither of them knew what was coming but the craziness was quickly thrust upon them. A girl from the *Irish Daily Star* arrived over in the early days of the Games and asked if she could stay there as the paper wanted to have a presence in the house for the fights. Mam obliged but little did she know the girl would be there every day. She didn't understand all this, the same way she never expected all of it. Before I left I gave Mam a little card and said, *"If any reporters come calling, ring that number and they'll solve any problems."* The number was for the Olympic Council but turned out to be of little use because even they didn't know what was hurtling down the tracks.

True to form, she never watched a single fight. Instead she sat out on the wall in the back garden and had a cup of tea every time I was on. It was just as well because there was no room inside the house. One reporter even had to crawl out the window to get to the toilet because it was too full in the hall. She didn't know most of the people in the house but she never asked questions either. But she did know little Gavin from across the road. Early on in the tournament she asked if he'd do her a favour and get the newspapers each morning because she wanted to collect memories from the Games. In return, she made sure there was a seat right in front of the television for Gavin each time I entered the ring. He had pride of place in the living room while celebrities and politicians scrambled just to get a glimpse of the box.

With each win came more chaos. By the time of the semi-final when a medal was guaranteed, some guy from Spar in Castleknock rang to say he'd supply the food for the house for the last two fights for publicity. He brought so much that the entire estate was fed. There was a kid's corner with two young lads from our road in charge of the plastic cups and drinks while out the front, the adults were queuing just to get in.

RTÉ started getting interested too and arrived over with a satellite truck and wanted to bring it into the driveway. But my brother Willie's Passat was already parked there and my Mam can't drive. She had to give the keys to the guy from RTÉ and told him to move it back when he was finished. Meanwhile, inside, all these tripods for various cameras were taped to the ground. She looked around and announced to them all, *"You'd think the fight was actually on in the living room."*

Maybe all of that added to the tension because she had been fine up until the semi-finals. But that morning she was up in the bathroom throwing her guts up, and while she stood over the toilet Brian Cowen rang the house. Bernie answered and told him to *"hold on there a minute"*, while she shouted up to Mam to say that the Taoiseach was on the phone. Mam, still vomiting, mumbled back, *"Taoiseach who?"*

By the time of the fight, the house was chaotic. In fact, before the first bell in that last-four fight Mam tried to get to her customary position in the back garden but couldn't get through the house so she sat it out in the front garden instead, and listened to cheers and groans as points went for and against me. When the final bell went, the roof nearly came off the house and Joe Stack from RTÉ came up to her and asked about doing an interview in front of the local pub, Boomers, that evening. She still talks about how she could feel her legs buckling as a camera was stuck in her face for a live chat on the *Six-One News*. But at least by the final, my brother Paul had come back home and she didn't care what happened once he was here. She wasn't on her own anymore.

The night before the gold medal bout Mam's sister came up from Kilkenny too, and they had a quiet meal with some friends. They came home early though and thought they had some calm before the storm of the next day until the then Minister for Sport Martin Cullen arrived over to wish the family well. Her sister was mortified when Mam gave Cullen an old, stained mug filled with tea and shoved the carton of milk in his direction. But he wasn't deterred and stayed for over an hour. Finally they got to bed but the next morning when Mam wandered down to the living room at about 6am to get a head start on preparations, Michael Carruth was already sitting there on the sofa with his Olympic tie on. He was on his way to RTÉ studios to do the fight analysis on the final but he wanted to wish her luck before he left. The only question she had was, *"How on Earth did he get in?"*

There was the usual routine in my house for the final. As the cameras were set up, Spar arrived over with another kitchen full of food and the house filled to bursting point. A fella passed the window before I was on and said, *"Mrs Egan, what score is the fight?"* She told him that it hadn't even started but asked if the guy was hungry. She then filled a roll with a fry, wrapped it up and he ran down the road with it to get his bus to wherever he was off to. That was how the Olympics brought people together here in the community. It was a brief return to an attitude that had long departed from Irish life.

Given what was to happen afterwards, it was ironic that she had a rule in the house that there was to be no alcohol during the fights. She didn't want it to turn into a drunken occasion and had made up her mind it was for the kids in the area. On the morning of the final everyone thought that the local boozer, *Boomers*, would be open and selling alcohol. They weren't allowed as it turned out and everyone descended on the house but she still never budged. Rules were rules.

As for me? I was unaware of all that went on in the house until I came home. Instead I was living in a different reality. The best reality I've ever known where the sort of peace I find in dribs and drabs and in relaxed moments, like here at the table, was as abundant as the air.

****

My own Olympic experience began long before Mam was overwrought or the country got excited. For me it started the day we went to collect our team gear out at the Hilton Hotel near Dublin Airport. For some it might have seemed like just a mundane routine in the build-up to the Games but I'd been waiting so long for that moment and suffered a lot to get to that point. So to see the rings on a tracksuit that belonged to me was special. We took a lift up to a room as a team with Billy and Zaur and all the stuff was waiting for us there. There were these big Asics bags with *Team Ireland* written beside our names along with these suits for the opening ceremony from John Rocha. The only downer was that the boots which I still have upstairs are the right length, a size 10, except you could fit my two feet into one of them. I don't know who measured them, but it was a small glitch and didn't take away from the experience.

The boxing team then travelled from Dublin to Frankfurt and on to Beijing, well before the rest of the Irish athletes because we had a camp organised. There were four other boxers. Darren Sutherland was as always minding his money. Paddy Barnes is the smallest big man you'll ever come across. Grumpy and argumentative, he's fiery and the closer he gets to the weight the worse he gets and when he's dieting he won't talk to anyone and just hates everything. His confidence is sky-high though and he would never back down from anyone as the rest of the world found out at those Olympics.

There was John Joe Nevin who is just a class act. He came on the scene at the second qualifier in Pescara and made it to the Olympics straight away. I was looking at him then and was shaking my head thinking, *I've gone for years, desperately trying and trying, fight after fight, tournament after tournament, Olympics after Olympics. And he comes from nowhere and did the business.'* I was delighted for him though. He's a very quiet guy, goes with the flow, potters around and keeps to himself. But in the ring he is super; great on his feet and very hard to hit. And there was Johnny Joyce too. He is really dedicated and is witty and one for slagging. But he's a great trainer and a polite guy too. But at the time there was trouble between the families of the Nevins and the Joyces. Johnny didn't care too much about what was happening, and made occasional conversation with John Joe. But even so, they wouldn't talk unless they had to which was a pity because Joyce is easy to get on with and made the rest of us laugh.

There was a day in Beijing where Joyce was on his way out the door and Darren roared at him,

"Hey Johnny, don't do anything I wouldn't do."

"Like what?" says Johnny, *"spend money?"*

The five of us and the coaches landed in Beijing and dropped off all our gear there and arranged our accreditation. After that, as we were hanging around, we took a tour down towards the Olympic Village, even though it wasn't open yet. We could see the buildings, there was all this security and thousands of volunteers. It was amazing and brought a tingle of excitement. We were staying in a hotel there on our short stopover, a huge place and you needed to see it to believe it. The amount of staff was incredible. There are so many people in China, it seems they have to give them all a job. I was sitting having some dinner one evening, a knife came off the table and hit the floor, and about 10 staff ran over. I thought they were going to attack me but they were just looking for something to do. I said it was fine and I could pick it up but they were insistent and just so nice.

It was one extreme to the other because we left there and flew up to Vladivostok in Russia for a camp, which lasted for 10 days. It's only a two-and-a-half hour flight up from Beijing, but it's a tough, run-down port town. A real dive with a few ships loading in an old naval harbour. The hotel was a bit of a kip and there was armed security on the door but it was a nice 10-minute stroll down to the gym, and there was a little bit of a beach beside the walkway. And as we had come to realise about Russia over the years with the High Performance Unit, even there in this city that time seemed to forget, the facilities for the boxers were superb. There was this huge room, divided into six with ropes and it was just full of rings and quality fighters.

While we were there, a team from Venezuela turned up to train with the Russians but they were refused because they'd never been invited. We saw them walking around the place training on their own. But we got the invite through Zaur and he was vital as always because the Russians are very bureaucratic. Because of Zaur we had full access and there were 70 senior Russian boxers there including their Olympic team and another six fighters in each weight division. We actually couldn't pick out who was rated number one or four or seven because they all seemed as good as each other. The standard was savage and every day we were sparring a different guy in our weight. Those boys were there to break us up, they didn't care that we were going to the Olympics and six of the seven were probably taking their anger out because they hadn't made the Russian team.

We sparred away and every day was tough and that did us a lot of good. On the last day I sparred the great Artur Beterbiyev, the now double European champion and 2009 world champion. He's known as the hardest puncher in amateur boxing and he's simply a beast of a man. When I won the bronze in the Europeans in 2006, he beat me in the semis, stopped me on the points rule although the politics were stinking. But I had four rounds with him in the training camp and I wanted to really test myself.

Zaur had said when we got to Vladivostok that we would do as much hard work as we could there and then we wouldn't throw a punch until our first fight in Beijing. He had that in his head, wanted us like animals getting into the Olympic ring, champing at the bit. So this was my last spar before the main event and I was flying, punching the head off Beterbiyev, mixing it with him. He caught me with one or two shots and shook me but if there was a judge there, I'd have easily been declared the winner.

After that I told myself that I was ready for the biggest stage. How could I not be when I was after getting on top of one of the world's finest boxers?

We had a camera there, taping the rounds I did with him, and when I looked back at it I could see I was hitting him with three or fours shots in a row. Zaur even looked at me like there was something special and told me that I looked in great shape. And that was it then. To have a good day before the break was really pleasing and from then on the confidence just built up. We flew back with the Russians to Beijing and our accreditation and all our bags were ready for us. We had everything done in minutes while there were loads of athletes turning up and waiting for hours in this blistering heat and humidity. Everything seemed to be coming together at the perfect moment.

The one bad aspect of that camp in Vladivostok in my mind involved the team manager, Jim Walsh. If you were to ask my personal opinion, he did a terrible job at it. The IABA assigned him to the job, but he was unpopular with many of the boxers. I don't think he really understood our needs and I think he could have done a lot more to help out at the training sessions.

He may as well have been in Timbuktu as in Beijing for the use he was to me. Himself and Darren Sutherland even had a few run-ins. The first time was at an exhibition. We were standing at the entrance to this huge hall, and Darren told him he'd *"knock him fucking out"*. And Darren never cursed. *"You will not,"* said Jim. *"What are you doing here? You're no use to the team,"* screamed Darren.

The second time was when we went to the Lord of the Dance, the Irish dancing show. Darren was straight down the line, he didn't have the Irish attitude. If there was something wrong, he'd say it to your face and it was a great trait for the most part. But that night he tried to climb over seats to get at Jim. Even Paddy Barnes turned on Jim one day in a dining hall, although it wasn't unusual to see Paddy lose his temper while he was losing weight.

Normally a team manager is just there to sort out problems.

But when there was one, Jim struggled to solve it. The only gear we hadn't got back in Dublin were the shorts and we were told they'd be delivered to China. They finally arrived and you should have seen these things. Both red and blue pairs were like silk hot pants. Darren liked his shorts baggy and long, and he was giving out but Jim kept telling him they'd be alright. We didn't want them and we just used them for training and in the end got a new proper set sent over.

The worst incident of the lot was when he interrupted training one day. Gary had asked specifically about gear before we left because we had to wear Asics but most of our stuff for training was O'Neills. But Gary was told by the Olympic Council that we could wear what we wanted while training. Next thing, midway through the tournament, we were out in front of our accommodation in the Olympic Village doing some drills when Jim came storming into the middle of a session, telling us we couldn't wear this and that. It was unhelpful to say the least.

If we needed something we should have just been able to call him. But he seemed to be causing more problems than the ones he was solving, and worse still was that he got accreditation, allowing him access to both the village and the arena. Now, I'm not saying that he shouldn't have got it, but even Gary Keegan didn't have such accreditation. He was on the outside looking in after everything he had achieved.

It was all numbers when it came to the passes handed out and it was one of the biggest disgraces I've ever come across. Gary was never a great sportsman but worked his way to an Olympics by using what he was good at. That was his big moment yet he was sitting in the rafters when he should have been there in the changing room. It was all down to the IABA. The first day he started the High Performance Unit, Billy even pulled him aside and warned him these things happen and for the 2004 Games told him to make sure he was team manager. Billy had been with Nicolas Cruz in 2000, training Michael Roche while Nicolas spent most of his time with Bernard Dunne. Roche was the only one who made it but when it came to accreditation on that occasion there was one coach, Nicolas, and a team manager who was an AIBA official. So there had been previous experience of this.

With the IABA and the High Performance Unit it was all about control and power which resulted in personality differences. This was a way of putting Gary back in his box but it could have also resulted in a big blow to the team if Gary hadn't been so selfless about it. He never let it affect the boxers and it was only the night before we left Vladivostok that he sat us down to talk about the next steps, because he always tried to map out what the sequence would be. On that occasion he told us the plan was that when we got to Beijing Airport, we would go with Billy and Zaur to the village, and he would go with Scott Murphy, the physio, somewhere else. *"Why aren't you coming with us?"* came the obvious question but he told us that didn't matter, that everything was organised and planned, that we'd be in the team accommodation and he would be 10 minutes away. *"I've an apartment set up, an oasis away from the pressure if any of you want to use it,"* was his explanation.

He thought that the Olympics were a test for us and if we were to achieve, we wouldn't need him at that point. In fact, if we did need him he was thinking he hadn't done this job. But because of all this he was faced with his own test. He negotiated for his two service providers, the psychologist Gerry Hussey and physio Scott, to be in with us every day. They were great to have there because Gerry had done so much work to get my head right in qualifying and Scott, aside from his physio work, was always good fun. When we were away for a long time he'd come up with table quizzes which Billy took far too seriously. But every morning in Beijing they'd have breakfast with Gary, he'd wave them off, and then sit there for hours by himself, flicking through channels feeling he was being denied an experience he had earned every bit as much as us, if not more.

But Gary should be proud because sometimes it can become too much about the coach or the manager and not about the players. There was a danger it would become like that with the row over accreditation, and become about his ego and what he was entitled to. He had a goal and a dream and it wasn't only to realise the ideal of putting Irish boxers onto podiums but also to try to realise his potential alongside that. For us to be world class, he and the support team had to be world class too. He had a chance to do that when he took over the High Performance Unit but the trimmings were supposed to be that he'd get the chance to walk into an Olympic Village and get the honour of managing his team in the Olympic environment.

In hindsight, the saving grace for him was the recognition that the major objective of putting Irish boxers on world podiums was ultimately achieved. And the second objective was then, by extension, achieved because our results meant he and the backroom team were recognised as world class. In short, he was a success even though he was missing out and that was very painful. But Billy and Zaur were exceptionally loyal and in a strange way, what happened possibly galvanised us as a team. We weren't going to be broken by that or anything else after what we'd all gone through to get there.

When Gary was alone in the apartment he was still within distance of what was happening but it got him thinking about all of the support team who didn't even get to go that far because they were back home. He felt selfish complaining, even if he had every right to, so he wrote them a text message. Eleven months to the day after the Olympics were over, he got a package posted to him from the team doctor, Jim Ryan. Jim was always black and white in his attitude and there was no bullshit about him. He had a hard edge but always delivered and he was in Vladivostok and said he really felt something.

All those months later he sent Gary a picture in a black frame of me, Darren and Paddy Barnes which was signed. But Gary discovered there was more as he turned it over to see if it had anything to hang by. On the back there was a note pasted, and as he read it, it seemed familiar. Then it clicked and he started crying. It was the text message he sent to the support team the night he was stuck outside the village on his own.

I went to see Gary in that same apartment during the Games and he didn't want to come to the boxing at first. I told him he had to come, that he had organised the High Performance Unit, got Zaur on board, broke down barriers and set up all these training camps abroad. He had got us that far. He had done everything. So finally he picked himself up and got tickets and came to see us. But that was hard and took guts because he even had to pay for his way out there and pay for his apartment.

Having experienced the Olympic Village, it made it worse because Gary then realised that he was missing something special. It was just a different world there; the most amazing place I've ever been. There was a running track. A 50-metre pool where I passed Michael Phelps one morning after his 20 omelettes, or whatever he claims to have for breakfast, getting ready to train. In fact, the only thing they didn't have were boxing rings and bags. They had a gym set up for us 40 minutes down the road but the Olympic lanes weren't open when we got there first so the traffic was terrible. We used it once, axed it and trained in the compound. We'd go outside the block we were staying in, get some pads and work away under the sun which helped us with the weight. We wanted to keep it simple and focus but it was hard not to spend your time looking around.

Everyone was in their colours and tracksuits and it was like a rainbow. There was a bus service going around all day, every day, and it was needed because of the size of the place. There were eight buildings to accommodate all the athletes. China and America had entire blocks, and those entire buildings were painted in their national flags. Meanwhile we had the corner of one building, stuck in beside Samoa, outside of which there was a little bicycle painted green, white and orange. We used to take it every morning and go to the launderette and we'd hand in our dirty clothes and they'd be returned eight hours later. A long way from the stinking hotel rooms we'd grown used to on our journey there. And everything was free. We had a keycard for the room and we'd just show it instead of money. Even with the vending machines you could shove the card in and take whatever you wanted.

Outside they had Chinese women, down on their knees, cutting the grass with their hands. And all these perfect hedges carved out to show an athlete playing a different sport. There were 10,000 athletes and 20,000 volunteers so everywhere you looked there was a Chinese person there to help you, always smiling and bowing down and they couldn't do enough for you.

The rooms were lovely too. I was supposed to share with Eoin Rheinisch but the canoeing was 100 miles down the road so he didn't stay there. Darren and John Joe Nevin were together, and I don't know how John Joe coped. By that stage I was scared to even go near a room Darren was staying in. Paddy Barnes and Johnny Joyce were in together as well but I was glad to be alone. I'd sit there flicking though all the different sports on the television and got settled very quickly. Not that it was hard because that place was like a wonderland. It just didn't seem real because everything was perfect.

There was an indoor gym across from us with everything in it. There was this endless line of treadmills and I made it my business to be at a specific end because there was an area in front where the Brazilian women's volleyball team used to warm up. I'd say I needed to make weight just as an excuse to be over there. And location was important not just because of the Brazilians, but because at the far end was a wrestling team from Kazakhstan that looked like midgets on steroids. They were training with these big rubber bands, muscles coming out of their muscles, with their Friar Tuck haircuts. You had the two extremes. There were all sorts.

You'd see the superstars floating about the place too. Rafael Nadal was in the village and there were people all over him looking for his autographs and photos. He got no peace. Darren Sutherland was over with him at one stage asking for a picture and I had the camera. Fair play to him, he obliged and it can't have been easy because every two minutes he had to stop and smile. The Williams sisters walked by and you could sit a pint glass on Serena's ass. I'm not into basketball but I saw the big Chinese guy Yao Ming walking past our block. He was enormous and all the other home athletes were running around after him and just staring in awe.

Every time we went into the canteen, our jaws dropped, even when we got familiar. It held 5,000 people and there were areas with every type of food you could imagine from Italian and French to Asian and Arabic. In the corner there was even a McDonalds where the US basketball 'Dream Team' were taking part in a photo shoot. They had all these burgers and chips piled in front of them but they didn't touch any of it. It was just for show and for some advertisements. In fact they were actually staying in a hotel outside the village.

But the more famous faces we saw, the more we had to keep reminding ourselves that for the duration of the Games, these people were just like us, trying to compete and trying to win. One day in the canteen John Joe Nevin went up to Billy and asked why he wasn't bothering with pictures or autographs. *"You forget I was an Olympian too,"* was Billy's answer, *"so if no one asks me for one, I won't ask them."* He then joked that he tried to get Usain Bolt to sign a piece of paper but couldn't catch up with him.

We tried harder and harder to keep our heads down and to keep to ourselves. There were just five of us with Billy and Zaur and the support group. The Irish Olympic team had their own physios who we weren't familiar with so we stuck with Scott and we did our bread-and-butter basics, just like we did back home. We kept to the same routine and tried to make it all as normal as possible. Later on we spoke to a few of the other Irish athletes but boxing was the first sport on at the Games so the track-and-field team weren't even out there in the early days. But while we may have been under the one flag, we were very much our own team.

Once the opening ceremony was over, our heads were immediately in the right place because of the attitude we brought, and there were other reasons to be delighted it was over too. The beige suits we got turned out to be a disaster in the heat over there. We went to a ceremonial function for the Irish athletes in this amphitheatre and you should have seen us after it. There were big sweat patches down our backs and on our arses that everyone could see. In that heat it was a crazy colour for a suit. I was on first in the boxing so I didn't go to the opening ceremony but Darren Sutherland went and when we weighed him after it, three kilos were gone. That three kilos turned the beige to charcoal with the eyes of the world on him.

I watched a good bit of boxing on the television in the early days because I wanted to see how the judges were scoring it. Were they awarding body shots, headshots, backhands, jabs? I was studying it. Sometimes in competitions the first day will give you a good indication but other times the main men call in the judges and say, *"Look, you aren't scoring enough of these or those."* Then it changes. But in Beijing they were scoring body shots and backhands and clean jabs. It was a high-scoring tournament, it was entertaining and it was what fans wanted. It was what I wanted too.

We were all sitting in the apartment when the draw came out and Billy came up and gave us all our opening bouts only. I drew a guy from the Virgin Islands called Julius Jackson. I'd beaten him at the World Championships when the referee stopped the contest so I knew it would be another handy one. But I had bigger worries. My brother Willie was out looking for tickets for himself and those that had made their way over. But because it was so early on in the Games, the touts were charging crazy money, chancing their arm. They met Pat Hickey from the Olympic Council on his way in and he couldn't even get them tickets. It was bad organisation but the lads kept ducking and diving and finally got in for an okay price to see me win 22-2. I came out of the ring and walked down to this barrier where all the media were, and Marty Morrissey was there. I told him I was delighted with the win and said that I was the first man in and I'd be the last man out. That's how confident and determined I was.

The routine of fight mornings stayed the same after that. I'd get up early and go outside of the village to the hotel where the weigh in was, have my medical, go back and have breakfast and rest up. But normally at a World Championship, it all lasts for a week and you'd have five fights in that time. However, this was stretched out over two weeks so there was a lot of hanging about. After that first fight, I had five days off but kept things simple, relaxed and took it easy. That was exactly what we were told beforehand. Don't be in awe of athletes that you see and forget about the occasion.

I remind my Mam of how I rang her after the first fight and asked her if everything was okay. *"You said it was,"* I laugh now. *"Well I didn't want to worry you and I couldn't say that it was already crazy here,"* she smiles back.

Instead she left me to focus on my next opponent, who was Bahram Muzaffer from Turkey. I'd never fought him before which was unusual given how long I'd been around the circuit and for that reason alone he could have been my bogeyman. But my frame of mind was telling me I'm good enough to beat him if I fight my fight. It was like when I fought Weiss, the German in the last qualifier. The two of us were even but I had the balls to beat him. And I was so confident in Beijing, none of the doubts that had plagued my career were there. I was feinting, throwing that body shot that scored most of my points, hurting him and in the end won 8-2 having never looked in trouble.

The funny thing was that Beterbiyev was beaten that same day by Zhang Xiaoping of China. I was in the showers afterwards beside him, happy with my day's work, and as he was leaving he looked at me and said, *"good luck"* in his broken English. That was the only time he ever said a thing to me, after all the camps we'd had. I realised there and then that he had a heart and wasn't just a machine. It was decent of him because he was favoured for a medal and being with the Russian team, there must have been a lot of pressure because they expect nothing but gold. It's little things like that which you remember and you appreciate.

When I came out of the boxing venue, it was straight onto the bus and back to the village. But with my Dad and brothers over there I used to go out to see them on the mornings I was off. I'd get a taxi to this Danish bar they were always in called The Den. I was wondering what they'd been up to and was feeding off them and getting the stories from them. And as the tournament progressed, every time I went there the Australian boxing team were in the corner because they'd been beaten. They were forever in the same spot with a bottle of Jagermeister. They were terrible men for drinking and my brothers were telling me they'd end up their session by running around in their jocks. They got barred at the end of every night but were always let back in. That shows you the process and how hard it is for us to qualify in Europe compared to other continents, but at least the Aussies were wishing me luck each time I was in there.

Next fight up and it was medal time. A win against Washington Silva of Brazil and I'd be through to the semi-finals and guaranteed a bronze. When we were out in the Philippines before the World Championships in 2005, I sparred him and did well. Even though it was only one round, it was a positive mental footnote I had in my head. Come fight time, the memory bank was working, I knew he liked to throw big hooks and go all in with his shots. But none of them connected, I won 8-0 and was assured of a podium place.

I was thinking for a second this couldn't be true but I quickly shook off any feelings of doubt. I was feeling so happy and fit, I couldn't wait to get back into the ring. I was in my prime and I deserved to be on the podium. I believed in my ability and my results showed as much. I felt whoever I was in with, I'd beat them. Paddy Barnes said recently, *"What's wrong with you Kenny, you aren't boxing the way you used to. If you boxed the way you did in the Olympics, then no one would touch you."* He was right. Whatever about the dip in form brought on by my personal problems in more recent times, back then I felt unstoppable and was doing all the simple things so well. Just feinting, scoring and getting out of the danger zone with an increased lead and without a glove being laid on me.

I remind Mam of how I rang her after that fight as well and wondered if things were coming to the boil here yet. *"You said it was all under control,"* I laugh again. *"Well I didn't want to worry you and I couldn't say that it was already crazy here,"* she smiles back, repeating the same words she said a few seconds ago.

Zaur was making sure his personal situation wasn't affecting me or the rest of the team either. In Vladivostok, he saw on the internet that there was huge tension between Russia and Georgia. On August 5, when we flew to Beijing ahead of the opening ceremony, his wife and son returned to Georgia. The Olympics began on August 8 and by then, in his town of Poti there were 1,000 tanks and dead bodies everywhere. The Russians had invaded South Ossetia and closed down all communications. He couldn't make contact with his family. All he knew was that 16 people had been killed close to his home including a very talented boxer he used to coach. So he was thinking the worst, but he never said a word. He was looking after his five boxers and that was his number one priority. He was on Skype any spare minute he had but he never involved any of us and I didn't even know about it all until after the Games. But away from us he couldn't sleep and even started smoking again.

Eventually a friend he had contacted in Tbilisi, who is great at computers, tracked them down via their mobile signals. They had fled to the mountains where his wife's sister lives. From that moment a weight lifted from him. It can't have been healthy having that in his head but with that sorted there were other things filling his mind. He got back to telling me about a dream he had a year before the Olympics, where I met a Russian in the final and beat him for a gold medal. The only problem with it was that Beterbiyev had been knocked out so it wouldn't be a Russian I'd be facing in the final, but I still fancied getting to there because next up was Tony Jeffries of England in the last four.

Before the semi-finals we went down to the hotel where the Irish Paralympians were staying, waiting to move into the village. Myself, Darren and Paddy had medals secured but the whole team went as a unit and the five of us talked to them about believing in themselves and we talked about enjoying the sport you are involved in. It was nice to be asked to speak because people need to respect the lengths they go to as athletes and realise that they are just as serious as we are about our sport. Plus it was a brief escape from the pressure. But the minute I left them behind, I was back focused on the job and on Jeffries.

In 2008 I had retained my EU title out in Poland and it was Jeffries that I beat in the final. In fact, I always knew I had the beating of him because his style suited me perfectly. Outside the ring he is a really good guy and he'd always make a point of talking to you. But inside the ring I liked him too. On one of the days before that fight, I wandered down to an internet building that was in the village and was reading on a site online which said that he was going to withdraw from the fight. That gave me even more confidence because while it turned out not to be true, it got me thinking that he feared me and I had this guy's number. Sometimes you get into the ring and think it'll be 50-50. Not on that occasion though.

I don't think even his own team believed in him either because of what happened next. It wasn't the only Ireland-England semi-final, with Darren having qualified to face James DeGale and after the Games Billy told me about a conversation he had. He said he had been approached by someone claiming to represent the Great British boxing team and a deal was suggested where we'd go one for one. This person even said they'd let Billy pick which one he wanted to win but he was having none of it though. Besides, we were expecting to win both of those fights.

There was a huge Irish crowd there for my fight, loads of 'Boomers Bar on Tour' flags and everyone was singing. I like to look back on that day because people ask if I got nervous but I can't say that was the case. Instead, it was just a happy time in my life, where everything was good, there were no problems in my head and I was just soaking up my surroundings. I was boxing well, having fun, posing in the ring after bouts and becoming a success all at once. Plus, there wasn't a drink in sight and I didn't need one because the emotions were all strong and all positive. It was heaven.

I was on a roll too as three wins out of three became four out of four. I caught Jeffries with a body shot early in that fight and he grimaced. I knew I'd hurt him and I kept doing damage, not only because of the way I was fighting but also because he was too slow for my style and never stood a chance. I won that 10-3 and afterwards as I was talking to Marty Morrissey when I looked up to see who was in the other semi-final because I hadn't a notion due to our one-fight-at-a-time philosophy in the camp. Zhang of China was in the process of being given a countback win over Yerkebulan Shynaliyev of Kazakhstan, who had been a world bronze medallist the previous year and was a super operator. I was delighted because if I had of picked who I wanted to win it was the Chinese fighter. He hadn't proven himself to the same extent as Shynaliyev and was taller, whereas the Kazakhstan fighter was small and compact and a southpaw. But it never dawned on me I would be fighting a Chinese boxer in China. It didn't seem to matter because the scoring had been correct all the way through the tournament and I just presumed that honesty would continue.

I went into the dressing room carrying the same smile I had on my face across the Olympics and there was this big, massive security guard standing literally behind me. He wouldn't move and his facial expression wouldn't move but he was in my way as I tried to get changed. So I pulled down my shorts, was stark naked and my arse was brushing against the guy. *"Sorry mate,"* I said and the dressing room erupted laughing. Even Gary had gotten in by this stage. Gerry Hussey gave him his accreditation and insisted he go but Gary wasn't sure because he thought the other security guards might look at the picture, stop him from coming in and march him out of the place. He already felt like a leper and couldn't avoid that feeling that he was being treated like a piece of dirt so he couldn't handle any more humiliation. But Gerry insisted and Gary made it in. He was starving as he always was on away trips; he never ate when stressed.

As well as Gary feeling a part of it all, my brother Willie was there too and gave me a massive hug, nearly breaking a few ribs in the process. I was delighted by the fact that so many people from my home estate had travelled over. That was really overwhelming. I could have lost my first fight but they still worked overtime and long hours, scrimped and saved what they could, and flew out. A lot actually had to return home because they had their flights booked around the quarter-final stage. My brothers were on that list too but Rory, the owner of Boomers, coughed up money for them to stay and just Paul returned home before the final. I believe Rory spent mad money out there and not just on the flights. Another night he brought 20 lads out to a fancy restaurant and treated them all. Granted, I'm sure he made his money back after the Games.

The only downside to it all was that I was the only one who had made it to a final. John Joe Nevin lost out to a Mongolian, Enkhbatyn Badar-Uugan, in the last 16 and had no complaints. Johnny Joyce, meanwhile, was heartbroken because in the first round he beat Gyula Kate, who he'd lost to on a couple of occasions before. That had been the best performance of his career but in the next round he lost a countback to Felix Diaz of the Dominican Republic, having been a couple of points up with seconds left.

Paddy Barnes had made it to the medals but was equally disgusted, and let everyone know. On my way to the stadium to fight Jeffries, I caught a glimpse of his semi-final on a television in a hotel window. I was looking at the score and knew he was gone. In the end he lost to Zou Shiming 15-0. He came out to the media after that and said bronze is for losers. But that's how competitive he is. He hates losing and that wasn't his first or last outburst. I can still remember him spitting fire into a microphone after a fight at the 2009 World Championships and saying it's not the athletes that need drug testing, it's the judges.

He was just too early in his progression to get the better of Shiming and bronze was a remarkable result. But for a long time after that I was winding him up by telling him that bronze was for losers and my silver made me the number one Irish boxer. Then he went over to Moscow last year and won gold in the European Championships and returned the compliment.

The biggest disappointment of the lot though was Darren's bronze because he should have beaten James DeGale. In the previous round he looked good enough for gold when he took apart the silver medallist from Chicago, Alfonso Blanco, 11-1. But when he guaranteed himself a medal he changed. And before the semi-final he had a two-hour warm-up when it should have been short. He couldn't sit down and he couldn't sit still. He'd beaten DeGale before but even his body language after that semi-final defeat said it all. He was too happy with being in a semi-final when he was good enough to win it all out.

But that's not to take away from what the team achieved. I was in a final and the way the results happened meant that even if I lost, we'd have all been beaten by the eventual gold medallists in our weights. But I had no intention of being beaten. After the semi-final I walked into the canteen and a relay team there had silver medals around their necks. I went to look and Zaur pulled me back. *"No,"* he said, *"You will get a gold, they are silver."* He didn't say that to build me up, instead he had a genuine belief in me and so did I. The others had belief in me too. The night before the final Darren came into my room and looked into my eyes and told me to do the business the next day. I even went to bed the night before the final with a smile on my face, not because the worst I could get out of it was a silver medal, but because I felt I could win the final and win it well.

It was interesting to see the Olympic Village as the Games progressed. McDonald's was empty the first week, but by the second week it was full of beaten athletes. They were fed up with healthy food and were eating two or three burgers at a time. And day after day there were less tracksuits and flips flops, less colours and less hope in the faces of those wandering around. As time passed more and more were eliminated and were in clothes for going out. High heels and mini-skirts. Shirts and shoes. Later on I'd be desperate to be part of any session going, but at that time being an athlete that was successful was fulfilling all my needs. I was still there in my team gear and on this day three years ago I left my room and headed for an Olympic final, still in my Ireland colours, still carrying my gear bag.

As I was heading out of the village to the weigh in, Ronaldinho came in with a teammate singing and laughing and joking, hat on sideways at seven in the morning, locked. The soccer final had been the previous day and he was obviously out after that. I didn't have my phone or camera so I shouted out, *"How are ya,"* and he cheered back and nearly fell over. It was madness. But everyone was there to win medals, regardless of bank balances. He'd only got a bronze. I wanted to go two better.

At the weigh-in, I saw Zhang up close for the first time. He was very friendly, smiling away. He was big as well and must have been tight on the weight so I was telling myself to work this guy hard and tire him out quickly because he would have been dehydrated from the night before. With that in my head I went back to the village for a few hours before the fight, was up in the apartment with a couple of hours to go before the biggest moment of my life. I had the laptop open in front of me and the boys came in, Paddy Barnes looks over at the screen and let's a roar of laughter out of him.

"He's in an Olympic final in a couple of hours and he's watching porn," he told the lads. But surely it's about whatever relaxes you? I wasn't going to sit there and worry myself to death so what better way to take my mind off it all.

Finally the time came to put away the laptop and head for the stadium. I got into the dressing room and was doing the same 15-minute warm-up I did for all the other fights. We got these deadly robes with the number eight on the side of the hood because eight is a lucky number in China. I put it on and went and waited behind the curtain. Zhang went out first and it was deafening. There was a massive crowd there, almost a full house but when I walked out, I could hear the little group of Irish singing *"Ole, Ole, Ole"*. It reminded me of the World Cup with the underdogs making themselves heard.

I was in great shape mentally which was more important than physically after all my slip-ups. I felt so good. I was calm and believed. It couldn't have come at a better time. A lot of athletes who train all their lives get it wrong for those Olympics weeks, they don't even make their personal best. There was a lot of negativity among other athletes in the Irish camp and some had started complaining before they even competed. We didn't want to hear any of those excuses; the five boxers were there for each other, there to perform and we had our own group. That left me in a perfect state to win gold.

Billy told me to keep focused, keep feinting, get the points and at 8.52am Irish time, the same time that's on the kitchen clock now, the bell rang. He was big and long and rangy as I thought, but he was fast and he wasn't throwing the straight right I was expecting. Instead, there as a bit of a hook in it which meant the timing was a little different and that put me off. We were going at it, and he got in with a couple of shots in the opening round, and I got him back with a decent right. But I knew myself I had started too slow and did too much looking. I went back to the corner and asked Billy how I was fixed.

"Right Ken, you are two down."

"That's not too bad," I told myself, *"I can pull that back because I still have the belief and the fitness."*

"Ready to go, Ken, ready to go," Billy said as I headed back out for the second.

And I had a good second round. I had it back to a point when I landed with a clean shot but I heard the Chinese going crazy and for a split second I thought about it. That wasn't a good sign, even if I was only 5-3 down at the halfway point. But there was a good pace to the fight, and I had a super third round, caught him with right hooks, milled him with left hands, thought I was taking control. But the home crowd were cheering and I was saying to myself, *"He is getting points here"*. I got back to the corner expecting to be told that I was ahead but Billy just said, *"Right Ken, you are still two down."*

Zaur looked at me and I could see it in his face that I had to throw everything at him to get this fight, the judges were just holding it back from me a little. And as I went out for the final round he shouted at me, *"Kenny, try everything."* I went back out and he was running and I was finding it hard to close the ring down. When I did corner him off, he was rangy and holding. His tactics were very good, he was sneaky with his right and he wasn't letting me land my left to the body as much. I like to be ahead and counter but no matter what I did in round three, the judges wouldn't let me ahead and that meant I couldn't close it out in round four. The final bell rang and it was 11-7 when it should have been a lot closer.

I just dropped to my knees at that moment, not only because I'd lost but because I wanted those Games to last forever. I was so content and enjoying life but suddenly the bell tolled and the show was over and I was heading into the unknown. If you'd offered me a silver medal at the start I'd have taken it with both hands, but I was so close to being an Olympic champion. I knelt on the canvas and just told myself, *"I can't do anything else now, I can't try anymore. The journey is over. Where do I go?"* I gave Billy a hug, went over to Zhang's corner and he was jumping around with the crowd going bananas. In all that noise for me it was just quiet. *"How could I replace this?"*

My humour turned because of that empty feeling and I had to go to a press conference which Zhang was at as well. I was sitting there disgusted listening to the media asking stupid questions. I told them if that fight was anywhere else in the world I'd have won by a couple of points. They asked him the same question and he said he felt comfortable in every round and was better but that I was a great fighter. I didn't dislike him but I know there is human error on the part of the judges and the only wonder is if it was intentional or not. To this day I still have my doubts about that because coincidences have a limit.

After that I just got out of there and went to O'Shea's, an Irish bar in Beijing, where my family had congregated. There was a giant Irish flag, the size of the room, and there was a song everyone was singing (to the tune of *'Can't Take My Eyes Off You'*).

"Oh Kenny Egan, you are the light of my life,
"Oh Kenny Egan I'd let you shag my wife,
"Oh Kenny Egan I want to box like you too."

Lads with their girlfriends there were belting this out and I was mortified. The best part of the lot though was that I met an Irish guy there who was in a bad way and he called me over and said, *"Egan, I've got a present for you."* I thought he was drunk and it would be something stupid but when I got back home to *Boomers* I was presented with the blue corner pad from the same ring that was used for my final. Seemingly this guy was running down the street with it in Beijing. How he stole it I still don't know.

There was just the closing ceremony left and I was supposed to carry the flag but I got drug-tested and I made it to the stadium late so they gave it to Johnny Joyce instead. But just to be there at all was incredible — to be standing in this searing heat in the middle of the Bird's Nest, cameras going off everywhere. It was amazing. We went on the piss that night even though we were leaving the next day and John Joe Nevin got well gargled. We got some menus and since he could barely see, we asked him what he wanted.

"I'll have the steak and the burger."

"No, which one?"

"I'll have the steak and the burger, I told you."

We got him both, but he finished neither, fell asleep on his plate and that was it. The end of Beijing.

The homecoming was great too but looking back, having been through so much, it was just postponing the inevitable silence and loneliness and search for something else that gets the adrenaline rushing. I didn't know that at the time though.

Even though we had the medals, we were stuck down the back of economy for the flight home, and the lads from the Olympic Council were living it up in first class. I didn't want to cause a scene, I'm not that type of person, but I couldn't understand it. But no matter how sore our limbs were from a long trip home with no leg room, Dublin brought a freshness to all of us. I didn't think it would have caused as much of a stir as it did. There was a small flag out the cockpit window and I was first off the plane. As I stuck my head out, I was shocked. There were loads of people on the tarmac and it's like they were look-ing at me differently, like there was an aura around me. People were telling me that I was amazing, but I was saying back, *"I'm human, I just trained hard for this."*

I've come through that arrivals area many times with a medal around my neck and just my mother and a few friends were there. But this was the Olympics, it's what it was all about, it's what people watch, it's why they care. It was mobbed that day and everyone was cheering *"Kenny! Kenny!"* That was the start of creating a different person. And inside in the terminal Mam and my brother Paul got called over by the head of secu-rity to follow him up to the VIP Lounge. Paul said he needed to go to the toilet first and this guy offered to escort him. It'll show you where we were coming from that Mam thought there was something wrong and they were going to throw him out.

As for us, we sat down first with Martin Cullen and then made our way through to the main arrivals area. There were banners everywhere. All the photographers wanted was the three guys with their medals but I said, *"Wait, we are a team."* It had to be the five boxers because, while a lot of people think it's an individual sport, without a team we wouldn't have gotten so far and done so well. From there we got ushered out by the airport police towards the car park, where there was a bus hooked up for us.

The plan was to go to Clondalkin but we decided to go through Neilstown first because that's where the club is, but it was espe-cially for Noel Humpston's wife. She even turned up to see us all on this open-top bus and off we went through Clondalkin Vil-lage and down towards Boomers. I was looking around laugh-ing, thinking I never thought I'd see all this in the Kip In The Dip. Kids were screaming. Adults were hanging off lampposts. People you met all through your life, people you drank with, bought your shopping off, women you were with in nightclubs, they were all there going crazy.

We went into Boomers and I've never seen a place as busy. Even the car park was full. I got dragged over to an RTÉ microphone and I said a few words, told them that everyone should take up a sport because it keeps kids off the street. I was rambling but everyone picked up on that. It was strange that people suddenly cared what I had to say because I don't be thinking about what I'm saying half the time, but as long as I wasn't cursing I'm okay because I was brought up around a lot of bad language. When I finished up there, one man had come up from Cork and said he had watched me on the television. I took out the medal and he held it in his hand and started crying. I was wondering how a medal could have this kind of effect. I think it made him proud to be Irish. It was very strange. It wasn't the first time that happened either. I really was trying to tell people that, *'okay, I worked hard for it, but it's not the be all and end all'*. But they wouldn't listen. I was saying that I'll be here tomorrow and the next day, there's no need for this panic. But there were people touching me as if it was going to heal the limp in their leg.

Finally, I made it upstairs to the function room, which was closed off. I went there to relax with my girlfriend at the time, Karen. Mam and Dad, Bernard Dunne and Mick Carruth were all there and crucially there was space beside them so I took a breather. When you are being mauled and touched you get a little uncomfortable. I went back downstairs for half-an-hour, gave the nod to the missus and went back to the house. Peace and quiet. I've often thought about this since — you have all these people that want to pat you on the back, shake your hand, all this noise and excitement and this rush. But the minute you close that front door, it's just you and you have to deal with that withdrawal. It was nice that first time to get home and I was thinking a lot of doors would open so I could just relax. But if I hated the excitement at first, pretty quickly I came to depend on being around people and hysteria, on being the centre of attention.

The next morning I was only out of bed and the kitchen was full of people with notepads and Dictaphones. They took a picture of a fry. The headline the next day was *'Kenny Egan looks forward to his mother's cooking'*. A picture of me with a fry? Did they want to take a picture of me going to the toilet for the first time as well? It was ridiculous.

Letters were coming through the door daily, in their hundreds. The postman would come down with letters with no address on the envelope, just saying *'Kenny Egan'.* Even one Sunday morning I went down and he was there and told me that there were so many letters that he was passing by on his day off and decided he'd better get rid of some of them. There was a school in Mayo and each person in the class had to write a letter about me. Mam had the names of all the kids and we got photographs for every one of them. Each letter we wrote back was individually addressed to the child. Mam even rang the teacher, thanked her and said there's a batch of post going to the school so to let her know if we left any of them out. We didn't miss one.

Mam said that if it meant that much to people that they wrote to us, we had to go to the trouble to write back. So we sat for hours here at this table in our kitchen, returning every one of them and were flat out signing stuff. There were a couple of begging letters too, because a lot of people thought I was going to be a millionaire. Parents were writing saying they had six kids and couldn't feed them, others said they needed donations for a relative to have an operation in America.

But slowly things changed. The press didn't want to see me smiling anymore and they started looking for dirt. They went after so many negative stories about me that during the worst days of my drinking Billy was going to put all the clippings on a table to show me what I was doing and there was enough of it to have an effect. People get bored of you being a hero and they want to bring you down. Weird letters started dropping through to the door. I was doing a radio interview one day and was asked how things were. *"All is well in the world,"* I said, but later that week someone wrote to me saying how dare I say such a thing when there was so much trouble out there.

Another guy wrote to me: *"Ken, I strongly recommend a Kerry Blue dog as a companion. They don't suffer from any canine diseases. They are great anti-burglar dogs. The only people that they al-*

low to play with them are their owners. They will guard any babies in the family until the death. My old Kerry Blue pal Rocky died at the age of 24 and that is very old for a dog. Rocky was a great anti-burglar dog. You comb their thick curly coats at least once a day. They are great companions to have out walking." Lunatics.

I got a text from a friend here in Clondalkin saying that there was graffiti down by the shops. *"Kenny Egan is a kiddy fiddler."* There was more at the top of the hill. *"Kenny and Tony Egan are perverts."* My first thought was to go up with a bucket and scrub this huge red writing off a white wall but finally I said I'd just leave it because if I react they'd do it again. It was a Friday, the council were off until the Monday but the staff of Boomers actually went and cleaned it off in the end.

Incidents like those made it very obvious that there were two paths in front of me and the way things turned and the way people turned on me so quickly made it obvious which way to go. But I didn't. I went the other way. I had been given so much attention that I couldn't just close the door of the house, switch on the television and look around at emptiness. I wanted more noise and excitement and adrenaline. I wanted to replicate the feeling I'd gotten in Beijing. Even though it was impossible, I went down the wrong path and kept going in the hope there might eventually be those moments of perfection awaiting me.

****

Right now there is silence in my life though and I've learned to live with it. I glance up at the clock and it reads 9.05. It's the time my Olympic final finished, my Olympic experience ended, and a new and destructive me was created. The house has emptied and the silence persists, following on awkwardly from Mam's question.

"You won't go back on it, will you Kenneth?"

Those words echo around my mind but finally the suspense is broken, not by the gurgle of tea filling a cup, but by an answer that has finally crawled to the forefront of my mind. But unlike the last few years where drink made me lie, this time I tell the truth to both Mam and to myself.

I know there are temptations and there always will be. After I lost my senior crown to Joe Ward earlier this year I was feeling particularly low and that's the closest I've come. I was in the car, considering just driving down the country to some small village, checking into a B&B and wandering into an old man's pub with a nice Guinness where no one recognises me. There I could do what I used to. But I've a sponsor now, a guy called Des who I met in the gym in CityWest, and he said no matter what happens, before I am ever about to take a sip from that first pint, just ring him. I told him I would, so I give Mam the best answer I can in this empty kitchen with just the two of us sitting at the table.

"You won't go back on it, will you Kenneth?"

"I hope not, Mam. I really hope not."

Career Record

IRISH SENIOR CHAMPIONSHIPS

2001 - MIDDLEWEIGHT
Quarter-final - beat Kevin Walsh (St Colman's, Cork) 21-14
Semi-final - beat Michael McAllister (Belfast ABC) 13-7
Final - beat Conall Carmichael (Holy Trinity, Belfast) 11-6

2002 - MIDDLEWEIGHT
Quarter-final - beat Leon Senior (Crumlin BC, Dublin) 14-13
Semi-final - beat Keith Whelan (Saviours Crystal, Waterford) 19-9
Final - beat Marvin Lee (Oughterard, Galway) 15-10

2003 - LIGHT-HEAVYWEIGHT
Quarter-final - beat Donnacha Cuttriss (St Colman's, Cork) RSC2
Semi-final - beat Michael McDonough (Brosna, Offaly) 10-4
Final - beat Conall Carmichael (Holy Trinity, Belfast) 16-4

2004 (staged December 2003 to allow for Olympic qualifiers) - LIGHT-HEAVYWEIGHT
Semi-final- beat Shane Dalton (Sunnyside, Cork) RSC3
Final - beat Marvin Lee (Oughterard, Galway) 8-2

2005 - LIGHT-HEAVYWEIGHT
Semi-final - beat Leon Senior (Crumlin BC, Dublin) 23-6
Final - beat Darren O'Neill (Paulstown, Kilkenny) 27-7

2006 - LIGHT-HEAVYWEIGHT
Final - beat Darren O'Neill (Paulstown, Kilkenny) 21-12

2007 - LIGHT-HEAVYWEIGHT
Final - beat Willie Mitchell (Dromore, Tyrone) RSC1

2008 - LIGHT-HEAVYWEIGHT
Final - beat Ciarán Curtis (Dealgan, Dundalk) 19-4

2009 - LIGHT-HEAVYWEIGHT
Semi-final - beat Denis Hogan (Grangecon, Wicklow) 16-3
Final - beat Tommy McCarthy (Oliver Plunkett's, Belfast) 9-5

2010 - LIGHT-HEAVYWEIGHT
Quarter-final - beat Disha Gezim (St Matthew's, Dublin) RSC3
Semi-final - beat Denis Hogan (Grangecon, Wicklow) 21-2
Final - beat Tommy McCarthy (Oliver Plunkett's, Belfast) 9-5

2011 - LIGHT-HEAVYWEIGHT
Semi-final - beat Thomas Roohan (Ballinacarrow, Sligo) RTD2
Final - lost to Joe Ward (Mullingar, Westmeath) 11-6

***

EU CHAMPIONSHIPS
(all contested at light-heavyweight)

2003 - STRASBOURG, FRANCE
Semi-final - beat John Dovi (France) 19-19
(29-24 on countback)
Final - lost to Tarhan Yardarm (Turkey) 18-12

2004 - MADRID, SPAIN
Round one - lost to Aleksy Kuziemski (Poland) 37-21

2005 - CAGLIARI, ITALY
Round one - beat Kevin Piquet (France) RSC3
Quarter-final - beat Yildirim Tarhan (Turkey) RSC2
Semi-final - beat Istvan Szucs (Hungary) 28-18
Final - beat Mario Sivolija (Croatia) 48-38

2006 - PECS, HUNGARY
Quarter-final - beat Tervel Pulev (Bulgaria) 18-17
Semi-final - lost to Constantin Bejenaru (Romania) 32-12

2007 - DUBLIN, IRELAND
Quarter-final - beat Imre Szello (Hungary) 17-7
Semi-final - beat Mario Sivolija (Croatia) W/O
Final - beat Constantin Bejenaru (Romania) 23-17

2008 - CETNIEWO, POLAND
Semi-final - beat Caner Sayak (Turkey) 27-9
Final - beat Tony Jeffries (England) RSC4

2009 - ODENSE, DENMARK
Round One - beat Constantin Bejenaru (Romania) 18-4
Quarter-final - beat Erik Skoglund (Sweden) 10-6
Semi-final - lost to Imre Szello (Hungary 7-6

***

EUROPEAN CHAMPIONSHIPS
(all contested at light-heavyweight)

2004 - PULA, CROATIA
(also first qualifier for 2008 Olympics)
Round one - lost to Yildirim Tarhan (Turkey) 28-13

2006 - PLOVDIV, BULGARIA
Round one - beat Robert Woge (Germany) RSC2
Quarter-final - beat Mamadou Diambang (France) RSC3
Semi-final - lost to Artur Beterbiyev (Russia) RSC2

2008 - LIVERPOOL, ENGLAND
Did not compete due to the proximity of the tournament to Olympic Games.

2010 - MOSCOW, RUSSIA
Round one - beat Simone Fiori (Italy) 3-2
Round two - beat Aleksander Ramo (Albania) 15-2
Quarter-final - beat Ainar Karlson (Estonia) 7-4
Semi-final - lost to Abdelkader Bouhenia (France) 11-9

***

WORLD CHAMPIONSHIPS

2001 - BELFAST, NORTHERN IRELAND
- Middleweight
Round one - beat Youssef El Awad (Denmark) 17-5
Round two - beat Miroslav Krepstul (Lithuania) 33-13
Quarter-final - lost to Yordanis Despaigne (Cuba) 28-8

2003 - BANGKOK, THAILAND
- Light-heavyweight
Round one - beat Donatas Jasevicius (Lithuania) 20-9
Round two - beat Beibut Shumenov (Kazakhstan) 23-17
Quarter-final - lost to Evgeny Makarenko (Russia) 27-13

2005 - MIANYANG, CHINA
- Light-heavyweight
Round one - beat Kymatbek Byskulov (Kyrgyzstan) RSC3
Round two - lost to Babacar Kamara (Sweden) 35-26

2007 - CHICAGO, USA
(also first qualifier for 2008 Olympics)
- Light-heavyweight
Round one - beat Julius Jackson (Virgin Islands) RSC2
Round two - beat Julio Castillo (Ecuador) 16–10
Round three - lost to Marijo Sivolija (Croatia) 17–9

2009 - MILAN, ITALY
- Light-heavyweight
Round one - bye
Round two - beat Mohammad Qadir Sultani (Afghanistan) RSC3
Round three - beat Jeysson Monroy Varela (Colombia) 16-7
Quarter-final - lost to Abdelkader Bouhenia (France) 17-9

***

2004 OLYMPIC QUALIFIERS
(all contested at light-heavyweight)

FIRST QUALIFIER - PULA, CROATIA
(also 2004 European Championships)
Round one - lost to Yildirim Tarhan (Turkey) 28-13

SECOND QUALIFIER - PLOVDIV, BULGARIA
Round one - beat Babacar Kamara (Sweden) 35-17
Quarter-final - lost to Semiotas Daugirdas (Lithuania) 33-16

THIRD QUALIFIER - BAKU, AZERBAIJAN
Round one - beat Mario Duro (Spain) RSC3
Quarter-final - lost to Babacar Kamara (Sweden) 27-21

***

2008 OLYMPIC QUALIIFIERS

(all contested at light-heavyweight)

FIRST QUALIFIER - CHICAGO, USA

(also 2007 World Championships)
Round one - beat Julius Jackson (Virgin Islands) RSC2
Round two - beat Julio Castillo (Ecuador) 16–10
Round three - lost to Marijo Sivolija (Croatia) 17–9

SECOND QUALIFIER - PESCARA, ITALY

Round one - beat Myasnik Sargsyan (Armenia) RSC3
Quarter-final - beat Emil Krastev (Bulgaria) 29–8
Semi-final - lost to Ramazan Magomedov (Belarus) 17–13

THIRD QUALIFIER - ATHENS, GREECE

Round one- beat Alessandro Sinacore (Italy) 23–14
Quarter-final - beat Daniel Kooij (Holland) 13–4
Semi-final - beat Gottlieb Weiss (Germany) 21–11
Final - beat Kennedy Katende (Sweden) 15–10

***

OLYMPIC GAMES

(all contested at light-heavyweight)

2008 - BEIJING, CHINA

Round one - beat Julius Jackson (Virgin Islands) 22–2
Round two - beat Bahram Muzaffer (Turkey) 10–2
Quarter-final - beat Washington Silva (Brazil) 8–0
Semi-final - beat Tony Jeffries (Great Britain) 10–3
Final - lost to Xiaoping Zhang (China) 11–7

Index